OYSTER HEARTS PRESS

A Perspective on Spiritual Warfare:
The Choices We Make

Jonathan "Jonbo" Owen

12/10/2024

*I have set before you life and death, blessings and curses.
Now choose life, so that you and your children may live.*

(Deuteronomy 30:19)

In John 17:21 Jesus prayed that we would be one as He and the Father are one. He continually emphasized "If you have seen me you have seen the Father", "I only speak..." "I only do..." the will of the Father. This book looks at how we are created in the image of God as three separate persons, and how each has its appetite and agenda. How we become rooted in the world system and the need to align ourselves to the Word of God through New Birth, renewal of the mind, and awareness of the conflict of flow from the Spirit vs. a direct response to input from the world system.

A Perspective on Spiritual Warfare: The Choices We Make

Copyright © - TX 9-473-139 (02-27-2025)
Jonathan "Jonbo" Owen - All rights reserved.
DeFuniak Springs, Florida
ISBN: 979-8-218-57051-4
LCCN: 2024926240
No portion of this book may be reproduced in any form without written permission from the publisher or author, except as permitted by U.S. copyright law.

This publication is designed to provide accurate and authoritative information regarding the subject matter covered. It is sold with the understanding that neither the author nor the publisher is engaged in rendering legal, investment, accounting, or other professional services. While the publisher and author have used their best efforts in preparing this book, they make no representations or warranties with respect to the accuracy or completeness of the contents of this book and specifically disclaim any implied warranties of merchantability or fitness for a particular purpose. No warranty may be created or extended by sales representatives or written sales materials. The advice and strategies contained herein may not be suitable for your situation. You should consult with a professional when appropriate. Neither the publisher nor the author shall be liable for any loss of profit or any other commercial damages, including but not limited to special, incidental, consequential, personal, or other damages.

Book Cover by Jonathan "Jonbo" Owen
Author and Editor: Jonathan "Jonbo" Owen
Illustrations by Jonathan "Jonbo" Owen [Unless otherwise listed per graphic]

First Edition 2025

FOREWORD

I have been blessed by my long friendship with Jonathan Owen. We both hail from the same town in Michigan, enjoyed long careers as professional musicians, share a love for the Lord, and now Jon joins me as a published author.

Jon's special insight comes from years of serving around the globe as a missionary. God called him in this season to write this book with the help of the Holy Spirit that dwells in him. In it, Jon shares with us his extraordinary experiences, particularly involving God speaking through him with prophetic words and answering specific prayers with miracles he personally witnessed.

I recommend this inspiring book to all those who seek wisdom, a closer walk with Jesus, and the spiritual armor with which to battle against the very real forces of darkness arrayed against us. It is beautifully written, filled with unique discernments, and contains great wit as well.

James A. Watkins

COVER SYMBOLOGY 8
DEDICATION AND CREDITS 11
INTRODUCTION: 15
Let's Get Personal 15
Testimony 30
Reliability of the Bible 34
Why Study the Pre-Nicene Fathers? 41
A HISTORY OF WAR 47
AS WE ARE ONE 65
In His Image 65
Phil, Shep, and Hap 65
A Threefold Cord is Not Quickly Broken (Ecc. 4:12) 67
The Trinity Confirmed 71
Jesus - The Flesh 72
The Father - Soul/Mind 76
The Holy Spirit - Comforter, Teacher 79
FIRST ROOTS 89
Dominant Sphere 89
Fruit 92
All That is in the World 95
Who Wears the Crown? 97
LIKE A TREE PLANTED 105
Unless a Seed Dies 105
BAPTIZED - TREE OF LIFE 113
Spiritual Hunger 113

- The Tree of Life - NEW BIRTH 114
- Pluck Out Phil's Eye? 136

BLOODLINE 139

- Circumcision 139
- Stone - Dust - Flesh 140
- Regarding "Original Sin" 142
- ...All That is in the World. 147
- A Question on the Geneology of Jesus 149

COVENANTS FULFILLED 159

- Jesus Fulfilled All Conditional Covenants 160
- Jesus Was More Than a Prophet or Teacher 167
- "son of man" vs. "Son of Man" 169
- The Temptation of Christ Victorious 170
- Parallels 173
- The Substitute Lamb 174

BETTER COVENANT? 183

- In The Faith 183
- I Will Magnify 184
- Personal Shortcomings 185
- Lest I Be Disqualified 192
- Eye for an Eye vs A Better Way 198

VOICES 201

- Where Did That Thought Come From? 201
- "Feed Me" 202
- Buffet or Buffet 203
- Can We Hear Evil Spirits? 204

Simeon the Sorcerer Tried to Buy the Holy Spirit - Acts 8 210
  Practicing God's Voice 213
  Practicing His Presence 215
  My Sheep Hear My Voice 217
  Interactions 219
  McDonald's 221

AWESOME VOICE **225**

  Voice of God: Direct or Echoes? 226
  Sound Spectrum 234
  God is Pure Light (1 John 1:5 TPT) 235

A MIND FOR BATTLE **243**

  A New Mindset 243
  High Places 245
  Flesh, Eyes, Pride - Warfare 249
  "Why could we not cast him out?" 256
  More on Fasting - Empty Phil 259
  Talents 262
  Battle Strategies 265

CARRY THE KINGDOM **275**

  A "Garden of Eden" in Your Heart 275

POINTS OF KINGDOM CONTACT **289**

  Hands 292
  Feet 298
  Mouth 305

SPEAK A RIVER OF LIFE **323**

  Prayer 323

MIRACLES: HOME & FIELD **349**

    TONGUES - MAURY, EL SALVADOR 363

    ACTS TWO EXPERIENCE 370

    ANGEL UNAWARES? 379

THOUGHT LIFE - OR DEATH? **385**

    LEAVEN/YEAST 386

    HEART GARDEN 390

    IDENTIFY AND ISOLATE 392

    BREAKING THE CONNECTION 399

    NEW HABITS 401

NEW HABITS **405**

    HABIT ONE: PRACTICING GOD'S PRESENCE 405

    FOR SUCH A TIME AS THIS 413

BEYOND THE GATE **427**

A SPIRITUAL LEGACY **437**

EXTRAS **445**

Cover Symbology

The three spheres represent how we are created in God's image as triune beings - Spirit, Soul, and Body - with attributes reflective of the Holy Spirit, Father God, and Jesus.

I have named the spheres after their attributes.
 Left to Right.
Spirit is Shep (Shepherd). Nurturing, guiding, comforting.
Soul/Mind is Hap (Happy). He wants to be happy and keep everyone else happy. He is the arbitrator between Shep and Phil. As such, he is the "boss" and needs to relinquish his crown to the Lordship of Jesus.
Flesh is Phil (Fill). Phil wants to "Feel" good and "Fill" himself with food, pleasure, etc. He is the one most impacted by the world as he has been directly connected since birth via the five senses. So, inherently, he is also the only point of direct contact our spirit and soul have with the world.

As the Garden of Eden had a Tree of Life and a Tree of the Knowledge of Good and Evil we have two trees bearing fruit in the garden of our hearts. One is rooted in the wisdom and thinking of the world system inducing us to take the position of god and determine our actions accordingly. This produces fruit consistent with what the Scripture considers works of the flesh. The heart is stone. Throughout scripture, God announces that someday He will take our stony hearts and make them into flesh. He will take the law that was chiseled in stone and "write it on our hearts". The green tree on the left - is the Tree of Life planted in the Spirit of God at New Birth and producing fruit of the Spirit. This was made possible through the blood Jesus shed on the cross.

We have a choice to eat from the Tree of Life led by the Spirit of God. Or, act as our god by feeding off the world system and making life choices accordingly. The fruits of each way are listed below. We have a choice. The command is to "Choose Life".

Regarding the background:
The right is dust, earth, and chaos while the left is light and sky signifying heaven and spiritual light or insight.

Regarding the logos:
My production company is "Out of Mind Productions".

My spiritual products, including this book, are "OysterHearts".

Oyster♥Hearts

A good man, out of the good treasure of the heart, bringeth forth good things (Matthew 12:35)

Pearls are formed when an irritant, such as a grain of sand enters and becomes trapped in the shell of a mollusk, like an oyster. To protect itself, the oyster secretes and layers substances around the irritant to smooth out the roughness and stop the irritation eventually forming a treasure, a pearl.

In the same way, as we read the Word of God some passages demand more attention than others and we find ourselves meditating on these, studying them, cross-referencing, and ultimately producing a treasure, a "pearl" to share with others.
Thus, we are "Oyster Hearts".

Dedication and Credits

Many people come to mind that I would like to mention. I have 15+ people in my "Interactions" Excel file who have been reading along with my writings. My reentry church, Abundant Love Fellowship in Cahokia, Illinois, and Pastor Tim Ritzel. Many of whom became like a second family to me. Jack and Sherrie Harris with whom I worked in India. They invited me to teach at their pastor's school and entrusted me to return alone the next year to set up and train three film teams showing the Jesus Film in India - Daya Sagar. It is the first Jesus film produced and directed in India with a full Indian cast in Hindi, the national language.

I especially would like to thank my sister, Laurie. More sensible and spiritual than she could ever imagine. Our many conversations led to the writing of this book. She has also been very helpful in the editing process.

My parents, Walden and Beverly Owen who "raised up a child in the way he should go". If I had to name one person it would be my maternal grandmother, Ida Keith who introduced my family to...

A Legacy of Faith

One of my earliest memories of stories about my "Peep Eye" Gramma is a supernatural intervention. My Grandmother was dying of tuberculosis. She had three young children, Aunt Jeannie, Aunt

Juanita, and Aunt Rani. In her words, "Then one night something happened - something strange and wonderful."

"Neal had gone to work, but I was afraid to go to bed because when I fell asleep, I stopped breathing. I knelt beside the bed and prayed all night long.

"What will become of my babies?" I asked God. "If I die, who will take care of them?" I had

overheard my husband tell someone that "if she dies, I'll have to put the kids in an orphanage." (she had been raised as an orphan)

"Jeannie, you and Nita and Lorraine come pray with me and keep me awake," I told my daughters, ages 4,3 and 2. "Don't let me go to sleep. if I do, wake me up."

They did pray, but they were just little girls and couldn't stay awake. Suddenly, sometime during the night, a light appeared up near the ceiling in the corner of the bedroom. It grew brighter and brighter, and then a voice spoke to me. "you will get well, but it will come slowly." And then it faded away.

There was a message of hope. A promise I could trust. I would get well. My God knew all about me and He was here with me in my difficulties. I went to sleep and woke up the next morning feeling rested and strengthened.'

I AM INCLUDING THE FULL STORY AT THE END OF THIS BOOK. IT IS ENTITLED "JOURNEYS OF FAITH" BY IDA KEITH AS TOLD BY JEAN REDER.

INTRODUCTION: 15

- Let's Get Personal 15
  - *Listen to the Teacher* 15
  - *Running on Empty* 23
  - *Epiphany* 23
  - *Cribb School* 24
- Testimony 30
- Reliability of the Bible 34
  - *If God is "GOD", then He got His Book Written and Preserved the Way He wants it.* 37
- Why Study the Pre-Nicene Fathers? 41

Introduction:

Let's Get Personal

Listen to the Teacher

1986: One of the pastors, Pastor Moses, from the school in India where I was teaching asked me to come to his village in the mountains for a four-day crusade. I was very tired as I had taken an all-night 2nd class sleeper train ride and a five-hour bus trip to get there. Upon arrival, I was immediately asked to teach here, pray there, lay hands... " They would take me to someone's house and say, "Please play your trombone and do some tricks for the children, then teach." Or, they would say, "This person has been bedridden for three years." or, "This woman has had several miscarriages, please pray." After laying hands on the person, they would want me to teach.

I was completely drained. I didn't want to repeat the same message at each house. I tried to think of something different and specific to the situation. I especially wanted to vary the teaching as there was a crowd following me and I didn't want to sound like a parrot.

It was finally time for the crusade to start. As I prepared to enter the platform I was advised that the area was in the middle of a drought and the locals were concerned they would lose their crops. They asked me to pray for the drought to break. Nothing like a bit of added pressure. A pressure that I had to immediately turn over to God. I had no power over the weather and even less power over God. But, I could ask. More about that later in **Speak: A River of Life**.

As I was speaking my interpreter kept interrupting me saying "No, Pastor. Owen, you cannot say that. They will not understand." I told him, "Trust me. I know where I'm going. Just interpret." The interpreter and I finally got a flow going only to be interrupted by Pastor Moses. He pulled me aside and told me that the interpreter was not translating my words. He was preaching a sermon of his own. I told him to go sit down and asked Pastor Moses to interpret for me. He was reluctant at first saying he was not qualified to interpret. I told him, "You speak the language. The people know you. You trust me. Just interpret, please." The night went much better.

At the end of the night, I told God "I need a good interpreter." He said, "So do I."

This was one of the most freeing things I have experienced in ministry. Since that day, my focus has been to listen and learn His voice. Speaking what I believe He is saying. I would never say "Thus saith the Lord." Instead, I would say, "I believe this is what the Lord is saying."

This is what I term prophecy. Speaking God's heart and wisdom for that person for that moment. I have experienced this to be spot on many, many times.

Years later, while working with Youth With A Mission, I was asked to help run the book table at a worship conference. A friend, Kent Henry, whom I hadn't seen in years was teaching so I took some time off from the book table to attend. The place was packed so I stood just inside the back entrance to watch. The teaching was excellent. At the end of his teaching, Kent recognized me in the back and called me up to minister in the prayer line. The person standing with me to minister kept jumping in with the prayer, running down a list of points from Kent's teaching. After he ran down the same list for about five people I interrupted and said, "Let me do this one." I wanted to speak about what God might have to say to this person. Not, run down a checklist of what that person probably already had in his notes from the teaching.

I told the man there seemed to be some type of issue going on with a relative of his.
He looked unimpressed.
I said, "I think it is your cousin."
He broke down crying, saying "Thank you God." and walked away with his hands up praising God.

My "prayer partner" was sharing what he had just heard Kent speak. He basically ran down a list of points from the teaching. I have known Kent Henry for years and what he speaks, and what he teaches is God-inspired and for the moment (Rhema). He is a Psalmist and a teacher. We need the same grace-instilled words to come out of our mouths.

Words direct from the fountain of Living Water. Not from the cistern of our mind.

"My people have committed two sins: They have forsaken me, the spring of living water, and have dug their own cisterns, broken cisterns that cannot hold water. (Jeremiah 2:13)

I plan to speak more about this in my section on prayer.

We can speak the Word of God and we can speak the "WORD" of God. You might call this semantics. I call it a distinction between speaking a memorized or instilled piece of scripture versus a current, in-the-moment God-inspired Holy Spirit-powered word that carries grace for the need of the moment. I have heard the distinction made between Rhema and logos many times. My friend, Robert Zimmerman in his book "Hope for the Hopeless: Finding Your Miracle in Plain Sight" gives one of the best explanations I have seen. The following is an excerpt from Rob's book. BTW: I highly recommend this book to everyone. It is one of the best books I have read in a long time containing many insights that could only have come directly from the Spirit of God. I am quoting from his book.

> **Page 83-86 "Hope for the Hopeless: Finding Your Miracle in Plain Sight"**
> One thing all English versions have in common is the limitation of the English language capturing the full meaning of certain words that have multiple meanings. Take, for instance, love. When describing love, the Greeks

use eros for romantic love, storge for family love, philia for brotherly love, and agape for divine or God's love. All of these concepts are neatly wrapped up in the one English word love.

The same is true for the word "*word*". The Greek words used in the Scripture are logos for spoken, unchanging, applicable to all people and all situations. Another is rhema, which seems to describe more of the moment, narrowly applicable, catered to the situation, in the now. Both appear throughout the Scriptures in Greek translations. It should be noted that theologians are divided as to the significance of the use of one versus the other. My own belief is that the split usage is by design and that understanding the context of each is important in the Christian walk.

Here are some examples of verses that use the word logos in the Greek:

In the beginning was the LOGOS, and the LOGOS was with God, and the LOGOS was God. (John 1:1)

Be diligent to present yourself approved to God, a worker who does not need to be ashamed, rightly dividing the LOGOS of truth. (2 Timothy 2:15)

The next three examples are verses I have used in this

book. The first example comes from the parable of the sower of seed (1 Would Be John Wayne chapter).

Now the parable is this: The seed is the LOGOS of God... (Luke 8:11)

The second is from Paul's (presumably) letter to the Hebrews (Perspective chapter):

For the LOGOS of God is living and powerful, and sharper than any two-edged sword, piercing even to the division of soul and spirit, and of joints and marrow, and is a discerner of the thoughts and intents of the heart. (Hebrews 4:12)

The last example is from Peter's first epistle (I Would Be John Wayne chapter):

...having been born again, not of corruptible seed but incorruptible, through the LOGOS of God which lives and abides forever... (1 Peter 1:23)

The second usage, rhema, is subtly different and requires the presence of two or more witnesses to its validity within the Scripture.

in the mouth of two or three witnesses shall every RHEMA be established

(2 Corinthians 13:1)

When Jesus first meets Simon Peter. He tells him to put his net out on the other side of the boat. Within Peter's response is a rhema use of word.

But Simon answered and said to Him, 'Master, we have toiled all night and caught nothing nevertheless, at Your RHEMA I will let down the net.' (Luke 5:5)

Staying in Luke's Gospel, when God told John that he was to preach repentance as a forerunner of the Messiah, Luke said, "The RHEMA of God came unto John."
(Luke 3:2)

In the book of Acts, Peter recalled a message he had received from the Lord,

"Then remembered I the RHEMA of the Lord, how He said, John indeed baptized with water; but ye shall be baptized with the Holy Spirit." (Acts 11:16)

When the angel Gabriel told Mary she would have a child Lake wrote:

Then Mary said, 'Behold the maidservant of the Lord! Let it be to me according to And the angel departed from her. (Luke 1:38)

When Jesus told His disciples that He is the vine and we are the branches, John wrote:

"If you abide in Me, and My RHEMAs abide in you, you will ask what you desire, and it shall be done for you." (John 15:7)

Finally, when Jesus went into the wilderness to be tempted by Satan, among other temptations, Satan urged Jesus to turn rocks into bread. Recall that Jesus had been fasting for forty days and was hungry. Here was the Lord's response: It is written, 'Man shall not live by bread alone, but by every RHEMA that proceeds from the mouth of God.' (Matthew 4:4).

This verse speaks volumes to me that God is still speaking to His people. We are to live by every rhema from His mouth, every fresh word spoken to our spirit, every divinely inspired instruction from Him. I believe God, through the Holy Spirit, speaks to us a lot more often than we realize. It is in times of quietness and prayer that we usually hear His still small voice.

END QUOTE

So I tell you this, and insist on it in the Lord, that you must no longer live as the Gentiles do, in the futility of their thinking. (Ephesians 4:17)

For now, we must realize that in our Western mindset of secular thought, we tend to speak from a checklist of gathered knowledge. We form a plan of what we think God wants to say and speak it out as prayer or as counsel. We need to "Listen to the Teacher" and speak His rhema. Our gathered knowledge of Scripture and experience is good only so far as it allows our renewed minds to not hinder the Spring of Living Water.

I believe this is what Paul was referencing regarding prophesying in the church. It might be more general in a body situation. But, sharing the heart of God with power is needed for all those in the congregation - believers, non-believers, ALL.

Running on Empty

You might ask, "If you have seen God work so often and in so many ways why don't you see them, now?" That's a great question and the purpose of this book.

First, I never stopped seeing God's involvement in my life. I can look back on my entire life and see his fingerprints all over it. As I read my journals, I see a common concern throughout. I did not want to come back home and become filled up and distracted by the world. Bills, jobs, TV, swimming pools, barbeques, etc. These are all distractions. The "Old Wine" of the world is very appealing and familiar. Jesus warned of the cares of this life in His Parable of the Seed.

Epiphany

My sister, Laurie, and I were speaking of this very thing at her home in 2017.

Why is it that we don't seem to have the motivation to continue on our journey with Christ at the level we desire? You read a book or hear a sermon and have an epiphany. You are determined to follow this new inspiration. Maybe you just read an inspiring book on world-changing prayer. "I am going to get up early and pray for an hour each day." You set the alarm. You fall asleep after praying for five minutes. "I'll pray the other 55 minutes before I go to sleep tonight." Yeah, right.

Why do we run out of epiphany? Why do we run out of power to do good? First of all, you are doing this in your strength. Not God's strength. You're doing this in your work. You're not depending on God's grace. But how do you stay in God's grace? How do you keep a focus on that? How do you find and keep the flow of God's grace working in your daily life? You aren't turning evil. You just want to stay more God-focused. It's like you get in there, you plug in your battery, you charge it, and run off into the world. Pretty soon all the motivation, all that "spiritual" energy is gone.

" My people have committed two sins: They have forsaken me, the spring of living water, and have dug their own cisterns, broken cisterns that cannot hold water." (Jeremiah 2:11-9) The cisterns are our "batteries". We get all charged up and ready to take on the gates of hell. At some point, though, we all end up running out of juice. Our "battery" is drained.

Cribb School

I have seen miracles many times in the past. The first visual miracle I ever saw was back in the early 70s. The Jesus movement was just catching on in our area. My father's church, Coloma Circle Church, was meeting at Cribb School North of Watervliet, Michigan on M-140.

We were just realizing that God has made provision for healing prayer. That it didn't end with the Apostles. It is for today. Specific prayer would be offered by the elders and my father at the end of each service.

One Sunday morning a guy from our church, I don't remember his name, interrupted the service early on stating he needed prayer right now and couldn't wait until the service was over. On the way to church his car was overheating so he pulled over to check. As he opened the radiator cap a burst of steam escaped and scalded his arm. His arm was hurting so bad that he either needed prayer now or he needed to go to the hospital.

My father, Walden Owen called him up. The man removed the cloth from around his forearm. It had a solid red blister from elbow to wrist. We were very new to this. Walden put olive oil on the guy's forehead, referenced several scriptures including James where it says to come before the elders for healing prayer, closed his eyes, placed his hands on the guy's head, and began to pray.

I was sitting in the front row about five feet away.

If you can imagine pulling a long glove off your arm, you can get a picture of the healing as the red was swept away - elbow to wrist to reveal a white, healed arm.

There was a gasp from the congregation and a shout of joy from the man in response to the release from pain. We all had just seen miraculous healing right in front of our eyes.

Unfortunately, my dad had closed his eyes to pray, like a good Baptist boy, and was the only one in the room who didn't see it. He promised himself never to close his eyes in prayer in a situation like that ever again.

I posted this on Facebook a while back and got quite a response from friends who also witnessed it. (thirteen people responded)

Here are a few responses from that Facebook posting.

Dale Owen
I've told this story before but here it is again. It was 1971 or 72 when this occurred. On a Sunday morning at church one of our friends came in with his left arm blistered from his elbow up to his wrist. His car had overheated on the way in and without thinking he popped the radiator cap and the steam got him good. Very painful.
During the church service, we gathered around him and prayed for him. We asked God to heal his arm. There were probably around twelve to fifteen of us praying, my father Walden Owen the pastor of our church was among those of us praying as well.
I was there, I saw this with my own two eyes. As we were praying it was as if an invisible hand touched his arm and slowly from his elbow up to his wrist created a defining

healing line that traveled upward as the raw blistered skin became healthy, un-blistered skin.

Hold your left arm up with your forearm facing out. Place your finger right at your elbow and slide it up to your wrist counting one one thousand, two one thousand, and count that way up to ten.

That is the exact way it happened.

My poor dad who was raised Baptist kept his eyes closed while he prayed because that is what good Baptists do when they pray. He didn't get to see what us 'renegades' had just observed. He heard us all yelling with excitement and opened his eyes to see the final result.

Again, I saw this with my own two eyes. God is all-powerful and He loves us.

My brother Jon is writing a book about some of the amazing miracles we experienced at Circle Church.

One of which was my brother Jon speaking perfect French to a French girl...while he doesn't speak a lick of French, except that the Holy Spirit spoke thru my brother Jon. Those were amazing days AND I tell you this....it's about to start happening again and already is happening in many places. This evil world has done enough damage and God will do mighty things to open as many eyes as He can to the Truth.

(there ya go..my "every once in a while" serious side)

Robert Sliter

...I was a witness to that miracle, one of many...I was just a kid but it affected me...

Fritz Flowers

I remember it well, the first miracle healing, new to me too! TyJ

Back to Jon

Since that time I have seen and experienced many more miracles.

What was going on in my life during those and other times when signs and wonders were manifesting? What was I doing? What were we doing? Doing right? Doing wrong? I began to look through some of my journals. Journals from India, the Dominican Republic, El Salvador, Guatemala, etc. I began remembering times when God spoke through me. Specific prayers answered. Not just on the mission field but at home.

I asked God, how does that work? How can we keep that flow going? The flow from the spirit? Because we've got to live by the Spirit and not the world. The Lord gave me the diagram I am using as a basis for the teaching. As I continued reading the Scriptures I began to notice things in a new light. I began emailing verses to myself with various topics and collecting them in folders - Two Trees, Baptism, New Birth, Renewing the Mind, etc.

I finished reading my Bible and started over. I would finish and start again. Each time I would have more pieces to the puzzle. Like an oyster producing a pearl; a treasure was forming in my heart.
(Matthew 12:35)

I began working on this in 2017. But, looking back through my journals, I was surprised to see how much of this I had taught at the Pastor's School in India back in 1986. I'll be sharing journal entries, scriptures, experiences, and scientific information that I've gathered over the past years throughout this book.

Note: At the time I began writing this book I was reading the New International Version (NIV). Upon checking the copywrite information for the NIV I learned that it is held by Biblica, Inc.
The copywrite allows for a certain percentage or number of references before I need to file for permission to use.

As I state in the book, after years of reading multiple versions I have come to the determination that it is the Holy Spirit who leads us into truth, not one particular version.

I left these references as they stand rather than go back and add NIV to each.
If there is no reference given (i.e. KJV, ESV) the default will be NIV.

Testimony

I grew up in the Baptist Church as a pastor's kid. Friends and I would talk about involvement in the church and sort of come to a consensus. You try to be good. Go to church. Attend Sunday school. Show up every chance you get. Sunday morning. Sunday night. Wednesday or Thursday evenings. Don't smoke, drink, cuss, chew, or run around with those that do.

Level Two: If you're really into church, you can be an usher or a deacon.
Level Three: Be a Sunday School Teacher.
If you are really into serving God, you could be a pastor or a missionary.

But the ultimate level was to be an evangelist.

These traveling evangelists would come to the church and preach. We called them Rallies. They would last several evenings and end on a Sunday morning. Many of them would preach hellfire. I got saved so many times out of fear I cannot count them. That is until my father took me into his study and led me to a personal relationship with Jesus Christ. Not out of fear but understanding.
These evangelists would tell great stories about what they did when they were out "in the world". I did this and I did that and I was a bad person. Then I found Jesus. Don't go out and do "This" and "That". Just stay in church and be good.

My friends and I would say, "This guy has built up a great testimony here. And now he's in the church being blessed by God, being looked up to as a "Super" Christian. He is singing and preaching on the stage with his beautiful wife playing the piano. He has a great ministry. Maybe we should go out and become evangelists."

So, when I had an opportunity to get out on the road - touring nightclubs with different bands, I tried a few things to "build up my testimony" because I wanted to be able to relate. You know - "been there, done that." If someone says, You don't know what it's like. Oh yeah, I've experienced that, I've done that.

I thought as long as I was out there playing on the road, I might as well try a few things. But I noticed the more things I tried, the more distance I got from God. I reached the point where I felt like I was floundering. I was out in the ocean. I knew where the rock was. But, I was drifting farther and farther away and didn't know how to get connected back to that rock. I would pray, "Here I am again. God. Help me. I don't like this. I want to get back to that rock." I identified with that phrase from the Kansas song "How Far to the Point of No Return".

In 1983, I went through a divorce. It was time to find my way back. I didn't want to be an evangelist. I just wanted God.

I was playing in the Millennium Band and living in Cahokia, Illinois. One day I said, "God. I need a church. Show me where to go." That was on a Saturday night. The next morning I was tempted to put it off until the next week. I had been up really late the night before playing music. But, I was determined to make the change, now. I got in my car, a car that was being loaned to me by my drummer, Terry Kannewerf, and started driving.

I drove past a dilapidated-looking shopping center and noticed a church sign, "Abundant Love Fellowship". That sounded like a good name for a church. So, I pulled in. I figured they had probably moved because this shopping center looked pretty rough. I went up to the door to find out where the church had moved to and what time the services were. Lo and behold, the church was there. And they were having service. I decided to go in. As I walked through the door, tears started flowing down my face. A warmth hit me like I had not felt in a long time. I thought, "I'm home."

This church taught that the Word of God, the Bible isn't something you just memorize and try to live by. It is not a bunch of rules to follow. It's a living thing. It is the Living Word. Food for your soul. Food for your spirit. Nourishment. Seeds that you plant in the garden of your heart to produce a crop.

This church also believed in miracles, tongues and interpretation, and prophecy. They weren't out of line on these things. They believed in them, but they were very solid in Scripture and grounded in love. If the Bible said it, it was the truth. Forget about the "My aunty always said" or "I always thought this." The Bible was and is the final authority. As my roots grew in the church I became more and more involved. I was still playing in the band. But. I changed the way I performed. I had a new attitude. A new level of performance. The jokes I told on stage, the way I talked, and how I behaved changed. I wasn't an alcoholic, but I quit drinking. I didn't quit drinking because I was raised Baptist. It just wasn't expedient. I decided it was not helpful for this season of my life.

People started noticing, saying, "You're different. What happened? I hear you got religion." I would say, "No, I got a relationship. Not religion. A relationship with God. Relationship with Christ." We started having Bible studies in the clubs during the breaks between sets. People would ask a question. I would say, "I don't know. Let me find out. Let me ask my pastor. Let me study my Bible. I'll be at this club on such and such a day. Meet me there and I'll try to have an answer for you". So they would come in and I'd share with them what I learned and show it to them in the Bible.

Eventually, I decided that I needed to get out of the band. I needed to just get out of that environment. I spoke with my pastor and he said, "That's good because I've been feeling really strong to tell you this is a good time for you to leave the band. But I was concerned that you would do it on my word. I wanted you to make this decision because you felt God leading you. So, let's call this a confirmation." I gave six weeks' notice to the band to replace me. Now I'm looking for work.

The story is continued in **Miracles: at Home and in the Field.**

Reliability of the Bible

All Scripture is God-breathed and is useful for teaching, rebuking, correcting, and training in righteousness (2 Tim 3:16)

My first point in any consideration is belief in the veracity of the Bible. If God is the God purported by the Bible; then He got the book written, assembled, and preserved the way He wanted it. Whatever traditions or policies that don't adhere to or originate from this are extraneous and possibly fallacious.

I base my life spiritually on this fact. If it says it in the Word of God, then it's true. I don't care who says something different. Show it to me in plain scripture. I'm not going to go for someone who tickles my ears. I don't care if I was raised to believe one thing or how much I want to believe something else. If it's not in the Scripture, then it's moot. If it is not in the scripture I'm not saying it can't be true, but if it goes against Scripture, I say it is not correct. I can conjecture a lot of things. But it's just conjecture and not necessary for spiritual living.

God got His book written the way He wanted it and has been able to keep it that way or He is not God. He is God. One version is no better than another version. There are differences in the various versions available. But, whether it's a transliteration, a translation, or a paraphrase the "translators" are trying to do the best they can. Here are a few examples of how changing language and the meaning of words has given demand to newer translations of the Bible.

Around 1565-75 a new phrase was becoming popular with young people much to the consternation of their elders. Goodbye. This is a contraction of the phrase "God be with ye". The word gay has changed from something to the effect of "joyful", "carefree", "full of mirth", or "bright and showy" in the 12th century to being associated with immorality somewhere around the 17th century. The Oxford Dictionary defined it at that time to mean "addicted to pleasures". In the 19th century, it changed in referring to a woman as being a prostitute and to a man as someone who slept with a lot of women. Fast forward to today.

When the King James Bible was written in 1611 it was current with the language of the time. Two Bible translations were being used by the Protestants at the time - the Geneva Bible and the Bishop's Bible. King James disliked the Geneva Bible because the annotations in the margins were very Calvinistic and questioned the authority of the bishops and the king. The language of the Bishop's Bible was too grandiose and the translation work was inferior to the Geneva Bible. He told the translators to use the Bishop's Bible as a guide. The KJV was a revision of the Bishop's Bible that heavily followed the Geneva Bible's translation - sans the Calvinist notations.

I have read the Bible all the way through in enough different versions to realize that there's nothing in any of them that changes the purpose or message of the Word. And besides, it's not the King James Version or the living Bible that teaches you. It's the Holy Spirit that leads you into all truth. There are people in other countries who have had the Gospel of John translated into their language. That is the only scripture they have in their language. Yet they have eternal life. They serve a living God through Christ in a relationship with the Holy Spirit. And they don't know how to read King James or the New International Version.

As you read this book you will notice some scriptures have no reference to the version listed, i.e. KJV, ESV, Amplified. When I started writing this book I was reading the New International Version (NIV). Partway through my writing I decided to vary my reference sources in standing with my belief that it is the Holy Spirit and not a particular version of the Bible that is the teacher. Rather than go back and add NIV to what was already written I left those references stand.

Some doctrines are probably harmless such as baptism by immersion vs. sprinkle as long as it is a willful and knowledgeable act of obedience symbolic of dying to the world and being reborn in Christ. I am only stating that faith, purpose, and obedience override any particular church doctrine in my opinion.

Grace is only received by faith through the act of Christ Jesus' death/sacrifice on the cross and His resurrection. Jesus is alive!

There is no other mediator between man and God and no other path except through faith in Christ's sacrifice. Grace cannot be dispensed to men in any other way nor withheld by anyone on earth.

For it is by grace you have been saved, through faith, and this is not from yourselves, it is the gift of God. (Eph 2:8)

If God is "GOD", then He got His Book Written and Preserved the Way He wants it.

God Himself inscribed the original Ten Commandments on both sets of stone tablets. *(Exodus 32:15-16 and 34:1)*

If the boss dictates a letter to his secretary either in person, over the phone, or through a recorded message - would I be correct in assuming that the contents of the letter reflect the message of the boss?

God dictated the original laws and rituals to Moses beginning in Exodus 20 and Moses wrote them down. (for more read Deuteronomy and Leviticus). If you are wondering how Moses was able to write these down there are a few excellent videos on YouTube you can watch. **Did They Find the First Alphabetic Script; Proto-Sinaitic. Patterns of Evidence** and **Was Hebrew the First Alphabet? - Doug Petrovich (Conf Lecture).**

All scripture is given by inspiration of God, (2 Timothy 3:16-17 KJV)

I do not accept evolution because; regardless of how "scientists" gift-wrap it. Evolutionists state that millions of organisms lived-died-evolved. The Bible says there was no death until the fall of man. I will accept the Bible as true over anyone.

Intellectuals have derided Christians as being ignorant and superstitious because they thought the world was flat and you could fall off. This is because many "professed Christians" didn't want to look foolish and adopted these ideas from pagans.

In the oldest book of the Bible God speaks directly to *Job 26:7* and mentions that the world hangs over space. *Isaiah 40:22* says God is enthroned above the circle of the Earth.

This is a starting point of where I am in my faith and my relationship with God. The veracity of the written Word of God. What we need to know is in the Book. Anything beyond that may be exciting or interesting - but, if it is true or real - it will not contradict the Book.

Because two people differ in their views regarding how they interpret the Bible does not discredit the Bible. Most new denominations grew out of concern that the status quo had become corrupt or heretic and began with looking back to the Word. They then settled into their new doctrine and eventually stagnated as new generations perceived the doctrines as law and were no longer heartfelt. Another reason for different denominations is that people build their dogma and develop traditions or find personal interpretations of scripture, usually out of context, to promote their agenda or to fit their view of who God should be (Santa, Grandpa, Disinterested, Vengeful...). Or, they split off into a new group because of a different opinion.

"Every way of a man is right in his own eyes, but Yahweh weighs the hearts." (Proverbs 21:2)

I have read the life testimonies of many well-educated people who committed their lives to disproving the Bible only to end up believers. The fact of different denominations does not disprove anything regarding the Bible which is why I say "If you have a question, read the book". The Bible stresses that we are to renew our minds to the Word. The Bible speaks of a "wisdom of this world" vs. "Godly Wisdom". It all comes back to my initial stated premise.

If God is the God presented to us in the Bible; He got the book written, compiled, and preserved the way He wants it. It was written by men inspired by God and put down according to His direction. Like a boss dictating to his secretary. Something that is a standard accepted procedure in businesses all over the world but somehow incomprehensible regarding an almighty God capable of creating the world in six days.

If I have questions about different "beliefs" I go to the source - the Bible. It is my authority above any man-made teaching. I have read the Bible in King James Version, New King James Version, New American Standard Bible, Amplified, Douay-Rheims, Good News, J.B. Phillips New Testament, Living Bible, and the New International Version. I have seen no real difference in the basic message of the creation, the fall of man, God's promise of redemption, God's seeking to restore His relationship with mankind, the birth, death, resurrection, and ascension of Jesus, etc.

Some call it blind faith or ignorance. If they want to equate Scripture to a witch doctor reading tea leaves, I have no problem with that. That is on them.

The fact is, what I base my beliefs on is a lifetime of experience, study, and results.

Others don't need to agree with me, but I am not going to be intimidated from stating and standing by those beliefs. If God is not God; then I have lived and died to no detriment. If the Bible is true and there is only one path to salvation through the work of Jesus Christ on the cross then those who don't believe lose big time.

Christians are constantly being vilified for sharing what they believe to be the most vital and eternal truth there is - eternal life or death. I cannot count the number of discussions I have had with people who are fine with Buddhism, Hinduism, New Age, and many more "pathways"; but, stumble at Christianity. "You people think you have the only truth," I tell them to read the Gospels. Read the words of Jesus. I am kind of in a bind because I follow His teachings. I am a follower of Christ who said that He is the only way. If I believe there could be other ways, I am not following His teachings and am not a true Christian. They are free to believe as they wish, as am I.

We are all human with human imperfections and easily subject to those imperfections. This is one of the major premises of the Bible. Man is sinful and selfish. In all our self-absorption and personal failure we look at this critical fact of eternity and present this "Gospel of Christ" to others whom we believe to be walking into eternal damnation; then are ridiculed and attacked for caring. On top of that, we are called evil and heartless for adhering to the foundation of these truths and for resisting dilution and misrepresentation of that foundation.

I pray anyone sincerely seeking truth will find it.

Why Study the Pre-Nicene Fathers?

For anyone trying to say that the New Testament was manufactured or compiled by a group of men at the First Council of Nicea in 325 AD and is not consistent with the Apostles or early church fathers - take note.

Written thousands of years ago, what we Christians call the Old Testament and the Jews refer to as the Tanakh (Torah, Nevi'im, and Ketuvim) differ mostly in the order in which they are listed. There are a few other differences; but, the context is the same.

The canon of Scripture which we now see as the New Testament is greatly based on those known as the Pre-Nicene Fathers. These are men who personally knew or lived within one or two generations of the original disciples and Paul.

Irenaeus was a student of Polycarp, who was a disciple of the Apostle John. Iraneus quoted from 21 of the 27 of the books of the New Testament thus verifying those scriptures. He asserted that all four of the Gospels, Matthew, Mark, Luke, and John, were canonical scripture.

Justin Martyr referred to the four gospels around 150 AD, calling them the "memoirs of the apostles" and then quoting from all four.

The writings of these men reference much of today's canon of Scripture and were very influential to the decisions made by the Council of Nicaea in AD 325. Many of these writings are available to us today along with references to them by other historians. The content of these writings gives strong verification of the canon of Scripture that we call the New Testament. Polycarp is important in that he's a bridge to the original apostles themselves.

According to his student Irenaeus. Polycarp was a student of the Apostle John, and he knew the other apostles, although they went unnamed. Here's what Irenaeus wrote, he says. "But Polycarp also was not only instructed by apostles in converse with many who had seen Christ but also by apostles in Asia. Appointed bishop in the Church of Smyrna, whom I saw in my early youth, where he tarried on earth a very long time. And when, as a very old man gloriously and most notably suffering martyrdom, departed this life, having always taught the things he learned from the apostles in which the church has handed down, which alone are true." Irenaeus also, wrote, " For I have a more vivid recollection of what occurred at that time than of recent events (inasmuch as the experiences of childhood, keeping pace with the growth of the soul, become incorporated with it); so that I can even describe the place where the blessed Polycarp used to sit and discourse-his going out, too, and his coming in-his general mode of life and personal appearance, together with the discourses which he delivered to the people; also how he would speak of his familiar intercourse with John, and with the rest of those who had seen the Lord; and how he would call their words to remembrance. " (in his letter to Florinus)

So, if Polycarp is a direct link to the eyewitnesses of Jesus through the Apostle John, we can look at his writings and see if anything he says contradicts the New Testament documents. Does he respect the accounts or does he play fast and loose with them? Does he quote any of the non-canonical sources outside of the New Testament? These are things that would undermine our confidence that the New Testament writings are genuine and trustworthy. But on the flip side, if Polycarp shows that he values the New Testament texts and uses them frequently, then they pass the test of early use. So what New Testament books does Polycarp quote? And how many times?

Matthew four - Mark one. - Luke one - Acts two - Romans one
1 Corinthians four - 2 Corinthians four - Galatians three
Ephesians four - Philippians three - 1 and 2 Thessalonians one
1 and 2 Timothy three times each - Hebrews two - 1 Peter nine
1 John one - 3 John one.

That is 17 out of the 27 books in the New Testament way before the First Council of Nicea in AD 325. Remember, his student Irenaeus quoted from 21 of the 27 books. Let me address quickly that some skeptics have cried foul over the Church's claim that Polycarp knew John. After all, he doesn't quote from John's gospel, but the writer of First and Third John, clearly, in my opinion, is the writer of the Gospel of John. Moreover, Polycarp might have written other letters. We just have one of them. But, we do have that one.

If you read Polycarp's letter to the Philippians you can't get through more than a few sentences before he starts drawing from the Gospels and the epistles. He quotes from our New Testament 47 different times. And out of those times, the meaning of the text may be paraphrased, but it is never substantially changed. Polycarp also mentions Paul's martyrdom. He cites Paul's letters and he even calls them scripture. He says that he knows that the Philippians are already well-versed in the scriptures, and he continues to quote Paul. This is rather extraordinary because it shows us that in the early first century, the Gospels and epistles were already treated as the word of God. It's also interesting because if no one knew who had written these works, as some critics have alleged, then why would the early Christians have accepted them as authentic?

Repeatedly, Polycarp quotes from Jesus' Sermon on the Mount in Matthew and Luke. And, he also says that Jesus came in the flesh. That he was a servant to all. That Jesus died on the cross. That He bore our sins. He was raised from the dead. He was glorified. He's our high priest. That we're saved by grace through faith. And that Jesus will judge the living in the dead.

Polycarp refuted the Gnostic notion that the incarnation, death, and resurrection of Jesus were all just imaginary episodes, and were just made up of essentially ethical and mythical significance. These were historical happenings, according to Polycarp. And notably, Polycarp quotes zero heretics, and zero gospels outside of our New Testament and contradicts zero teachings of Jesus or the Apostles that we find in our Bible. Everything he says is consistent with the New Testament records. His followers attested to him knowing the Apostles and being a student of John himself. Polycarp said that anybody who perverts the teachings of the Apostles is the firstborn of Satan and He would rather die than deny the truth that he's so dearly held. He stated this last part when the magistrate, unwilling to send an 86-year-old man to his death asked him to renounce Christ. Polycarp answered, "Eighty-six years have I been His servant, and He hath done me no wrong." He was subsequently burned at the stake.

In short, Polycarp's witness is a really big deal. The importance of what we glean from his short letter to Philippi cannot be understated. You can read it free online at **https://www.christian-history.org/polycarps-philippian-epistle.html**. So when critics and skeptics ask, "How do you know the books and the Bible are the right ones?" give them the name, Polycarp.

While Polycarp isn't the only early evidence we have for the early use of the New Testament is one of the beginning links to a greater chain of unbroken testimony for our Bible.

Parts of this information were taken from: isjesusalive.com/polycarp and
(How Polycarp Gives us Evidence For the Early Use of the New Testament - TESTIFY) https://www.youtube.com/watch?v=SkFKQUzH4xI

A HISTORY OF WAR: 47

I Will Be Like God 47

You Can Be Like God 48

The Gene Pool 50

A Counteroffensive 51

A Bit of Lineage History 53

Idol Worship 55

A Holy People - Separated Unto God 57

A New Thing 58

What War? 60

A History of War

I Will Be Like God

God created the earth and our universe. He built a perfect ecosystem of land, air, and sea. He then created and populated it with all types of beautiful and interesting creatures. Last of all, God created man and woman. Adam and Eve. He created them in His image. He created them to be in relation with Him by placing his nature within them. Mankind was created in God's image and nature. God declared His creation very good and rested.

God created mankind for relationships. Not just any relationship. One that is so close as to be like one.

I pray that they will all be one, just as you and I are one—as you are in me, Father, and I am in you. And may they be in us so that the world will believe you sent me. "I have given them the glory you gave me, so they may be one as we are one. I am in them and you are in me. May they experience such perfect unity that the world will know that you sent me and that you love them as much as you love me.
(John 17:21-23 NLT)

Even after creating Adam God went above and beyond by creating Eve. Not as a separate being but one taken from Adam's body. *(Genesis 2:21-24)* God wanted to give mankind the very best opportunity for fulfillment in a relationship as possible.

Then the LORD God said, "It is not good for the man to be alone; I

*will make him a helper suitable for him." (Genesis 2:18 NASB)
from the beginning 'God made them male and female.'" And he said,
"'This explains why a man leaves his father and mother and is joined
to his wife, and the two are united into one.'
(Matthew 18:4-5 NLT)*

You can't program love. You cannot program obedience. To love you need to be able to choose not to love. To obey you need to be able to not obey. God created Adam and Eve with the ability to choose. Then, He placed them in the most beautiful life possible. Everything they could want or need was provided. They could live like this forever. But for this loving relationship to exist there needed to be an opportunity to make a choice. To use their free will. God made it so simple. He set them up for success. Everything is good. Everything is yes. Only one thing is "No". Do not eat from one tree. The Tree of the Knowledge of Good and Evil. Someone decided to rock the boat. Jealousy? I can't say. But, he decided to not only interrupt this relationship. He would usurp God's place in the relationship.

You Can Be Like God

We all know the story. The serpent tempted and deceived Eve. Eve gave the fruit to Adam who was not deceived. Adam took the fruit and ate. The choice had been made to turn their free will against God's word. To determine a separate path. The relationship was broken. Man questioned God and then rejected God's command thus breaking the bond. Embracing the serpent's lies he decided on a path of his determination taking the position of god of his life. But, is he a god? No. He only substituted the laws of the True God for the lies of another.

You are of your father the devil, and your will is to do your father's desires. He was a murderer from the beginning, and does not stand in the truth, because there is no truth in him. When he lies, he speaks out of his own character, for he is a liar and the father of lies. (John 8:44 ESV)

God immediately initiated a plan to restore the relationship. He promised a savior to come from the woman. One that would crush the serpent's head. That would defeat Satan's plan.

Satan didn't like that. Through the use of the same three points of temptation successfully used on Eve, he would become man's master. The lust of the eyes, the lust of the flesh, and the pride of life. Three deadly desires. As long as men follow these lies they will be under the influence of this deceiver and subject to him. as opposed to being in a relationship with the true God. With his newly gained influence and authority, he would align their thinking to his plan and stop any possibility of that special one being born. Beginning with the firstborn son, Cain killed his brother Abel.

For all that is in the world—the desires of the flesh and the desires of the eyes and pride of life—is not from the Father but is from the world. (1 John 2:16 ESV)

Satan continued developing this system of thought based on these three realms of desire. Drawing man further and further from the will of God into their own will and, ultimately into his will. Each person behaving as god brought them all under his will. He became their god - the "god of this world".

The Gene Pool

Seth was born and the progeny continued. *And it came to pass, when men began to multiply on the face of the earth, and daughters were born unto them, That the sons of God saw the daughters of men that they were fair; and they took them wives of all which they chose. (Genesis 6:1-2 KJV)*

Although the Scripture differentiates between sons of God and daughters of men; some people think it too far-fetched to think that angels mated with humans. They conflate sons of God with progeny from godly Seth vs. ungodly Cain. The problem here is the sons of God took wives of all they chose. Why would godly men from the line of Seth forcibly take women from the ungodly line of Cain? It would need to be the other way around. The ungodly sons of Cain took beautiful, godly daughters from the line of Seth. There is quite a distinction in Scripture between angels - sons of God, and sons and daughters of men. I will be talking more about this in **Covenants Fulfilled - "son of man" vs. "Son of Man"**.

If Satan could not stop mankind's multiplication maybe he could corrupt man to the point where no "Messiah" would be possible. Many angels found the daughters of Adam attractive. This was good. Let them mate with mankind and corrupt the gene pool.

The plan was going smoothly. The gene pool was becoming polluted. Every thought of mankind was evil. *(Genesis 6:5-17)*. Again, God stepped in. Not that He hadn't been involved all this time. God personally warned Cain to change his attitude. *(Genesis 4:6)* Even after Cain killed Abel the Lord placed a mark on him to protect him. God's interest in mankind never waned nor did His involvement.

A Counteroffensive

God selected a family of eight people. Noah, his three sons, and their wives. God began afresh by rescuing each kind of animal and this family of eight and placing them in an ark, Then He destroyed all living things on the earth that breathed through a worldwide flood. Satan continued his battle plan using his proven system of deceit and seduction. All that is in the world. The three deadly temptations.

We now come to the Tower of Babel. *(Genesis 11)* God had told mankind to spread out across the earth. They had another plan. *"Come, let's build ourselves a city, and a tower whose top will reach into heaven" (Genesis 11:4 NASB)*

I'm not sure of all the ramifications of the tower plan. But, God didn't like it. He was concerned that being united with one language was not good. *"And the Lord said, Behold, the people is one, and they have all one language; and this they begin to do: and now nothing will be restrained from them, which they have imagined to do."*
(Genesis 11:6 KJV)

God removed the original Adamic language giving each family group a unique tongue. No longer unified by a common language they dispersed by clan and spread out over the earth.

And the Lord said, Behold, the people is one, and they have all one language; and this they begin to do: and now nothing will be restrained from them, which they have imagined to do. Go to, let us go down, and there confound their language, that they may not understand one another's speech. (Genesis 11:6-7 KJV)

All of mankind is now descended from the sons of Noah - Shem, Ham, and Japheth. While the Scripture doesn't follow Japheth's genealogy beyond three generations Bill Cooper has written an excellent book titled "After the Flood" which traces the genealogies of Noah's sons via the writings of Nennius, Chronicles of the early Britons, and other non-Biblical historical genealogies. These include years and dates that line up very close to the timeline given in the Bible. Placing the age of the world at around 5,194 years from creation to Christ's birth.

> Page 70 from the book
>
> 'From the beginning of the world until the Flood (are) 2242 years.
>
> From the Flood until Abraham (are) 942 years.
>
> From Abraham to Moses (are) 640 years.
>
> From Moses to David (are) 500 years.
>
> From David to Nebuchadnezzar are 569 years.

From Adam until the migration to Babylonia (i.e. the Captivity of the Jews) are 4879 years.

From the migration to Babylonia until Christ are 566 years.

From Adam therefore until the Passion of Christ are 5228 years.

From the Passion of Christ have been completed 796 years.

And from His Incarnation 831 years.'

(Translated by Bill Cooper from Nennius, chvs 1-4 Written around the end of the 8th century AD)

Cooper even traces descendants of Japheth to China in Appendix 12 "The Descent from Japheth of the Miautso People of China". Speaking of China, there is a great video on YouTube tracing the Chinese alphabet to creation and the flood. Perfectly in line with the canon of Scripture. Search: God in Ancient China: Chinese characters and how they relate to the Book of Genesis - Scott Sacker.
or (https://youtu.be/DA-AkJzpKmg?si=BZa2jhBjfdOe-3-a)

A Bit of Lineage History

We do know that not soon after the flood the line of Ham became corrupted. Among his descendants are the Canaanites (Canaan), Egyptians (Mizraim), and Cush who was the father of Nimrod founder of Babel.

What we are interested in is Shem's lineage. From Shem, we get the term Semites or Semitic people. Farther down the line we have Eber. Also known as Heber. Shem's great-grandson. You guessed it. He is the father of the Hebrew language. Most likely, when God dispersed the nations at Babel each lineage was given a unique language. So, the descendants of Eber/Heber would have been the first to speak Hebrew.

The story of Babel in Genesis Chapter Eleven names seventy descendants of Noah each of which most likely spawned a clan. Each of them spoke its language (*Genesis 10:32*).
The Midrash states that God divided mankind into 70 nations with a ministering angel assigned to each. This could explain the Prince of Persia and the Prince of Greece from *Daniel 10:13-21*. We also know that Michael is the Archangel who oversees Israel.
(*Daniel 10:13, Jude 9*).
(https://www.chabad.org/library/article_cdo/aid/5258600/jewish/Where-Did-the-70-Nations-Come-From.htm)

The gift of tongues at Pentecost may have been a reversal of the curse of Babel which was intended to separate and disperse mankind to stop them from becoming united in a purpose at odds with God's command to *Be fruitful, and multiply, and replenish the earth. (Genesis 9:1 KJV)*. This is the same edict God had given Adam and Eve in the Garden before the Fall and the same one Jesus gave the disciples to *"Go ye therefore, and teach all nations, baptizing them in the name of the Father, and of the Son, and of the Holy Ghost: Teaching them to observe all things whatsoever I have commanded you:" (Matthew*

28:19-20 KJV), "all the world" (Mark 16:15 KJV)," in Jerusalem, and in all Judea and Samaria, and to the end of the earth."(Acts 1:8 KJV) before His ascension.

Idol Worship

There were giants in the earth in those days; and also after that, when the sons of God came in unto the daughters of men, and they bare children to them, the same became mighty men which were of old, men of renown. (Genesis 6:4 KJV)

These guys were a real problem. Even after the flood according to the Book of Exodus, they were a major part of the corruption of man. Continuing to corrupt the gene pool. Now, instigating idol worship. God said if the Israelites allowed the Canaanites to remain alive, *"they will teach you to follow all the detestable things they do in worshiping their gods" (Deut. 20:18 NIV84)*.

Although the flood killed every land-dwelling and air-breathing thing living on the face of the earth (*Genesis 7:22*) Nephilim or their descendants existed after the flood. It has been conjectured by some that all the Nephilim were not destroyed by the flood as being a hybrid of angels and humans they may not have needed to depend on breathing air. Or, as a second attempt to corrupt the gene pool another group of angels repeated the process of mating with humans. This seems pretty far-fetched at first look. But, as they had already been deceived into believing they could overthrow God this may have been a desperate attempt to reinitiate the corruption of the gene pool. There is a third explanation I have heard that mankind had been so infiltrated by Nephilim genetics that one or more of the surviving wives (most likely Ham's wife) carried and passed on those genes producing a new wave of giants.

Just as every culture in the world carries a version of a worldwide flood. We see in Roman, Greek, Norse, Hindu, and many other cultures references to gods and demons mating with humans producing such progeny as giants, satyrs, centaurs, chimera, and other "mythical?" creatures.

I believe there was more than one incursion of angels mating with humans. A close reading of the KJV alongside Strong's reads like this. *There were giants in the earth in those days and also after that when the sons of God came in unto the daughters of men and they bare children to them the same became mighty men which were of old men of renown (Genesis 6:4 KJV with Strong's)*

Regardless of how - they were back and needed to be removed from the earth. The inhabitants of Canaan had been corrupted by the Nephilim both in their gene pool and in idol worship which is why all of them needed to be destroyed - man, woman, and child. Israel was forbidden to allow them to live or intermarry. He didn't have a problem with the surrounding nations because they were not corrupted in this manner.

When thou comest nigh unto a city to fight against it, then proclaim peace unto it. And it shall be, if it make thee answer of peace, and open unto thee, then it shall be, that all the people that is found therein shall be tributaries unto thee, and they shall serve thee. And if it will make no peace with thee, but will make war against thee, then thou shalt besiege it: And when the Lord thy God hath delivered it into thine hands, thou shalt smite every male thereof with the edge of the sword: But the women, and the little ones, and the cattle, and all that is in the city, even all the spoil thereof, shalt thou take unto thyself; and thou shalt eat the spoil of thine enemies, which the Lord thy God hath given thee. Thus shalt thou do unto all the cities which are very far off from thee, which are not of the cities of these nations. (Deuteronomy 20:10-15 KJV)

God, through Israel, began to systematically decimate the giant population beginning with Moses, then Joshua, and later on we see David killing Goliath who had four brothers. Talking about faith, David picked up five stones. He didn't consider that he might miss. He was ready to take out all four of Goliath's brothers. Several other giants are also mentioned. God wanted to make an end to all traces of the giants.

A Holy People - Separated Unto God

As God continued unfolding His plan to redeem and return mankind to a relationship with Him He called out a nation through Abram/Abraham to lift His name among all nations as a demonstration of his power and goodness. As a sign of separation from the rest of the world, God made a covenant with Abraham. A covenant of circumcision. The lineage leading from Adam and Eve to the promised Son of Man who would crush the serpent's head was being guarded and meticulously documented to keep the line pure.

In another level of separation, God established a covenant with Israel. He gave them the Ten Commandments with the Sabbath as a sign of the covenant. *(Exodus 31:16-17)*

He also laid out a specific system of rituals of acceptable worship, cleanliness, and moral behavior in Leviticus and Deuteronomy.

The genetic line was being protected and a systematic teaching of God's law was being prepared for the arrival of the Son of Man - the Messiah. A set of prophecies and conditions were laid out to confirm the arrival of the Promised One. At the proper time.

But when the fullness of the time had come, God sent forth His Son, born of a woman, born under the law, (Galatians 4:4 KJV)

Jesus fulfilled each covenant and prophecy and gave us a new covenant. A covenant for the restoration of mankind back to the Godhead.

A New Thing

A new thing never before seen. God writing His law on people's hearts.

Behold, the days come, saith the Lord, that I will make a new covenant with the house of Israel, and with the house of Judah: Not according to the covenant that I made with their fathers in the day that I took them by the hand to bring them out of the land of Egypt; which my covenant they brake, although I was an husband unto them, saith the Lord: But this shall be the covenant that I will make with the house of Israel; After those days, saith the Lord, I will put my law in their inward parts, and write it in their hearts; and will be their God, and they shall be my people. (Jeremiah 31:31-33 KJV)

Those who enter into this new and better covenant undergo a second birth. A birth into the Spirit of God as new creatures. A new creation. (*2 Corinthians 5:17*)

Whereas previously God would place His Spirit on individuals - the Judges and the Prophets and place His presence in the Tabernacle and the Temple, He now dwells within these new creations. Each new creation is a tabernacle of God. Each one is a priest of God. With their spirits planted in the Spirit of God and God's Spirit dwelling in them. *I will not leave you comfortless: I will come to you. Yet a little while, and the world seeth me no more; but ye see me: because I live, ye shall live also. At that day ye shall know that I am in my Father, and ye in me, and I in you. (John 14:18-20 KJV)*

Each of these new creations is blessed and commissioned to carry the Kingdom of God as an ambassador to the world.

And He said to them, "Go into all the world and preach the gospel to every creature. (Mark 16:15 KJV)

What War?

The battle will continue until the Final Trump. We have an accuser and an Advocate. A liar and the Truth. It is a battle of two kingdoms. The same power that raised Christ from the dead. The same power that made the universe and sustains all things by the power of His Word dwells in you.

There are no bystanders. You have been in this battle since your conception. You can amble through life as a walking wounded or you can take up the armor and fight.

EPHESIANS 6: 12-13...

For everyone who has been born of God overcomes the world. And this is the victory that has overcome the world— our faith. (1 John 5:4 ESV)

Finally, be strong in the Lord and in the strength of his might. Put on the whole armor of God, that you may be able to stand against the schemes of the devil. For we do not wrestle against flesh and blood, but against the rulers, against the authorities, against the cosmic powers over this present darkness, against the spiritual forces of evil in the heavenly places.

Therefore take up the whole armor of God, that you may be able to withstand in the evil day, and having done all, to stand firm.
(Ephesians 6:10-13 ESV)

I call heaven and earth to record this day against you, that I have set before you life and death, blessing and cursing: therefore choose life, that both thou and thy seed may live:
(Deuteronomy 30:19 KJV)

Choose Life

AS WE ARE ONE: 65

- In His Image 65
- Phil, Shep, and Hap 65
- A Threefold Cord is Not Quickly Broken (Ecc. 4:12) 67
  - Trinity in Unity 68
- The Trinity Confirmed 71
  - One as They Are One 72
- Jesus - The Flesh 72
  - Who is Jesus 72
  - Jesus Was One With the Father 74
- The Father - Soul/Mind 76
  - A Father 76
  - The Judge 77
  - Forgiving 78
  - Giving 78
  - Covenant Maker 79
- The Holy Spirit - Comforter, Teacher 79
  - "You Shall Receive Power" 81
  - A Spiritual Cornucopia 84

AS WE ARE ONE: In His Image

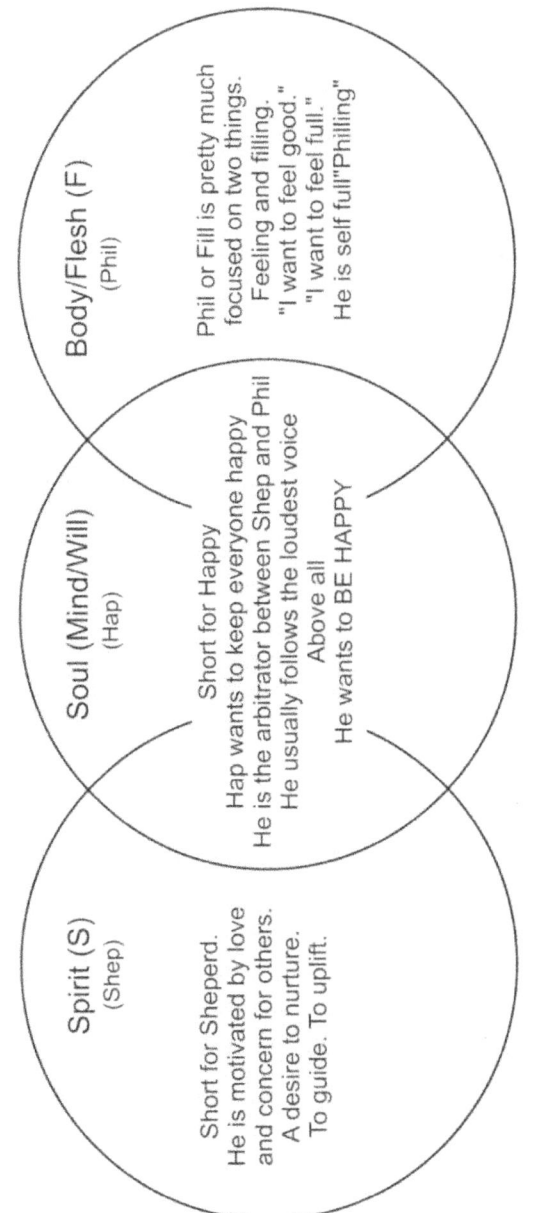

Each of these three individuals is a complete expression of ourselves in the spiritual, soulish, and physical realm; just as the Holy Spirit is the total expression of God in the spiritual realm, the Father in the realm of the soul, and Jesus is the total expression of God in the physical realm. We are triune beings.

We inherently carry the same natures as the GodHead; but, unfortunately, due to the fall, these characteristics manifest in a distorted and self-centered manner influenced by and based on the reasoning of a fallen worldview.

As We Are One

In His Image

And God said, Let us make man in our image, after our likeness:(Genesis 1:26 KJV))

As I am finishing this section on the oneness of the Trinity of the Godhead my friend Dean Harvey posted this on Facebook yesterday.

> All the acts of Jesus were expressions of His Father for all humanity to see...The writer of Hebrews called Jesus the exact representation of His Father's nature (Heb. 1:3). The life of Jesus was the most complete and accurate revelation of the Father ever seen in the world. "If you have seen Me you have seen My Father" (John 14:9). It is still true. It is the heart of the perfect Father to give life to humankind (John 10:10) and destroy all the works of the destroyer (1 John 3:8). The Holy Spirit is the One who reveals the heart of the Father to and through us (John 16:12-15).
> *Bill and Beni Johnson, Mornings and Evenings, page 167.*

Phil, Shep, and Hap

For the word of God is living and active and sharper than any double-edged sword, piercing even to the point of dividing soul from spirit, and joints from marrow; it is able to judge the desires and thoughts of the heart. (Hebrews 4:12 KJV)

Looking out the window on such a beautiful day, you decide to clock out from work and take your packed lunch to a nearby park. As you prepare to eat you notice a hungry-looking person digging through a trash can a small distance from you.

A thought comes to give your lunch to that person. You look down at your waistline and think they need the food more than you. As you prepare to go over and offer your lunch to this person, a voice inside screams out, "That's mine. Who do you think you are giving away my food?"

You now have an argument going on inside between two distinct and different personalities. Each with its own motivation and temperament. Should I give my lunch to this hungry person or keep it for THIS hungry person? A third person steps in. "Let's give one of the sandwiches and the apple. We'll keep the other sandwich and the chips." An agreement is made and the situation is resolved.

We have just witnessed three distinct personalities within ourselves. Each has its own set of motivations, appetite, and temperament. To better identify these three within me; I have named them according to their personalities. When the thought to give away the lunch was brought up Phil had a fit. He is pretty much focused on two things. Feeling and filling. "I want to feel good." "I want to feel full." This is why I call him Phil (Fill). He is self "full-Philling". The person who wanted to give our lunch to the hungry individual I call Shep. This is short for Shepherd. He is motivated by love and concern for others. A desire to nurture. To guide. To uplift. Our third person. The one who steps in and arbitrates between the other two is Hap. This guy wants to be happy and keep everyone else happy. He will actively arbitrate to achieve this goal.

Phil (flesh)
Shep (spirit)
Hap (mind/soul)

Each of these three individuals is a complete expression of ourselves in the spiritual, soulish, and physical realm; just as the Holy Spirit is the total expression of the Godhead in the spiritual realm, the Father is the total expression of the Godhead in the soul, and Jesus is the total expression of the Godhead in the physical realm.
We are triune beings.
*"May God himself, the God of peace, sanctify you through and through. May your whole **spirit, soul and body** be kept blameless at the coming of our Lord Jesus Christ. The one who calls you is faithful, and he will do it." (1 Thessalonians 5:23-24)*

A Threefold Cord is Not Quickly Broken (Ecc. 4:12)

Just as God is three distinct persons as one individual; in the same way we, created in the image of God, are a unique trinity consisting of three distinct individuals. Each with an independent personality, temperament, appetite, and motivations - yet, functioning as one being.

We inherently carry the same natures as the Godhead; but, unfortunately, due to the fall, these characteristics manifest in a distorted and self-centered manner influenced by and based on the reasoning of a fallen worldview. A worldview developed and promoted by the god of this world.

Wherein in time past ye walked according to the course of this world, according to the prince of the power of the air, the spirit that now worketh in the children of disobedience: (Ephesians 2:2)
Therefore seeing we have this ministry, as we have received mercy, we faint not; But have renounced the hidden things of dishonesty, not walking in craftiness, nor handling the word of God deceitfully; but by manifestation of the truth commending ourselves to every man's conscience in the sight of God. But if our gospel be hid, it is hid to them that are lost: In whom the god of this world hath blinded the minds of them which believe not, lest the light of the glorious gospels of Christ, who is the image of God, should shine unto them.
(2 Corinthians 4:1-4)

Trinity in Unity

" And now I am no more in the world, but these are in the world, and I come to thee. Holy Father, keep through thine own name those whom thou hast given me, that they may be one, as we are. " (John 17:11)

Jesus is the body - God, the Father is the soul and the Holy Spirit is the spirit. They are three and yet they are one. We are also a body/flesh, a soul/mind, and a spirit. Due to the "Fall" and resultant sinful nature our flesh rebels against our spirit with our mind vacillating between the two. We are three personalities.

Many people are in such disunity between the three that their minds do not even associate with their spirit at all. Especially in our current Westernized secular society. Some people with a more dominant spirit might be drawn to that realm by performing acts of asceticism or using drugs in an attempt to reach it. But this concept originating from the world system will only bring about a perverted consciousness of the spirit which potentially opens a channel for involvement by other spirits not of God.

Neither pray I for these alone, but for them also which shall believe on me through their word; That they all may be one; as thou, Father, art in me, and I in thee, that they also may be one in us: that the world may believe that thou hast sent me. (John 17:20-21 KJV)
Jesus, the Flesh, was submitted to God (the mind the soul) in every way. He did only what he saw the Father doing and only said what He heard the Father say. He agreed with both the Father and the Spirit. They were in unity. Jesus prayed that we would be one as He and the Father are one. He promised when He left that He would send the Spirit to help us. *(John 14:15-31)*

Could this mean that our spirit, soul, and flesh should be in agreement with each other as three separate personalities able to disagree (as we so often witness in our lives); yet, working together in agreement as one?

Each of our "persons" is struggling for dominance. Phil (flesh) has his appetites and motivations as do Hap (mind/soul) and Shep (spirit). The spirit of someone who has not received salvation usually will not have much more of a voice than a conscience. Once born again, this voice will become active and will promote thinking in line with the Spirit of God producing life. As our renewed spirit grows so will its voice. The struggle for dominance will increase as Phil and Shep push their agenda with Hap caught in the middle trying to make peace between the other two while maintaining some semblance of control.

I do not understand what I do. For what I want to do I do not do, but what I hate I do. And if I do what I do not want to do, I agree that the law is good. As it is, it is no longer I myself who do it, but it is sin living in me. For I know that good itself does not dwell in me, that is, in my sinful nature. For I have the desire to do what is good, but I cannot carry it out. For I do not do the good I want to do, but the evil I do not want to do—this I keep on doing. Now if I do what I do not want to do, it is no longer I who do it, but it is sin living in me that does it. So I find this law at work: Although I want to do good, evil is right there with me. For in my inner being I delight in God's law; but I see another law at work in me, waging war against the law of my mind and making me a prisoner of the law of sin at work within me. (Rom. 7:15-23)

The Trinity Confirmed

Trinity of the Godhead

*Then Jesus came to them and said, "All authority in heaven and on earth has been given to me. Therefore go and make disciples of all nations, baptizing them in the name of the **Father** and of the **Son** and of the **Holy Spirit**, and teaching them to obey everything I have commanded you. And surely I am with you always, to the very end of the age." (Matthew 38:18-20)*

*For there are three that bear record in heaven, the **Father**, the **Word**, and the **Holy Ghost**: and these three are one. (1 John 5:7)*

I prefer the term Holy Spirit. He is not a ghost.

*"For this reason, I kneel before the **Father**, from whom every family in heaven and on earth derives its name. I pray that out of his glorious riches, he may strengthen you with power through his **Spirit** in your inner being, so that **Christ** may dwell in your hearts through faith. And I pray that you, being rooted and established in love, may have power, together with all the Lord's holy people, to grasp how wide and long and high and deep is the love of Christ, and to know this love that surpasses knowledge—that you may be filled to the measure of all the fullness of God." (Ephesians 3:14-19)*

Human Trinity

May God himself, the God of peace, sanctify you through and through.

*May your whole **spirit**, **soul and body** be kept blameless at the coming of our Lord Jesus Christ. The one who calls you is faithful, and he will do it. (I Thessalonians 5:23-24)*

One as They Are One

Jesus prayed *"I do not ask for these only, but also for those who will believe in me through their word, that they may all be one, just as you, Father, are in me, and I in you, that they also may be in us, so that the world may believe that you have sent me. The glory that you have given me I have given to them, that they may be one even as we are one, I in them and you in me, that they may become perfectly one, so that the world may know that you sent me and loved them even as you loved me. (John 17:20-23 ESV)*

Let's first look at some of the characteristics of the "Godhead" Trinity. This is by no means meant to be a comprehensive look.

Jesus - The Flesh

Who is Jesus

He was not just a traveling rabbi - a great teacher. Not just a good man, a miracle worker, or a prophet.

*Now the earth was formless and void, and darkness was over the surface of the deep. And the **Spirit of God was hovering** over the surface of the waters. And **God said**, "Let there be light," **and there was light**. (Genesis 1:2-3)*

*Then spake Jesus again unto them, saying, **I am the light of the world**:*

*he that followeth me shall not walk in darkness, but shall have **the light of life***. (John 8:12 KJV)

Jesus is that light. He is the Light of the World.

...yet for us there is one God, the Father, from whom are all things and we exist for Him, and one Lord, Jesus Christ, by whom are all things, and we exist through Him. (1 Corinthians 8:6 LSB)

*In the beginning was the Word, and the Word was with God, and the Word was God. The same was in the beginning with God. All things were made by him; and without him was not any thing made that was made. **In him was life; and the life was the light of men**. And **the light shineth in darkness**;" (John 1:1-5)*

Jesus is the Word that established the universe.

And the Word was made flesh, and dwelt among us (John 1:14)

Jesus fulfilled the Law and every covenant [see **Covenants Fulfilled**]

The Law was not something to be used against each other. An *"Eye for an eye"* in Leviticus Chapter 24 was not to give license for revenge. It was given to set a limit on revenge.

Jesus demonstrated the spirit of the law vs. the letter of the law by standing against man-made religion and precepts while focusing on its purpose.

Jesus sought out the lost. He healed the sick. He restored sight to the blind and caused the lame to walk. He raised the dead. He crushed the deeds of the evil one.

"On a Sabbath Jesus was teaching in one of the synagogues, and a

woman was there who had been crippled by a spirit for eighteen years. She was bent over and could not straighten up at all. When Jesus saw her, he called her forward and said to her, "Woman, you are set free from your infirmity." Then he put his hands on her, and immediately she straightened up and praised God. Indignant because Jesus had healed on the Sabbath, the synagogue leader said to the people, "There are six days for work. So come and be healed on those days, not on the Sabbath." The Lord answered him, "You hypocrites! Doesn't each of you on the Sabbath untie your ox or donkey from the stall and lead it out to give it water? Then should not this woman, a daughter of Abraham, whom Satan has kept bound for eighteen long years, be set free on the Sabbath day from what bound her?"
(Luke 13:10-16)

Ultimately, Jesus gave His life to open the gate of redemption for all mankind.
"For God so loved the world, that he gave his only begotten Son, that whosoever believeth in him should not perish, but have everlasting life. For God sent not his Son into the world to condemn the world; but that the world through him might be saved." (John 3:16-17)

Jesus Was One With the Father
"I and my Father are one." (John 10:30)
"I have come in my Father's name,..." (John 5:43)
"I seek not to please myself but him who sent me." (John 5:30)
It was because Jesus did such things on the Sabbath day [healed a

lame man] *that the Jews persecuted him. But Jesus' answer to them was this, "My Father is still at work and therefore I work as well." This remark made the Jews all the more determined to kill him, because not only did he break the Sabbath but he referred to God as his own Father, so putting himself on equal terms with God.*
Jesus makes His tremendous claim.
Jesus said to them, "I assure you that the Son can do nothing of his own accord, but only what he sees the Father doing. What the Son does is always modelled on what the Father does, for the Father loves the Son and shows him everything that he does himself, Yes, and he will show him even greater things than these to fill you with wonder. For just as the Father raises the dead and makes them live, so does the Son give life to any man he chooses. The Father is no man's judge: he has put judgment entirely into the Son's hands, so that all men may honour the Son equally with the Father. The man who does not honour the Son does not honour the Father who sent him.
(John 5:16-23 J.B. Phillips New Testament)
Jesus answered: "Don't you know me, Philip, even after I have been among you such a long time? Anyone who has seen me has seen the Father. How can you say, 'Show us the Father'? Don't you believe that I am in the Father, and that the Father is in me? The words I say to you I do not speak on my own authority. Rather, it is the Father, living in me, who is doing his work. Believe me when I say that I am in the Father and the Father is in me; or at least believe on the evidence of the works themselves. (John 14:9-11)

Unfortunately, we will never achieve this level of unity in our trinity. Phil, our flesh is unregenerate due to the fall and will never reconcile.

The Father - Soul/Mind

*"...but let the one who boasts boast of this, that he understands and knows Me, that I am the L*ORD *who exercises <u>mercy</u>, <u>justice</u>, and <u>righteousness</u> on the earth; for I delight in these things," declares the L*ORD*." (Jeremiah 9:24)*

A Father

"The Lord is like a father to his children, tender and compassionate to those who fear him" (Psalm 103:13)
For God so loved the world that he gave his one and only Son, that whoever believes in him shall not perish but have eternal life. (John 3:16)
Jesus answered and said unto him, He who loves me will keep my words, and my Father will love him, and we will come unto him and dwell with him. (John 14:23 Jubilee Bible 2000)
Look at the birds of the air, that they do not sow, nor reap nor gather into barns, and yet your heavenly Father feeds them. Are you not worth much more than they? (Matthew 6:26 LSB)

Jesus contrasted the spiritual leaders as having a different father. Not the same father as Abraham,
Jesus said to them, "If God were your Father, you would love me, for I have come here from God. I have not come on my own; God sent

me. Why is my language not clear to you? Because you are unable to hear what I say. You belong to your father, the devil, and you want to carry out your father's desires. He was a murderer from the beginning, not holding to the truth, for there is no truth in him. When he lies, he speaks his native language, for he is a liar and the father of lies. (John 8:42-44)

The Judge

You have feared the sword, and I will bring the sword upon you, declares the Lord God. And I will bring you out of the midst of it, and give you into the hands of foreigners, and execute judgments upon you. You shall fall by the sword. I will judge you at the border of Israel, and you shall know that I am the Lord. This city shall not be your cauldron, nor shall you be the meat in the midst of it. I will judge you at the border of Israel, and you shall know that I am the Lord. For you have not walked in my statutes, nor obeyed my rules, but have acted according to the rules of the nations that are around you (Ezekiel 11:8-12 ESV)

"I looked for someone among them who would build up the wall and stand before me in the gap on behalf of the land so I would not have to destroy it, but I found no one. So I will pour out my wrath on them and consume them with my fiery anger, bringing down on their own heads all they have done, declares the Sovereign LORD." (Ezekiel 22:30-31) Let God arise, let his enemies be scattered: let them also that hate him flee before him. (Psalm 68:1 KJV)

Forgiving

He is a loving Father. But, He is also just and must judge according to the law. This is where God, in His infinite wisdom displays the balance between justice and mercy.

He saw that there was no one, he was appalled that there was no one to intervene; so his own arm achieved salvation for him, and his own righteousness sustained him. (Isaiah 59:16)

If we confess our sins, he is faithful and just to forgive us our sins, and to cleanse us from all unrighteousness. (1 John 1:9 AKJV)

"The Redeemer will come to Zion, to those in Jacob who repent of their sins," declares the LORD. (v20)

Jesus fulfilled that redemption at the cross.

Giving

Is there anyone among you who, if his son asks for bread, will give him a stone? Or if he asks for a fish, will give him a snake? If you then, although you are evil, know how to give good gifts to your children, how much more will your Father in heaven give good gifts to those who ask him! In everything, treat others as you would want them to treat you, for this fulfills the law and the prophets. (Matthew 7:9-12 NET)

Fear not, little flock; for it is your Father's good pleasure to give you the kingdom. (Luke 12:32 AKJV)

Covenant Maker

God made covenants with Adam and Eve, Noah, Abraham, Moses and Israel, King David, and the Better Covenant with all who believe and confess Jesus as Lord.

The Holy Spirit - Comforter, Teacher

"For this reason I kneel before the Father, from whom every family in heaven and on earth derives its name. I pray that out of his glorious riches he may strengthen you with **power through his Spirit in your inner being***, so that Christ may dwell in your hearts through faith. (Ephesians 3:14-17)*

Could the Spirit of God seem so mysterious because we are so unfamiliar with the concept of a spiritual realm?

The Oxford Dictionary defines mystery as "something that is difficult or impossible to understand or explain". When explaining the new birth to Nicodemus Jesus compared the Spirit to the wind. *The wind blows wherever it pleases. You hear its sound, but you cannot tell where it comes from or where it is going. So it is with everyone born of the Spirit. (John 3:8)*

The word used here is pneuma which can be translated as spirit, Spirit, or wind. In this context, He could have been inferring Ezekiel's dry bones vision *(Ezekiel 37:1-14)* where the wind blows across a valley of dry bones and brings them to life. Just as we can see the effects of the wind but don't understand everything about it we might not completely comprehend how the Holy Spirit works but we can see the results and effects of those workings. *(John 3:5-8)*

The Holy Spirit has been given to us as an advocate.
And I will ask the Father, and he will give you another Advocate, who will never leave you. (John 14:16 NLT)
But when the Father sends the Advocate as my representative—that is, the Holy Spirit—he will teach you everything and will remind you of everything I have told you (John 14:26 NLT)
He is all that and more. Much, much more.
The Holy Spirit searches our hearts *(Romans 8:27)*
Speaks mysteries *(1 Corinthians 14:2)*
He knows the heart and mind of God *(1 Corinthians 2:11)*
He is the part of God that communes with our spirit. He is the voice that intercedes for us when we don't know how to pray.
(Romans 8:26-27)
It is His voice that gives us our guidance.

Before Jesus ascended He said *"I have much more to tell you <u>but you cannot bear it now</u>. Yet when that one I have spoken to you about comes—the Spirit of truth—he will guide you into everything that is true. (John 16:12 J.B.Phillips New Testament)*
The Contemporary English Version says *"but right now it would be more than you could understand."*
Jesus had information He wanted to share with His disciples but they

wouldn't be able to comprehend it. Their spirits were not yet awakened via New Birth. They could only receive His information through their flesh and process it in their soul. They needed the Spirit of God to interact with their spirit to communicate to their minds. Affirming the written Word.

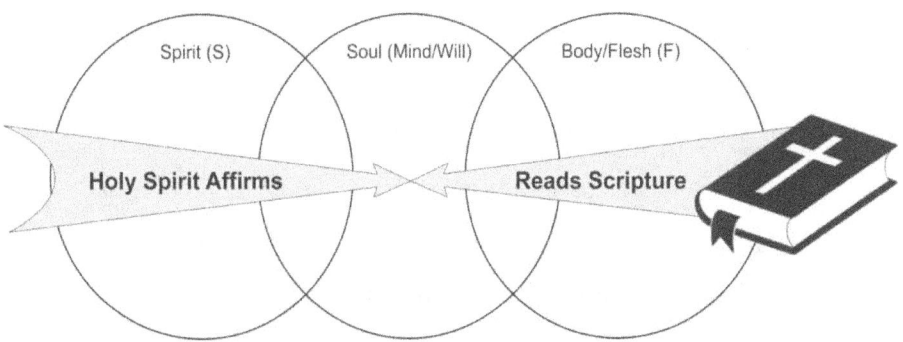

But the Comforter, which is the Holy Ghost, whom the Father will send in my name, he shall teach you all things, and bring all things to your remembrance, whatsoever I have said unto you.
(John 14:26 KJV)

"You Shall Receive Power"

I recently read "The Road to Ground Zero: Finding God's Will" by Fred Bishop. This is an excellent read and pertinent to anyone in, or hoping to enter effective ministry for Christ.

> The answer had arrived! It was not in intellect, not in education, it was in the message of Jesus Christ. He said,

"Tarry in Jerusalem until the Holy Ghost comes upon you" *(see Luke 24:44)*. Pentecost had come for me, and my life would never be the same.

When I got home I could not wait to relay to Jan what had happened to me. Excitedly I began spinning the tale and, as I am prone to do, soon got sidetracked by telling long stories and beating around the bush. She finally tired of waiting on me and said, "Fred, did you get baptized in the Holy Spirit or not?" The answer was an emphatic, "Yes!" "For two years I have been praying that Fred would experience the victory in his life that I had since receiving the baptism of the Spirit in Fort Worth. When Fred finally received the Spirit for himself his whole outlook on the ministry changed overnight. He started letting God lead him, rather than hoping God would fit into all his ideas and programs. I think the experience answered a lot of questions he had, and for the first time in his life he was ready for effective ministry." - Jan Bishop.

Something had happened to me that summer of 1972, in a life-changing sense.

(The Road to Ground Zero: Finding God's Will" by Fred Bishop - Page 33)

But ye shall receive power, after that the Holy Ghost is come upon you: and ye shall be witnesses unto me both in Jerusalem, and in all

Judaea, and in Samaria, and unto the uttermost part of the earth. (Acts 1:8 KJV)

Every letter Paul wrote was addressed to a certain finite group or church - *"to all in Rome"*, *"to the churches in Galatia"*, *"to God's holy people in Ephesus"*, and even 2 Corinthians is addressed to *"the Church of God in Corinth"*. All of Paul's letters except one.

Unto the church of God which is at Corinth, to them that are sanctified in Christ Jesus, called to be saints, with all that in every place call upon the name of Jesus Christ our Lord, both their's and our's: (1 Corinthians 1:2 KJV)

This is the letter that specifically speaks of spiritual gifts such as prophecy, miracles, healing, tongues, and interpretation of tongues. Supernatural manifestations of the Holy Spirit's power through committed believers. *" all that in every place call upon the name of Jesus Christ our Lord"*

In recent history, many theologians have determined that the supernatural workings of the Holy Spirit are not for today based on one section of Scripture from 1 Corinthians.

Charity never faileth: but whether there be prophecies, they shall fail; whether there be tongues, they shall cease; whether there be knowledge, it shall vanish away. For we know in part, and we prophesy in part. But when that which is perfect is come, then that which is in part shall be done away. (1 Corinthians 13:8-10)

They say that which is perfect has come referring to the canon of scripture we call the Bible.

They have been telling us that since the completion of the Old and New Testament tongues, knowledge, and prophecy are no longer relevant.

Just as the act of baptism has been reduced to a ceremony of infant baptism where the child is incapable of faith or as a public statement of receiving Christ as Savior but lacking emphasis on death to the flesh and resurrection in Christ as Lord. So, the power of the Holy Spirit in our daily lives has been reduced to the level of our conscience.

If you are sanctified in Christ Jesus and call upon the name of Jesus Christ our Lord then you are qualified for the supernatural power of the Holy Spirit to work through you.

A Spiritual Cornucopia

Have you noticed that the more time you spend with someone, the more you will tend to pick up their behavior? The Holy Spirit produces behavior traits that are representative of Jesus. Wisdom, Understanding, Counsel, Fortitude, and Knowledge, are all essences of the Holy Spirit. They are His aroma. An aroma of life to life. He is in us and our spirit is placed in Him.

To the one we are the savour of death unto death; and to the other the savour of life unto life. And who is sufficient for these things?
(2 Corinthians 2:16 KJV)

Love, Joy, Peace, etc. are traits of the Holy Spirit's personality. The apostle Paul referred to these as the fruit of the Spirit. *"The fruit of the Spirit is **love, joy, peace, patience, kindness, goodness, faithfulness, gentleness, and self-control**" (Galatians 5:22-23, NLT)*

The results of how I treat someone can be referred to as the fruit of my actions. The words I speak as the fruit of my mouth. In this sense, we are called to be a veritable cornucopia of spiritual food to a spiritually starving world.

And Jesus said unto them, I am the bread of life: he that cometh to me shall never hunger; and he that believeth on me shall never thirst. (John 6:35 KJV)

For I was an hungred, and ye gave me meat: I was thirsty, and ye gave me drink: I was a stranger, and ye took me in: Naked, and ye clothed me: I was sick, and ye visited me: I was in prison, and ye came unto me. Then shall the righteous answer him, saying, Lord, when saw we thee an hungred, and fed thee? Or thirsty, and gave thee drink? When saw we thee a stranger, and took thee in? or naked, and clothed thee? Or when saw we thee sick or in prison, and came unto thee? And the King shall answer and say unto them, Verily I say unto you, Inasmuch as ye have done it unto one of the least of these my brethren, ye have done it unto me. (Matthew 25:35-40 KJV)

And if thou draw out thy soul to the hungry, and satisfy the afflicted soul; then shall thy light rise in obscurity, and thy darkness be as the noon day: (Isaiah 58:10 KJV)

FIRST ROOTS: 89

- DOMINANT SPHERE 89
- FRUIT 92
- ALL THAT IS IN THE WORLD 95
- WHO WEARS THE CROWN? 97
  - *Heaven or Hell?* 97
  - *This Product Kills 99.9% Bacteria* 99

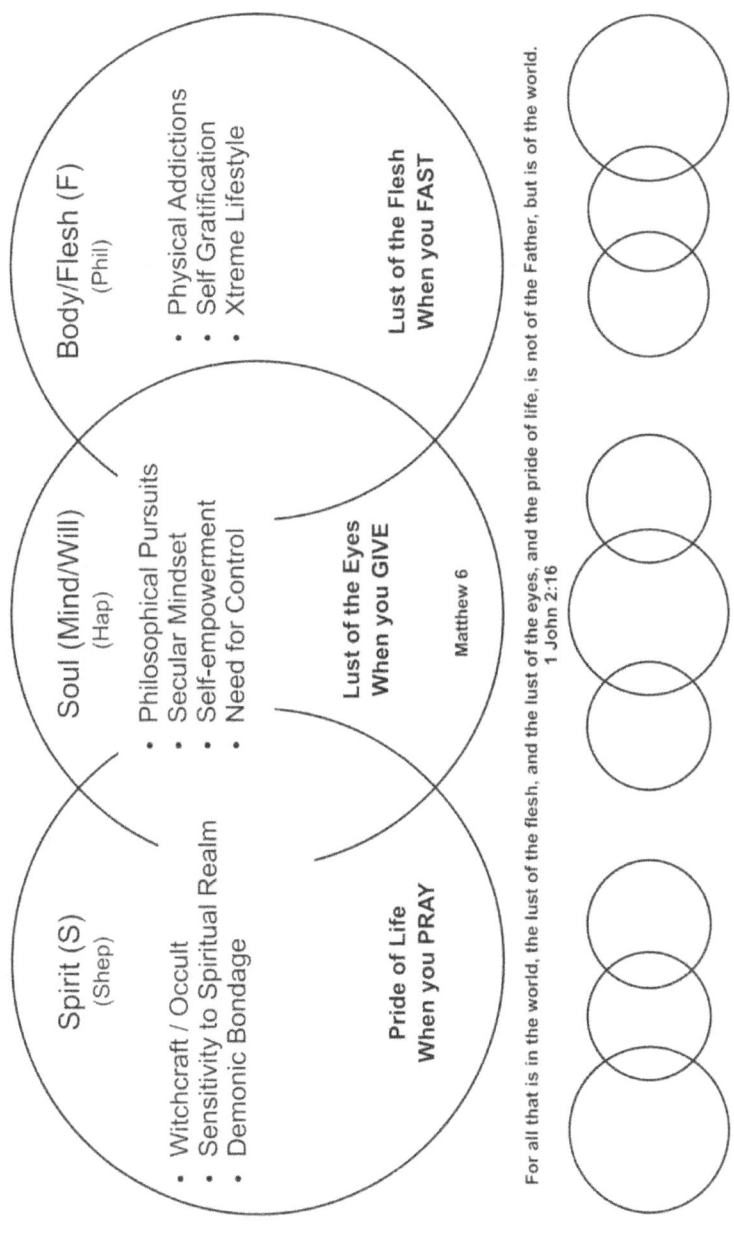

First Roots

Dominant Sphere

Just as we exist as three different personalities in three different realms - spirit, soul, and flesh many people seem to have a "Dominant Sphere". I believe some people tend to be more dominant in their spirit. Others might have a more dominant soul. While still, others are more dominant in the realm of the flesh. That's just natural. Everyone is a unique creature. So it would not be unusual for someone to have an inherent tendency towards one realm or another. This could explain how some people are drawn to certain areas of study and possible extremes.

Here we form patterns according to our environment, upbringing, and sphere tendency to best control our life. Before "New Birth" the spirit is dormant or weak. It is like an unplanted seed. Just as you can distinguish a kernel of corn from a bean by its external attributes even though it has not been planted and the life inside activated; so, the human spirit carries the characteristics of the Spirit of God. They are inherent. But the spirit is weak due to the fall.

One who is spirit-dominant will tend to be drawn toward mysticism, cults, and demonic influence They are drawn to the spirit realm. Just as the flesh borders on the physical realm and is influenced by that realm.

A flesh-dominant would tend to develop addictions or become immersed in self-gratification. Even if not physically capable, they might be drawn to sports as an interest. When I say not capable, I mean you might be enthused with football. Not having the necessary physique to play yourself you find an interest in football statistics and are one of those fans who shaves his head weirdly and paints his face. You would be very avid about sports. This would be a "high place" for you. A strong point of interest.

A soul-dominant person? A "soul man" would be more into philosophy or intellectual pursuits to an excess. Also seeking justice would rank high on the scale. Seeing things with no gray zone, black and white, but defining a personal threshold of black versus white according to your judgment.
"every man did that which was right in his own eyes."
(Judges 21:25 KJV)

The soul would tend to seek a sense of justice, righteousness, et cetera because even in the fallen state it is going to reflect the attributes of God the Father. How this person expresses these aspirations will have a lot to do with upbringing and individual personality.
Unless he is raised in a scriptural context this "Soul Man" will base his behavior solely on input from the world system. Even with a church upbringing, he might twist those "Biblical" truths to fit a personal agenda or vendetta. This is how a hitman for the mafia could kill someone in cold blood yet cherish his family.

In our Western mindset, many tend to compartmentalize their lives into secular and spiritual. Actually, secular and religious since our thinking has been pushed so far away from belief in the supernatural. The supernatural is fine for movies but not for real life. Beyond that, the Golden Rule is just a societal more. Relative to personal conviction and immediate circumstance. "Instant Karma".

I have a former friend who was an avid church-goer. He professed Christianity. But, would lie and cheat on business deals. His defense? "Church is church. Business is business." This tendency to lean toward dominant spheres is not necessarily bad. It is, in fact, definitive of a person's uniqueness and calling. I am merely pointing toward the potential for extremes and susceptibility to misdirection and bondage.

TREE OF KNOWLEDGE: Evil Works

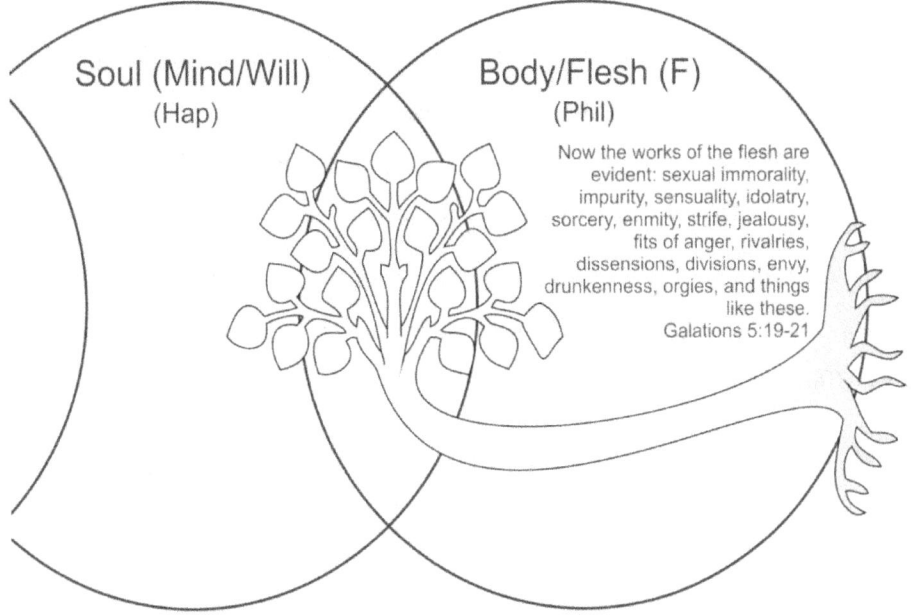

Soul (Mind/Will) (Hap)

Body/Flesh (F) (Phil)

Now the works of the flesh are evident: sexual immorality, impurity, sensuality, idolatry, sorcery, enmity, strife, jealousy, fits of anger, rivalries, dissensions, divisions, envy, drunkenness, orgies, and things like these.
Galations 5:19-21

Train up a child in the way he should go: and when he is old, he will not depart from it. (Proverbs 22:6 KJV)

Fruit

We talked about this earlier. About the world system of thought introduced and developed by the god of this world. Results from decisions made and acted on based on values taught by the world system could be considered fruit.

They will eat the fruit of their ways and be filled with the fruit of their schemes. (Proverbs 1:31)

The backslider in heart will be filled with the fruit of his ways, and a good man will be filled with the fruit of his ways. (Proverbs 14:14)

As the soul continues its interaction with the physical realm through the flesh and the senses you could say it becomes rooted in the world system producing a "Tree of the Knowledge of Good and Evil". This is the tree Adam and Eve were forbidden to eat from. This is the tree the serpent seduced Eve with by promising her *"You will not certainly die. For God knows that when you eat from it your eyes will be opened, and you will be like God, knowing good and evil." (Genesis 3:4-5)*

For all that is in the world, the lust of the flesh, and the lust of the eyes, and the pride of life, is not of the Father, but is of the world. (1 John 2:16)

The lust of the flesh would be of the physical realm. The pride of life in the spiritual realm. The lust of the eyes the soulish realm. They are not necessarily exclusive to one realm. As our personalities interact, their behaviors may become homogenized, and difficult to distinguish or identify one from another.

EXAMPLE: Pornography. As the flesh indulges visually on graphic images the soul joins in through fantasy compounding the snare of seduction, setting up behavioral patterns that are difficult to break. This would be a variant of covetousness. Illegitimate desire.

Thou shalt not covet thy neighbour's house, thou shalt not covet <u>thy neighbour's wife,</u> nor his manservant, nor his maidservant, nor his ox, nor his ass, nor any thing that is thy neighbour's.
(Exodus 20:17 KJV)
And it came to pass in an eveningtide, that David arose from off his bed, and walked upon the roof of the king's house: and from the roof he saw a woman washing herself; and the woman was very beautiful to look upon. And David sent and enquired after the woman. And one said, Is not this Bathsheba, the daughter of Eliam, the wife of Uriah the Hittite? And David sent messengers, and took her; and she came in unto him, and he lay with her; for she was purified from her uncleanness: and she returned unto her house. (2 Samuel 11:2-4 KJV) But every man is tempted, when he is drawn away of his own lust, and enticed. Then when lust hath conceived, it bringeth forth sin: and sin, when it is finished, bringeth forth death.
(James 1:14-15 KJV)
For out of the heart proceed evil thoughts, murders, adulteries, fornications, thefts, false witness, blasphemies:(Matthew 15:19 KJV)

FIRST ROOTS: All That is in the World

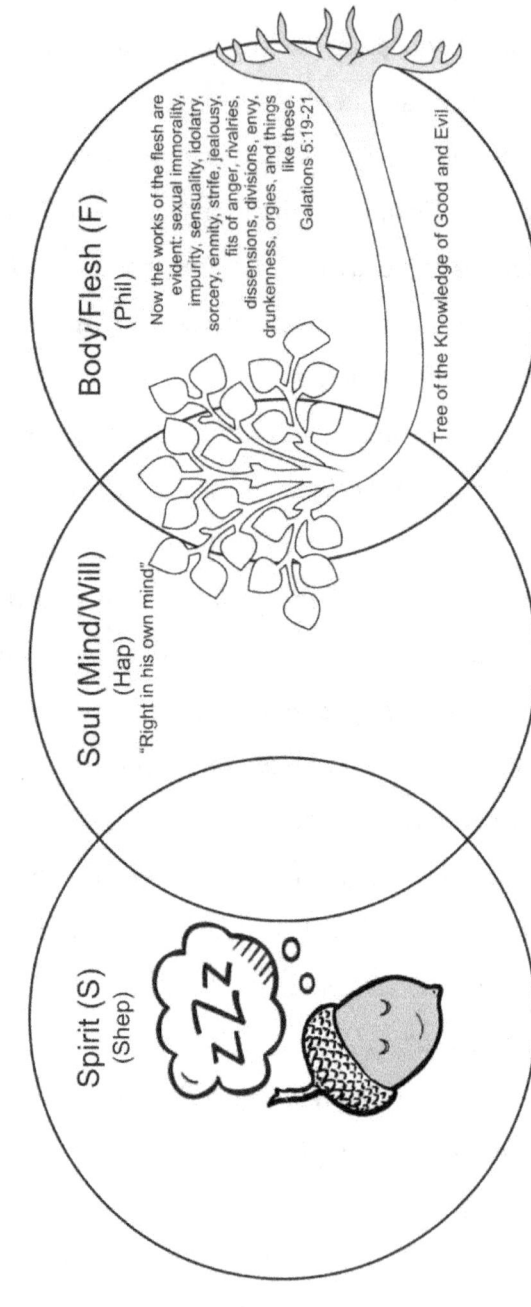

For all that is in the world, the lust of the flesh, and the lust of the eyes, and the pride of life, is not of the Father, but is of the world.
1 John 2:16

All That is in the World

Both Eve and Jesus were tempted in each of these three areas.
*When the woman saw that the fruit of the tree was **good for food*** [lust of the flesh] *and **pleasing to the eye*** [lust of the eyes], *and also **desirable for gaining wisdom*** [pride of life], *she took some and ate it. (Genesis 3:6)*

*After fasting forty days and forty nights, **he was hungry**. "If you are the Son of God, tell these stones to become **bread**." (v2-3)* [lust of the flesh]
Then the devil took him to the holy city and had him stand on the highest point of the temple. **"If you are the Son of God,"** *he said, "throw yourself down. For it is written:" 'He will command his angels concerning you, and they will lift you up in their hands, so that you will not strike your foot against a stone.' (v5-6)* [pride of life]
*Again, the devil took him to a very high mountain and **showed him all the kingdoms of the world and their splendor**. "All this I will give you," he said, "if you will bow down and worship me." (v8-9) (Matthew 4:1-11)* [lust of the eyes]

The human spirit would have an inherent understanding of the spiritual attributes, and nature of the Spirit of God. But again, it's dormant like an unplanted seed. So it has the characteristics of the Spirit of God but no valid, active input. Due to our secularized Western thinking, we tend to place the voice of our spirit as a part of our soul. Eliminating the concept of our having a spiritual dimension.

Let's take a look at some of the fruits of this "Tree of the Knowledge of Good and Evil.

Now the works of the flesh are evident sexual immorality, impurity, sensuality, idolatry, sorcery, enmity, strife, jealousy, fits of anger, rivalries, dissensions, divisions, envy, drunkenness, orgies and things like these. (Galatians 5:19-21)

This is the end point of indulging in the fruit of the world system. We might have the greatest motives for what we do for others. But, regardless of what those motives may be - "I want to do right? I want to be righteous. I want to change the world. I want to help people. I want to make the world a better place." it is all self-initiated and therefore self-indulgent.

In the fallen state, even the highest goals will still end up being self-indulgent because they are self-determined and self-motivated and end up self-gratifying. "Look how good I am. Look at what I did. I helped people. I'm a good person."

All that we can do in our own will is satisfy our flesh, gratify our eyes, or nurture our pride. We are determining our path to righteousness. Self-determining our rightness with God, with the world, and with ourselves.

All we like sheep have gone astray; we have turned every one to his own way; (Isaiah 53:6 KJV)

We end up in a self-seeking and selfish means to an end. Our best is like filthy rags.

But we are all as an unclean thing, and **all our righteousnesses are as filthy rags** *(Isaiah 64:6)*

But whatever were gains to me I now consider loss for the sake of Christ. What is more, I consider everything a loss because of the surpassing worth of knowing Christ Jesus my Lord, for whose sake I have lost all things. ***I consider them garbage****, that I may gain Christ and be found in him, not having a righteousness of my own that comes from the law, but that which is through faith in Christ (Philippians 3:7-9)*

Who Wears the Crown?

Heaven or Hell?

You can define hell however you want.

God created man to be in fellowship with him. Man defaulted and, as the serpent suggested, became like God.

For God knows that when you eat of it your eyes will be opened, and you will be like God, knowing good and evil." (Genesis 3:5)

Man *"ate of the fruit"* and became his own god. This choice put him on a path of eternity separate from God's purpose making him responsible for his own eternity.

Adam and Eve had a choice between two trees and which fruit they would eat. The Tree of Life or the Tree of the Knowledge of Good and Evil.

We have the same choice. At some point in every person's life, we become accountable for the decisions we make to be our god. To eat from the Tree of Life (rooted in the Spirit of God) or the Tree of the Knowledge of Good and Evil (rooted in the wisdom of this world and authored by the God of this world - Satan).

Hell is separation from the very attributes of God that we inherently seek - faith, hope, love, and more. Imagine the loneliest, most hopeless feeling you have experienced lasting for eternity. This is just a taste of separation from God. God is just, but He is also merciful and loving so He made provision to restore man to Himself by sending Jesus to live a life without rebellion or sin and take the punishment of separation from God and restore relationship.

But, we have to give up our "godhood" and accept Jesus not only as our Savior and restorer but, also as our Lord.

As I stated in the introduction, salvation is not going up to the altar after a call to "avoid hell" and, then living your life however you please.

The Greek word used most often in the New Testament for "faith" is pistis. It indicates a belief or conviction with the complementary idea of trust. Faith is not a mere intellectual stance, but a belief that leads to action. *"For as the body without the spirit is dead, so faith without works is dead also." (James 2:26 KJV)*

The choice is ours. Eternity with God or without.

This Product Kills 99.9% Bacteria

Unless our spirit is empowered by the Holy Spirit it will be ruled or overruled by our soul rooted in the world's system of thought which is antithetical to the Spirit of God and the law and rule of God.

"Beware lest any man spoil you through philosophy and vain deceit, after the tradition of men, after the rudiments of the world, and not after Christ." (Colossians 2:8 KJV)

So although someone may think what they are doing is good, they are righting wrongs, they are seeking justice, and even feeding the homeless. Unless it is motivated by the Spirit of God it has been approached on their terms and is still self-indulgent. It will fall short of the mark. Our very best will not achieve 100%

The sin of Sodom and Gomorrah was not just sexual perversity.
"Now this was the sin of your sister Sodom: She and her daughters were arrogant, overfed, and unconcerned; they did not help the poor and needy. They were haughty and did detestable things before me. Therefore I did away with them as you have seen." (Ezekiel 16:49-50)

Sodom and Gomorrah self-served. They spent it on themselves. This turned into an inward spiral that led to narcissism, self-conceit, self-indulgence, and ultimately to debauchery and the works of the flesh. This is the ultimate fruit of all self-indulgence regardless of motive. I say inward spiral because the roots of this tree draw its perceived truth from the world. It then produces a deceptive fruit upon which we feed. We respond, in turn, producing the fruit of our lips and of "our own way". Poison in - poison out. We are recycling poison. Fruit from the Tree of the Knowledge of Good and Evil, basing our behavior on the premise that we can determine good, placing us in the position of God.

However, there is hope. Because that spirit, that dormant spirit, that seed although fallen carries the characteristics of the Spirit of God with great potential and through New Birth can be activated and made alive.

Blessed is the one who does not walk in step with the wicked or stand in the way that sinners take or sit in the company of mockers, but whose delight is in the law of the LORD, and who meditates on his law day and night. That person is like a tree planted by streams of water, which yields its fruit in season and whose leaf does not wither— whatever they do prospers. (Psalm 1:1-3)

Our spirit becomes rooted in the Spirit of God like a tree planted.

LIKE A TREE PLANTED: 105

UNLESS A SEED DIES 105

   Acorn - Oak 105

   Tempera'MENTAL 106

   Breaking the Yoke 108

   Awake 111

BAPTIZED: Alive in Christ

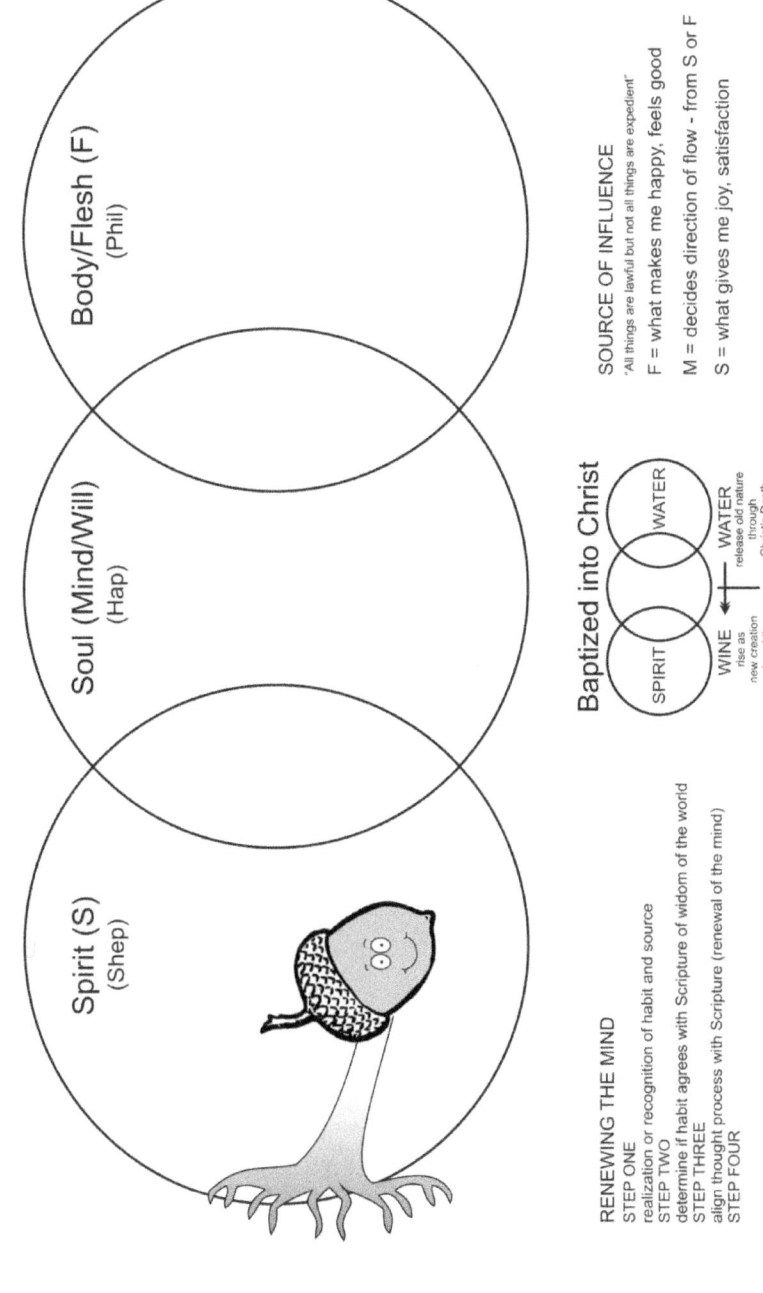

SOURCE OF INFLUENCE
"All things are lawful but not all things are expedient"
F = what makes me happy, feels good
M = decides direction of flow - from S or F
S = what gives me joy, satisfaction

Baptized into Christ

WATER
release old nature through
Christ's Death

WINE
rise as new creation in spirit

RENEWING THE MIND
STEP ONE
realization or recognition of habit and source
STEP TWO
determine if habit agrees with Scripture of widom of the world
STEP THREE
align thought process with Scripture (renewal of the mind)
STEP FOUR

Like a Tree Planted

Unless a Seed Dies

"Verily, verily, I say unto you, Except a corn of wheat fall into the ground and die, it abideth alone: but if it die, it bringeth forth much fruit." (John 12:24 KJV)

Acorn - Oak

I'm not sure how much time I spent researching this. It was the 70's and there was no internet that I knew of. No Google or YouTube to look things up. I had a Strong's Exhaustive Concordance of the Bible, Unger's Bible Dictionary, a Christian book store over in St. Louis, and my Bible. Oh, and the local library. I spent time researching what happens to an acorn when it becomes an oak tree. Does the shell just fall apart and become nothing? I wanted to experience a similar experience to that of an acorn. I wanted to "be like Christ". To be transformed into his image. To become an oak tree.

But, what would happen to me? Would I still have my personality? Would I become one of those hell, fire, and damnation-shouting preachers that always made me nervous? I used to cross the street to avoid them. And, I was a Christian. I studied. I read. I prayed. I pondered.

One day I had an epiphany. The acorn is only the potential state of an oak tree. What happens to the acorn is a moot point because the acorn is just an immature oak. It is only a container. A shell filled with oak tree potential.

Tempera'MENTAL"

I have always enjoyed who I am. I didn't like some of my behaviors and attitudes. But, my sense of humor is my favorite sense of humor. With my brother, Dale's running a close second. I had weaknesses. But, I also had many strengths. As an older teen, I had been presented with a personality test based on a study of four temperaments. The study came from a book by Tim LaHaye titled "The Spirit-Controlled Temperament" based on a teaching promoted by Hippocrates (c.460-c. 370 BC) and coined by the Greek physician Aelius Galenu. Hippocrates believed that certain human moods, emotions, and behaviors were caused by an excess or lack of body fluids (called "humours"), which he classified as blood, yellow bile, black bile, and phlegm. Hence the names. Each of which was responsible for different patterns in personalities, (Wikipedia)

Although the physical science was not correct the four personality types: sanguine, choleric, melancholic, and phlegmatic are still used today. We determined that I was Choleric and Sanguine. My Sanguine strengths were Sociable, Charismatic, and Optimistic. My Choleric strengths were Ambitious, Passionate, and Efficient. Not bad, eh? Unfortunately, I had weaknesses.

Impulsive, Shameless, Exaggerator, Aggressive, Impatient, and Argumentative. Hmmm.

Not good, eh?

You could almost place these in opposition to each other. Efficient v Impatient. Passionate v Argumentative. Ambitious v Aggressive. Optimistic v Impulsive. Charismatic v Shameless. Sociable v Exaggerator.

I used to tell people I didn't care if I led the parade, watched the parade, or marched in the parade. I wanted a good parade. If someone wasn't doing their part and the parade was failing I would be right in there upstaging and pushing them out of the way.

I once attended a large conference with a group of friends. The meeting had a set starting time and there were several other events that we also wanted to visit. Five minutes. Ten minutes. Almost twenty minutes had gone by from the start time. People were milling around talking, laughing. The event was nowhere near being called to order. It was time for this parade to start.

I walked up to the microphone and asked everyone to please begin moving toward their seats. We were about to begin. This was easy for me. I had been fronting bands and making announcements to large groups for years. As I continued speaking and calling the meeting to order a person I didn't know was motioning me to please come over to the side of the stage. This was his meeting. What did I think I was doing? I handed him the mic and said, "If this is your meeting you are doing a lousy job of running it." - Efficient v Impatient.

Yes. I needed my temperaments to be Spirit-controlled. I needed God to turn my weaknesses into strengths.

But, if I truly committed to Christ. If I was to die to myself and live as Christ what would happen to me? This may sound absurd. But, it was a real concern.

But you will receive power when the Holy Spirit comes on you; and you will be my witnesses in Jerusalem, and in all Judea and Samaria, and to the ends of the earth." (Acts 1:8 NIV)

Finally, my brethren, be strong in the Lord, and in the power of his might. (Ephesians 6:10 KJV)

The Lord is my strength and my shield; my heart trusted in him, and I am helped: therefore my heart greatly rejoiceth; and with my song will I praise him. The Lord is their strength, and he is the saving strength of his anointed. (Psalms 28:7-8 KJV)

Breaking the Yoke

Hold out your hand and extend your fingers down. Imagine these are extensions of your personality. If you turn your hand upward you will see the same profile except in a different posture. These are the same extensions of your hand only in a different direction. Are we focusing on the world or the spirit? Directing ourselves to the world will manifest in weakness while focusing on the Spirit of God will manifest our strengths.

You then, my child, be strengthened by the grace that is in Christ Jesus, (2 Timothy 2:1 ESV)

I heard so many stories growing up from evangelists who had "destroyed" their lives and returned. Many teachings were going around saying that our souls needed to be crushed so that God could use us. Why do we need to come to the end of ourselves to be used by God? I am currently working on a book dealing with this entitled "If-Then: The Pursuit of Our Heart".

Except a corn of wheat fall into the ground and die, it abideth alone: but if it die, it bringeth forth much fruit." (John 12:24 KJV)
We don't crush wheat or corn or mustard seeds when we plant. We place them in good soil with plenty of necessary nutrients. We water them and carefully remove any weeds that spring up.
He also that received seed among the thorns is he that heareth the word; and the care of this world, and the deceitfulness of riches, choke the word, and he becometh unfruitful. But he that received seed into the good ground is he that heareth the word, and understandeth it; which also beareth fruit, and bringeth forth, some an hundredfold, some sixty, some thirty. (Matthew 13:22-23 KJV)

And it shall come to pass in that day, that his burden shall be taken away from off thy shoulder, and his yoke from off thy neck, and the yoke shall be destroyed because of the anointing. (Isaiah 10:27 KJV)
The first time this verse became noticeable to me was while reading a book. The anointing in this particular case was described and compared to the oil flowing down from Aaron's beard upon his being anointed as a priest.
And he poured of the anointing oil upon Aaron's head, and anointed him, to sanctify him. (Leviticus 8:12 KJV)

It was a beautiful narrative comparing the power of the Holy Spirit bringing an anointing to a believer. I was preparing to teach about the power of the Holy Spirit and planned to use this concept as one of my main points. Something didn't settle right. So, I pulled out my Strong's Concordance. Hmm - the word translated as anointing here means fatness or grossness.

> (27) The yoke shall be destroyed because of the anointing . . .—The English, as it stands, is scarcely intelligible, but suggests the idea that the "anointing" was that which marked out the kings and priests of Judah as a consecrated people, and the remembrance of which would lead Jehovah to liberate them from bondage. Most commentators, however, render **"by reason of the fat," the implied figure being that of a bullock which grows so fat that the yoke will no longer go round his neck**, as the symbol of a people waxing strong and asserting its freedom. Comp. "Jeshurun waxed fat and kicked" (Deuteronomy 32:15).
> Ellicott's Commentary for English Readers

When the seed is placed in a proper environment the life inside is activated and begins to grow. As the life inside grows it becomes too large or "fat" for the shell to contain and bursts through the seed coat.

Although we have been created in the image of God as a triune being, due to the fall, our spirit is dormant. It is like a seed waiting to be planted. It contains the basic nature or characteristics of the Holy Spirit but has no real voice. We pretty much relegate our spirit to the level of a conscience. A small weak voice buried behind the cacophony of voices coming from the world.

Awake

Upon New Birth, the "seed" of our spirit is placed in the Spirit of God, and life is activated.

BAPTIZED - TREE OF LIFE: 113

- SPIRITUAL HUNGER 113
- THE TREE OF LIFE - NEW BIRTH 114
    - Water - Bread - Wine 114
    - Jesus the Word - The Spring of Living Water, The Bread of Life 114
    - Bread and Wine 115
    - Battle of the Leavens 116
    - Water/Wine 118
    - New Wine in New Wineskins 119
    - Flesh - No   Spirit - Yes 120
    - The Baptism of Jesus 121
    - To Fulfill All Righteousness 122
    - A Re-examination of Baptism 124
    - John's Baptism 134
    - Jesus' Baptism 135
- PLUCK OUT PHIL'S EYE? 136

Baptized - Tree of Life

Spiritual Hunger

We go through life trying to fill a void - glutting food, pursuing wealth, seeking knowledge, and moving from one relationship to another. Hoping to satisfy a deep-seated need. A deep craving. A hunger that just never seems to be satisfied.

A thirst that can never be quenched. A hunger deeper than our mind. A hunger that often leads to excess and extremism in an attempt to fill that void. It is a hunger that goes deep. Beyond our flesh. It is a hunger in our spirit.

We are trying to feed a withered, malnourished spirit. There is not enough nourishment in the entire world to truly satisfy that spiritual hunger. Even, the greatest dictators were not able to satisfy that hunger - always seeking more - power, glory, wealth, and indulgence.

We have an inherent need to fulfill, to satisfy God's law which, despite the fall, is embedded in our souls. Fulfillment of this law is unattainable in our fallen state. We hunger - we thirst for that feeling of rightness and oneness with God. Our souls cry out for a relationship with our creator.

There is only one thing that can truly satisfy this hunger.
"Come, all you who are thirsty, come to the waters; and you who have no money, come, buy and eat! Come, buy wine and milk without money

and without cost. Why spend money on what is not bread, and your labor on what does not satisfy? Listen, listen to me, and eat what is good, and you will delight in the richest of fare." (Isaiah 55:1-2)

The Tree of Life - NEW BIRTH

Water - Bread - Wine

Interestingly, Jesus' first recorded miracle was to change water to wine.

The Bible tells us that the earth was formed from water.
For they deliberately overlook this fact, that the heavens existed long ago, and the earth was formed out of water and through water by the word of God, (2 Peter 3:5)
Jesus told Nicodemus "no one can enter the kingdom unless he is born of water and of the Spirit (John 3:5)

Wine is often used in context with the Spirit of God. You could say that Jesus' first miracle was a foretaste of His purpose. To open up the ministry of the Holy Spirit through His redemptive act on the cross. To introduce the mystery of New Birth. Transforming those born of water into those born of the Spirit. From water to wine.

Jesus the Word - The Spring of Living Water, The Bread of Life
Jesus answered her, "If you knew the gift of God, and who it is that is saying to you, 'Give me a drink,' you would have asked him, and he would have given you living water." The woman said to him, "Sir, you have nothing to draw water with, and the well is deep. Where do you

get that living water? Are you greater than our father Jacob? He gave us the well and drank from it himself, as did his sons and his livestock." Jesus said to her, "Everyone who drinks of this water will be thirsty again, but whoever drinks of the water that I will give him will never be thirsty again. The water that I will give him will become in him a spring of water welling up to eternal life." (John 4:10-14)

On the last and greatest day of the festival, Jesus stood and said in a loud voice, "Let anyone who is thirsty come to me and drink. Whoever believes in me, as Scripture has said, rivers of living water will flow from within them." By this he meant the Spirit, whom those who believed in him were later to receive. Up to that time the Spirit had not been given, since Jesus had not yet been glorified. (John 7:37-39)

Then Jesus declared, "I am the bread of life. Whoever comes to me will never go hungry, and whoever believes in me will never be thirsty. (John 6:35)

Bread and Wine

I have been looking at events in Jesus' life that parallel Biblical types such as comparing wisdom to honey *(Proverbs 24:13-14),* teachings with milk *(1 Corinthians 3:2),* or water, wine, milk, and bread (Isaiah 55:1-2). Also, rituals such as Jesus' entry into Jerusalem on a donkey *(Zechariah 9:9),* and the Passover.

Many of these instances are obvious and universally taught. Let's look at a few connected to His final Passover and Feast of Unleavened Bread. The Last Supper.

From His entry into Jerusalem on a donkey, to His crucifixion outside the city, to His resurrection, and more; there is great comparison to His being the sacrificial lamb. The "Passover Lamb".

Jesus also identified Himself with the meal itself "
Now as they were eating, Jesus took bread, and after blessing it broke it and gave it to the disciples, and said, "Take, eat; this is my body." And he took a cup, and when he had given thanks he gave it to them, saying, "Drink of it, all of you, for this is my blood of the covenant, which is poured out for many for the forgiveness of sins. (Matthew 26:26-28)
Paul emphasizes this to the Church at Corinth.
For I received from the Lord what I also passed on to you: The Lord Jesus, on the night he was betrayed, took bread, and when he had given thanks, he broke it and said, "This is my body, which is for you; do this in remembrance of me." In the same way, after supper he took the cup, saying, "This cup is the new covenant in my blood; do this, whenever you drink it, in remembrance of me." For whenever you eat this bread and drink this cup, you proclaim the Lord's death until he comes. (1 Corinthians 11:23-26)

Battle of the Leavens

The Passover meal was eaten on the first day of the Feast of Unleavened Bread.
Now And on the first day of Unleavened Bread, when they sacrificed the Passover lamb, his disciples said to him, "Where will you have us

go and prepare for you to eat the Passover?" (Mark 14:12 KJV)
The two holidays were (and still are) considered a single celebration. In preparation for the Feast of Unleavened Bread, the Jews were commanded to remove all leaven from their homes.

For seven days you are to eat bread made without yeast. On the first day remove the yeast from your houses, for whoever eats anything with yeast in it from the first day through the seventh must be cut off from Israel. (Exodus 12:15)

Jesus' influence was growing with His teaching spreading like leaven in bread.

The chief priests and the teachers of the law heard this and began looking for a way to kill him, for they feared him, because the whole crowd was amazed at his teaching. (Mark 11:18)

It was getting to the point where even some of the leaders were beginning to secretly follow Him.

Yet at the same time many even among the leaders believed in him. But because of the Pharisees they would not openly acknowledge their faith for fear they would be put out of the synagogue (John 12:42)

The leaven of Jesus' (the Manna from Heaven) Kingdom teaching was in direct conflict with the leaven of the Pharisees and the Sadducees.

Then Jesus said unto them, Take heed and beware of the leaven of the Pharisees and of the Sadducees. And they reasoned among themselves, saying, It is because we have taken no bread. Which when Jesus perceived, he said unto them, O ye of little faith, why reason ye among

yourselves, because ye have brought no bread? Do ye not yet understand, neither remember the five loaves of the five thousand, and how many baskets ye took up? Neither the seven loaves of the four thousand, and how many baskets ye took up? How is it that ye do not understand that I spake it not to you concerning bread, that ye should beware of the leaven of the Pharisees and of the Sadducees?
Then understood they how that he bade them not beware of the leaven of bread, but of the doctrine of the Pharisees and of the Sadducees. (Matthew 16:6-12)

Jesus was tempted but He was never influenced by the leaven of the world.

For we do not have a high priest who is unable to empathize with our weaknesses, but we have one who has been tempted in every way, just as we are—yet he did not sin. (Hebrews 4:15 KJV)

He is the Bread of Life.

Water/Wine

The first step in "New Birth" is a transition from "born of water" to "born of the Spirit" (water to wine)

Jesus answered him, "Truly, truly, I say to you, unless one is born again he cannot see the kingdom of God." Nicodemus said to him, "How can a man be born when he is old? Can he enter a second time into his mother's womb and be born?" Jesus answered, "Truly, truly, I say to you, unless one is born of water and the Spirit, he cannot enter the kingdom of God. That which is born of the flesh is flesh, and that which is born of the Spirit is spirit. (John 3:3-6)

This is he who came by water and blood—Jesus Christ; not by the water only but by the water and the blood. And the Spirit is the one who testifies, because the Spirit is the truth. For there are three that testify: the Spirit and the water and the blood; and these three agree. (1 John 5:6-8)

For they deliberately overlook this fact, that the heavens existed long ago, and the earth was formed out of water and through water by the word of God, (2 Peter 3:5)

New Wine in New Wineskins

*And they said to him, "The disciples of John fast often and offer prayers, and so do the disciples of the Pharisees, but yours eat and drink." And Jesus said to them, "Can you make wedding guests fast while the bridegroom is with them? The days will come when the bridegroom is taken away from them, and then they will fast in those days." He also told them a parable: "No one tears a piece from a new garment and puts it on an old garment. If he does, he will tear the new, and the piece from the new will not match the old. And no one puts new wine into old wineskins. If he does, the new wine will burst the skins and it will be spilled, and the skins will be destroyed. But new wine must be put into fresh wineskins. And **no one after drinking old wine desires new, for he says, 'The old is good.'"** (Luke 5:33-39)*

Flesh - No   Spirit - Yes

We manifest the Kingdom to the world through our feet, mouths, and hands. Our behaviors manifest thoughts and intentions in the physical realm.

We believe in our hearts and confess with our mouths that Jesus is Lord as the step to salvation. Speaking it out makes our salvation manifest in the physical realm. In the same way, baptism as an act of faith is an outward step. A declaration to the world that we have committed to dying to the world and rising back to life in Christ Jesus. It is an outward manifestation of the decision to die to the flesh and live by the spirit. Burying our body in water, leaving it there, and rising to a new life in the Spirit.

The like figure whereunto even baptism doth also now save us (not the putting away of the filth of the flesh, but the answer of a good conscience toward God,) by the resurrection of Jesus Christ:
(1 Peter 3:21 KJV)

What is the requirement for baptism to be effective?
In Acts Chapter 8 Phillip was sent by the angel of the Lord to Gaza where he met an Ethiopian Eunuch reading Isaiah. The eunuch asked for help in understanding the text. Phillip read Isaiah thirty-three to him. The eunuch believed and asked a crucial question.

And as they went on their way, they came unto a certain water: and the eunuch said, See, here is water; what doth hinder me to be baptized? And Philip said, If thou believest with all thine heart, thou mayest. And he answered and said, I believe that Jesus Christ is the Son of God.(Acts 8:36-37 KJV)

The criteria? If you believe with all your heart baptism will be contiguous to salvation.

After Peter received instruction by way of the vision God gave him telling him to eat the animals on the sheet let down from heaven, many of which were unclean, he went to share the gospel with a Roman gentile centurion named Cornelius. *(Acts 10)*

While Peter yet spake these words, the Holy Ghost fell on all them which heard the word. And they of the circumcision which believed were astonished, as many as came with Peter, because that on the Gentiles also was poured out the gift of the Holy Ghost. For they heard them speak with tongues, and magnify God.
Then answered Peter, Can any man forbid water, that these should not be baptized, which have received the Holy Ghost as well as we? And he commanded them to be baptized in the name of the Lord. Then prayed they him to tarry certain days. (Acts 10:44-48 KJV)

The Baptism of Jesus

The link below gives three reasons for Jesus to be baptized:

- An initiation into Jesus' public ministry
- A time for God the Father to announce his approval of his Son
- An act of obedience to God the Father

source: https://blog.rose-publishing.com/2016/08/20/3-reasons-jesus-needed-to-be-baptized/#.Y6P1iH3MLRY

I believe there is a fourth reason. We are called to die in the flesh and live with Christ:

For if you live according to the flesh, you will die; but if by the Spirit you put to death the misdeeds of the body, you will live. (Romans 8:13) I have been crucified with Christ and I no longer live, but Christ lives in me. The life I now live in the body, I live by faith in the Son of God, who loved me and gave himself for me. (Galatians 2:20)

Baptism was the final step of Jesus dying to His flesh (born of water) through the act of baptism and rising to live by the Spirit of God:

To Fulfill All Righteousness

When we were baptized into his death, we were placed into the tomb with him. As Christ was brought back from death to life by the glorious power of the Father, so we, too, should live a new kind of life. If we've become united with him in a death like his, certainly we will also be united with him when we come back to life as he did. We know that the person we used to be was crucified with him to put an end to sin in our bodies. Because of this we are no longer slaves to sin.
(Romans 6:4-6 God's Word Translation)

Jesus was righteous but still believed it necessary that He be baptized. John the Baptist tried to deter him, saying, *"I need to be baptized by you, and do you come to me?"* Jesus replied, *"Let it be so now; it is proper for us to do this to fulfill all righteousness."* Then John consented. *(Matthew 3:14-15)*

As baptism for the believer is a putting down of the flesh unto death and rising to life in Christ; I believe Jesus' baptism was to release His flesh, although sinless, to the world. Considering His body dead and rising to life dependant solely on the Spirit of God and the written Word.

And Jesus, when he was baptized, went up straightway out of the water: and, lo, the heavens were opened unto him, and he saw the Spirit of God descending like a dove, and lighting upon him: This is my son in whom I am well-pleased, and Jesus was led to the wilderness to be tempted."(Matthew 3:16-17)

From here Jesus went into the wilderness to be tempted. After his victory over the flesh, Jesus began his Spirit-led ministry.

Now came the test. Satan saw this as an opportunity to try to seduce Jesus into embracing the power He had left behind to become a man and give in to the desires of His flesh. To return to His humanity. Jesus didn't fall for it. Jesus had committed His flesh to death. His finalization of death to self, that it was buried and he would live only to the Spirit was being challenged. It was a temptation for him to grasp the glory that He had before he came to earth as a man.

Have this mind among yourselves, which is yours in Christ Jesus, who, though he was in the form of God, did not count equality with God a thing to be grasped, but made himself nothing, taking the form of a servant, being born in the likeness of men. And being found in human form, he humbled himself by becoming obedient to the point of death, even death on a cross. (Philippians 2:5-8)

Pride. Hunger. The flesh reaches up and says, "This is in my power." Jesus knew who He was. He could have taken hold of and used that power for Himself. But it wasn't a power to serve Himself - *"a thing to be grasped"*.
It wasn't something for His soul. It wasn't something for His body. He was not to be self-serving. Jesus determined to trust the Word. To not pick up the Godhood He had laid aside. To continue to live as a man; but, to live by faith in the Word of God and led by the Spirit of God. As we, in His footsteps are called to live.

In the same way, we are called to trust in the Word of God. Thanks to Jesus' victory here and His sacrifice on the cross we now have the Spirit of God within us. Similarly, it is not to self-serve, name it, claim it, blab it, and grab it - bring things to ourselves. It is to be obedient and a blessing to others. It is in the heart of Christ.

Jesus continued to live by faith, trusting in the Word. Trusting that God would not let Him starve to death. He was not going to take matters into His own hands. He was to continue trusting God - *"Thy will be done"*.

A Re-examination of Baptism

Baptism is more to it than just an act of obedience. John the Baptist was surprised that Jesus felt the need for bäptism. Jesus said it was necessary *"to fulfill all righteousness "*.

Immediately after Jesus' baptism, the Holy Spirit rested on His shoulder in the form of a dove with God the Father voicing approval. *Then Jesus came from Galilee to the Jordan to be baptized by John. But John tried to deter him, saying, "I need to be baptized by you, and do you come to me?" Jesus replied, "Let it be so now; it is proper for us to do this to fulfill all righteousness." Then John consented. As soon as Jesus was baptized, he went up out of the water. At that moment heaven was opened, and he saw the Spirit of God descending like a dove and alighting on him. And a voice from heaven said, "This is my Son, whom I love; with him I am well pleased." (Matthew 3:13-17)*

Following this, Jesus went to the wilderness to be tempted and then began His ministry. I believe that, even though Jesus never sinned, something, either spiritual or in the realm of the soul, was accomplished that was *"necessary for righteousness"*. Something beyond a fond memory or public testimony.
To confirm this, I again, look to the warfare Satan has accomplished against the act of Baptism as an act of faith following salvation and being integral, but not necessary, to the salvation experience. In other words, salvation is by faith alone but you need to both believe in your heart and confess with your mouth to fully manifest your salvation into the world.

As you identify by faith with Christ's death and resurrection in your heart there is a need to move that act of faith into the physical realm. This is a crucial step in the process of death and resurrection in Christ Jesus.

Having been buried with him in baptism, you also have been raised with him through your faith in the power of God who raised him from the dead. And even though you were dead in your transgressions and in the uncircumcision of your flesh, he nevertheless made you alive with him, having forgiven all your transgressions.
(Col 2:12-13 NET Bible)

For Christ also suffered once for sins, the righteous for the unrighteous, to bring you to God. He was put to death in the body but made alive in the Spirit. After being made alive, he went and made proclamation to the imprisoned spirits— to those who were disobedient long ago when God waited patiently in the days of Noah while the ark was being built. In it only a few people, eight in all, were saved through water, and this water symbolizes baptism that now saves you also—not the removal of dirt from the body but the pledge of a clear conscience toward God. It saves you by the resurrection of Jesus Christ, who has gone into heaven and is at God's right hand— with angels, authorities and powers in submission to him
(1 Peter 3:18-22)

Therefore, brothers and sisters, since we have confidence to enter the Most Holy Place by the blood of Jesus, by a new and living way opened for us through the curtain, that is, his body, and since we have a great priest over the house of God, let us draw near to God with a sincere heart and with the full assurance that faith brings, having our hearts sprinkled to cleanse us from a guilty conscience and having our bodies washed with pure water (Hebrews 10:19-22)

There seems to be a major war against baptism taking it from an act of repentance and dying to the world to be resurrected in Christ and relegating it to something performed on a baby with no awareness on that child's part. This removes any semblance of repentance or act of faith on the part of the individual being baptized. I remember several people asking me in the past if they should be baptized again as a newborn Christian even though they had been baptized as a baby. This warfare was accomplished by the Catholic Church through the introduction of infant baptism. It was introduced in 431 AD, teaching that baptism regenerates the soul. According to the Catholic Church, by this Sacrament, they are made alive in Christ. Baptism, according to the Catholic Church absolves "original sin". The sin that all mankind is born into as a result of the fall of mankind in Genesis three.

> Now, when a child is born, it is born into the flesh. But the Bible tells us that the flesh is of no avail because of the consequences of original sin. That's why Jesus says we have to be born again. The first birth is birth of the flesh, but we need something more in order to have life.

What is that something more? The Bible tells us: Everyone must be born of the Spirit in order to have eternal life; it is the Spirit that gives life, not the flesh. And how do we receive the Spirit? The Bible tells us that we receive the Spirit by being born again—by being born of water and the Spirit—by being baptized. We find this in Ezekiel 36:25–27, John 3:3–5, Acts 2:38, and elsewhere. When we are baptized we put on Christ (cf. Gal. 3:27). We are buried with him in baptism (Rom. 6:4). We become members of the body of Christ (1 Cor. 12:13). We receive the Holy Spirit (Acts 2:38). We become a new creation in Christ (2 Cor. 5:17).

To sum up these last few paragraphs: Adam is the representative of the flesh. Christ is the representative of the Spirit. When we are born physically, born into the flesh, we are in Adam. When we are baptized—when we are born again, when we are born of the Spirit—we are in Christ. <u>Infants need to be baptized, just like anyone else, so that they can be "in Christ," so that they can put on Christ, so that they can become children of God, so that they can become members of the body of Christ, so that they can be granted eternal life.</u> (underline added for emphasis)

(https://www.catholic.com/magazine/print-edition/to-explain-infant-baptism-you-must-explain-original-sin)

- - -

Much of what is said in this article is very good. As we saw above, the difference is salvation is received through faith followed by baptism. A seven-day-old baby is just not capable of faith in Christ's redemption. No longer is baptism available as a step of faith following new birth because it is rendered moot as already having been ceremonially accomplished before reaching the age of reason. This is probably why so many people find themselves seeking re-baptism after accepting Christ later in life.

A heart decision is not complete without an outward manifestation, act, or behavior. We are told to believe with our hearts and confess with our mouths *(Romans 10:9-10)*. James states faith without works is dead *(James 2:17-26)*. In the same way, water baptism is an outward, external manifestation of the inward decision to die to the flesh. I think we need to place more emphasis on this in presenting the plan of salvation. Salvation, accepting Jesus as our Lord and Savior is not just fire insurance. It is a commitment to a spirit-led life and a decision to consider our flesh dead. Let's take another look.
Your whole self ruled by the flesh was put off when you were circumcised by Christ, having been buried with him in baptism, in which you were also raised with him through your faith in the working of God, who raised him from the dead. (Colossians 2:11-12)

This is the circumcision of the heart.
For the word of God is quick, and powerful, and sharper than any two-edged sword, piercing even to the <u>dividing asunder</u> of soul and

spirit, and <u>of the joints and marrow</u>, and is a discerner of the thoughts and intents of the heart. (Hebrews 4:12 KJV)

A severance, as you will from obligation to our flesh.

Likewise reckon ye also yourselves to be dead indeed unto sin, but alive unto God through Jesus Christ our Lord. (Romans 6:11 KJV)

Yes, our physical body is a temple of the Holy Spirit and we still need it. But, we are no longer subject to its desires if and when they come into conflict with our spirit and the Spirit of God.

What benefit did you reap at that time from the things you are now ashamed of? Those things result in death! (Romans 6:21 NIV)

This circumcision by baptism, this death to the flesh, and rising to life in the Spirit is our release from the Law of Sin. Death holds no power over us because we have already died. We are freed from the condemnation resulting from our failed attempt to fulfill the law and can enter into a new and better covenant as by faith we join with Christ in His death and resurrection.

Do you not know, brothers and sisters—for I am speaking to those who know the law—that the law has authority over someone only as long as that person lives? (Romans 7:1)

So, my brothers and sisters, you also died to the law through the body of Christ, that you might belong to another, to him who was raised from the dead, in order that we might bear fruit for God. For when we were in the realm of the flesh, the sinful passions aroused by the law were at work in us, so that we bore fruit for death. But now, by dying to what once bound us, we have been released from the law so that we serve in the new way of the Spirit, and not in the old way of the written code. (Romans 7:4-6)

We are now free. Christ has set us free. *(Galatians 5:1)*
What shall we say, then? Shall we go on sinning so that grace may increase? By no means! We are those who have died to sin; how can we live in it any longer? Or don't you know that all of us who were baptized into Christ Jesus were baptized into his death? We were therefore buried with him through baptism into death in order that, just as Christ was raised from the dead through the glory of the Father, we too may live a new life. For if we have been united with him in a death like his, we will certainly also be united with him in a resurrection like his. For we know that our old self was crucified with him so that the body ruled by sin might be done away with, that we should no longer be slaves to sin— because anyone who has died has been set free from sin. Now if we died with Christ, we believe that we will also live with him. For we know that since Christ was raised from the dead, he cannot die again; death no longer has mastery over him. The death he died, he died to sin once for all; but the life he lives, he lives to God. In the same way, count yourselves dead to sin but alive to God in Christ Jesus. Therefore do not let sin reign in your mortal body so that you obey its evil desires. Do not offer any part of yourself to sin as an instrument of wickedness, but rather offer yourselves to God as those who have been brought from death to life; and offer every part of yourself to him as an instrument of righteousness. For sin shall no

longer be your master, because you are not under the law, but under grace. (Romans 6:1-14)

Every instance of salvation in the New Testament is followed by the act of Baptism.

"Then he said (Ananias to Paul): 'The God of our ancestors has chosen you to know his will and to see the Righteous One and to hear words from his mouth. You will be his witness to all people of what you have seen and heard. And now what are you waiting for? **Get up, be baptized and wash your sins away**, *calling on his name.' (Acts 22:14-16)*

While Apollos was at Corinth, Paul took the road through the interior and arrived at Ephesus. There he found some disciples and asked them, "Did you receive the Holy Spirit when you believed?" They answered, "No, we have not even heard that there is a Holy Spirit." So Paul asked, "Then what baptism did you receive?" "John's baptism," they replied. Paul said, "John's baptism was a baptism of repentance. He told the people to believe in the one coming after him, that is, in Jesus." **On hearing this, they were baptized in the name of the Lord Jesus**. *When Paul placed his hands on them, the Holy Spirit came on them, and they spoke in tongues and prophesied. There were about twelve men in all. (Acts 19:1-7)*

Then Paul left the synagogue and went next door to the house of Titius Justus, a worshiper of God. **Crispus, the synagogue leader, and his** *entire household believed in the Lord; and many of the Corinthians who heard Paul believed and were baptized.* (Acts 18:7-8)

The jailer called for lights, rushed in and fell trembling before Paul and Silas. He then brought them out and asked, "Sirs, what must I do to be saved?" They replied, "Believe in the Lord Jesus, and you will be saved—you and your household." Then they spoke the word of the Lord to him and to all the others in his house. At that hour of the night the jailer took them and washed their wounds; **then immediately he and all his household were baptized**. *The jailer brought them into his house and set a meal before them; he was filled with joy because he had come to believe in God—he and his whole household.*
(Acts 16:29-34)

On the Sabbath we went outside the city gate to the river, where we expected to find a place of prayer. We sat down and began to speak to the women who had gathered there. One of those listening was a woman from the city of Thyatira named Lydia, a dealer in purple cloth. She was a worshiper of God. The Lord opened her heart to respond to Paul's message. **When she and the members of her household were baptized, she invited us to her home**. *"If you consider me a believer in the Lord," she said, "come and stay at my house." And she persuaded us.*
(Acts 16:13-15)

The eunuch asked Philip, "Tell me, please, who is the prophet talking about, himself or someone else?" Then Philip began with that very passage of Scripture and told him the good news about Jesus. As they traveled along the road, they came to some water and **the eunuch said, "Look, here is water. What can stand in the way of my being baptized?"** *And he gave orders to stop the chariot. Then both Philip and the eunuch went down into the water and Philip baptized him. When they came up out of the water, the Spirit of the Lord suddenly took Philip away, and the eunuch did not see him again, but went on his way rejoicing. Philip, however, appeared at Azotus and traveled about, preaching the gospel in all the towns until he reached Caesarea. (Acts 8:34-40)*

But when they believed Philip *as he proclaimed the good news of the kingdom of God and the name of Jesus Christ,* **they were baptized, both men and women.** *(Acts 8:12)*

Peter replied, **"Repent and be baptized***, every one of you, in the name of Jesus Christ for the forgiveness of your sins. And you will receive the gift of the Holy Spirit. The promise is for you and your children and for all who are far off—for all whom the Lord our God will call." With many other words he warned them; and he pleaded with them, "Save yourselves from this corrupt generation."* **Those who accepted his message were baptized***, and about three thousand were added to their number that day. (Acts 2:38-41)*

John's Baptism

urged preparation for the coming Kingdom of Heaven. *"Repent, for the kingdom of heaven is at hand." (Matthew 3:2 NASB)*

Jesus' Baptism

also symbolized His coming ministry as the suffering servant *(Isaiah 53)* the Righteous One *(Acts 7:52)* who would die for the sins of the world so that others could become righteous. Thus He *"fulfills all righteousness"*. It symbolized His future death.

During Christ's ministry, He used the figurative language of immersion as a symbol of His coming death and resurrection.

But Jesus said to them, "You do not know what you are asking for. Are you able to drink the cup that I drink, or to be baptized with the baptism with which I am baptized?" And they said to Him, "We are able." And Jesus said to them, "The cup that I drink you shall drink; and you shall be baptized with the baptism with which I am baptized. (Mark 10:38-39 NASB)

But I have a baptism to undergo, and how distressed I am until it is accomplished! (Luke 12:50 NASB)

Jesus' baptism laid out the path we should follow.

To count ourselves dead to sin and alive to God. *(Romans 6:11)*

We are now free from sin and have become slaves to righteousness *(Romans 6:7, 18, 20)*.

The Holy Spirit has regenerated us. *(Titus 3:5)* as a new creation with a new nature. *(Galatians 6:15)*

We are to put on our new nature and become like Him *(Colossians 3:10)*.

And continue the commission given to Adam and Eve, Noah's descendants, Abraham's descendants, and the Nation of Israel.

As with the original twelve disciples, we have an added upgrade. We have the Holy Spirit living in and working with us.

Go therefore and make disciples of all the nations, baptizing them in the name of the Father and the Son and the Holy Spirit . . .
(Matthew 28:19 NASB)

Pluck Out Phil's Eye?

If your hand or your foot causes you to stumble, cut it off and throw it away. It is better for you to enter life maimed or crippled than to have two hands or two feet and be thrown into eternal fire. And if your eye causes you to stumble, gouge it out and throw it away. It is better for you to enter life with one eye than to have two eyes and be thrown into the fire of hell. (Matthew 18:8-9)

The problem with this is whatever is offending me, whether it be covetousness, greed, lasciviousness, lust, or whatever I can pluck that eye out. I can pluck the other eye out. But, that offense is deeper than just your physical body. It goes all the way down to your actual flesh, your personality, and even into your soul. In other words, it is intrinsic to the nature of your flesh. Phil's appetite and nature.

This is why we have to Kill Phil. Or, as the Scripture puts it - die to the flesh

What shall we say then? Are we to continue in sin that grace may abound? By no means! How can we who died to sin still live in it? Do

you not know that all of us who have been baptized into Christ Jesus were baptized into his death? We were buried therefore with him by baptism into death, in order that, just as Christ was raised from the dead by the glory of the Father, we too might walk in newness of life. For if we have been united with him in a death like his, we shall certainly be united with him in a resurrection like his. We know that our old self[1] was crucified with him in order that the body of sin might be brought to nothing, so that we would no longer be enslaved to sin. For one who has died has been set free from sin. Now if we have died with Christ, we believe that we will also live with him. We know that Christ, being raised from the dead, will never die again; death no longer has dominion over him. For the death he died he died to sin, once for all, but the life he lives he lives to God. So you also must consider yourselves dead to sin and alive to God in Christ Jesus. Let not sin therefore reign in your mortal body, to make you obey its passions. Do not present your members to sin as instruments for unrighteousness, but present yourselves to God as those who have been brought from death to life, and your members to God as instruments for righteousness. For sin will have no dominion over you, since you are not under law but under grace. (Romans 6:1-14)

BLOODLINE: 139

CIRCUMCISION 139
STONE - DUST - FLESH 140
REGARDING "ORIGINAL SIN" 142
...ALL THAT IS IN THE WORLD. 147
A QUESTION ON THE GENEOLOGY OF JESUS 149
   The Two Lineages Compared 150
   Jehoiakim 151
   Coniah Cursed and Bypassed 154

Bloodline

Circumcision

Someone asked me once why God had the Jewish people perform circumcision on their sons. First and foremost, this was mandated directly by God as a stipulation in His covenant with Abraham. A sign of separation from the rest of the world.
Then God said to Abraham, "As for you, you must keep my covenant, you and your descendants after you for the generations to come. This is my covenant with you and your descendants after you, the covenant you are to keep: Every male among you shall be circumcised. You are to undergo circumcision, and it will be the sign of the covenant between me and you.(Genesis 17:9-11 KJV)

But, why would God choose such a strange thing? To remove a piece of flesh from the end of the penis? I think one reason might be a reflection on the promise that one day He would provide a seed by His Spirit and not through the flesh. Normally, the sperm/seed would pass through the foreskin during intercourse. In the case of circumcision, with the foreskin removed, we could say the seed was transferred but it did not pass through the flesh. The foreskin symbolizes the flesh. Jesus would be born as a human but not of human sperm/seed. Throughout the Scriptures, God refers to a circumcision of the heart.
And the LORD thy God will circumcise thine heart, and the heart of thy seed, to love the LORD thy God with all thine heart, and with all

thy soul, that thou mayest live.(Deuteronomy 30:6 KJV)
Circumcise yourselves to the LORD, and take away the foreskins of your heart, ye men of Judah and inhabitants of Jerusalem: lest my fury come forth like fire, and burn that none can quench it, because of the evil of your doings. (Jeremiah 4:4 KJV)

In our new covenant with Christ Paul contrasts physical circumcision with a separation of the flesh from the spirit. *For the word of God is living and active, sharper than any two-edged sword, piercing to the division of soul and of spirit, (Hebrews 4:12 ESV)*
No longer bound to the flesh but alive and obedient to the Spirit.
For we are the circumcision, which worship God in the spirit, and rejoice in Christ Jesus, and have no confidence in the flesh. (Philippians 3:3 KJV)

Stone - Dust - Flesh

God many times promises to replace our hearts of stone with a heart of flesh.
A new heart also will I give you, and a new spirit will I put within you: and I will take away the stony heart out of your flesh, and I will give you an heart of flesh. (Ezekiel 36:26 KJV)
How does He do this? I am not going to try to define the actual process.
I would rather look at it metaphorically and trust in His process.
Is not my word like as a fire? saith the LORD; and like a hammer that

breaketh the rock in pieces? (Jeremiah 23:29 KJV)

Like iron sharpens iron (*Proverbs 27:17*) the Word of God breaks the stubborn heart down to dust as it dies in Christ.

"In the sweat of thy face shalt thou eat bread till thou return unto the ground, for out of it wast thou taken; for dust thou art, and unto dust shalt thou return." (Genesis 3:19 KJV)

Then He resurrects it in Christ. Living flesh.

And the LORD God formed man of the dust of the ground, and breathed into his nostrils the breath of life; and man became a living soul. (Genesis 2:7 KJV)

We need to allow the Word of God to break the stone around our hearts so the Spirit of God can breathe His life into us and write His living commandments on the flesh of our hearts.

As we are reborn into the Body of Christ and become "new creatures" we are no longer sons of disobedience *(Eph 2:2)*. But we are still very susceptible to temptation and deception. Now the stony-heart made flesh is more ready for the Spirit of God to work in us.

In whom also ye are circumcised with the circumcision made without hands, in putting off the body of the sins of the flesh by the circumcision of Christ: Buried with him in baptism, wherein also ye are risen with him through the faith of the operation of God, who hath raised him from the dead. And you, being dead in your sins and the uncircumcision of your flesh, hath he quickened together with him, having forgiven you all trespasses; (Colossians 2:11-13 KJV)

Regarding "Original Sin"

I believe we are born with a spiritual "taint" or "flaw" of rebellion or disobedience produced by Adam's willful partaking of the fruit. Eve was deceived and the "flaw" passed down from her is a tendency or weakness to gullibility or deception.

We are born of a twice-tainted bloodline with disobedience and rebellion coming in through our father's bloodline (per Adam's disobedience) and susceptibility to deceit by way of Eve's yielding to temptation.

We are born flawed; but, not evil. Due to this flaw, we will at some point, "eat of the forbidden Tree" taking on the lordship of our life. "Becoming like God."

In becoming our god, sin is now active in us.

These "flaws" are passed down through the bloodline. As a result, thanks to Adam, we are born "sons of disobedience" with a tendency or bent toward rebellion. We are also born with a weakness toward temptation and deceit courtesy of Eve.

Something unique about conception is that the fetus develops from the egg while the placenta comes from the sperm.

Scientists discovered this years ago as a part of cloning research. Cloning two sperm could only create a placenta while cloning two eggs produced a fetus.

Placentas support the fetus and mother, but those organs grow according to blueprints from dad, according to new research. The study shows that the genes in a fetus that come from the father dominate in building the fetal side of the placenta. ScienceDaily Date: August 15, 2013 Source: Cornell University
(https://www.sciencedaily.com/releases/2013/08/130815133058.htm)
The sperm is responsible for creating the placenta and umbilical cord. So, technically, the placenta is *his* organ- growing in your body, supporting the baby you both created. How beautiful is that?
(https://sfbirthdoulaandplacentaencapsulationservices.com/birth-blog/2014/7/14/fun-facts-about-placentas)
Dad's genes build placentas, study shows
(https://news.cornell.edu/stories/2013/08/dad-s-genes-build-placentas-study-shows)
These results [in mice] led to an extraordinary conclusion. Paternal genes, inherited from the father, are responsible for making the placenta – maternal genes, inherited from the mother, are responsible for making the greater part of the embryo, especially its head and brain…
(http://www.thehumangenome.co.uk/THE_HUMAN_GENOME/Placenta.html)
Although the placenta develops inside the mother, the father actually helps to create the organ. When the sperm fertilizes the egg, a blastocyst is formed. This then becomes the placenta and the baby.

(https://www.huffingtonpost.ca/2016/06/14/placenta-facts_n_10398438.html)

As a result, the bloodline/placenta passes down through the father while the body/fetus comes from the mother. In other words, the body is maternal while the blood is paternal.

This is why Jesus had to be born of a virgin. When He was conceived God cut off the bloodline from Adam and introduced a fresh bloodline through the Holy Spirit while continuing the human bloodline through Mary who produced the fetus.

Remember God's first promise after the fall? An offspring would come from Eve and crush the serpent's head.

And the LORD God said unto the serpent, Because thou hast done this, thou art cursed above all cattle, and above every beast of the field; upon thy belly shalt thou go, and dust shalt thou eat all the days of thy life: And I will put enmity between thee and the woman, and between thy seed and her seed; it shall bruise thy head, and thou shalt bruise his heel. (Genesis 3:14-1 KJV)

As Jesus was born of a bloodline introduced through the Holy Spirit, He was fully God. He was also fully human through Mary's bloodline. Jesus was born able to be tempted and deceived but not prone to disobedience.

This is why the testing in the desert was crucial to Christ's ministry. He was presented with the same three temptations as Eve.

In the same way, at salvation our dormant human spirit "seed, so to speak" is planted/baptized/immersed in the Spirit of God, and new life activated.

Verily, verily, I say unto you, Except a corn of wheat fall into the ground and die, it abideth alone: but if it die, it bringeth forth much fruit. (John 12:24 KJV)

This new life is rooted in the Spirit of God.

"In Him we live and move and have our being" (Acts 17:28 KJV).

We become a new creature, a new creation. A member of this new family of the Second Adam - Jesus Christ. By faith, we live under the influence and cleansing of His blood; no longer obligated to our physical body, "our flesh". His Lordship is the switch that determines whether our life flow comes from the Spirit of God or the world and its influence.

Which of these is our source of influence? All that is in the world? The lust of the eyes? the lust of the flesh? The pride of life? We can say "metaphorically" that we now have two trees growing in the garden of our hearts. One tree is rooted in the world system, the world's wisdom - subject to the "god of this world". The "advising serpent". This would be the Tree of the Knowledge of Good and Evil. Rooted in the wisdom of this world, this tree bears evil fruit.

For from within, out of the heart of men, proceed evil thoughts, adulteries, fornications, murders, Thefts, covetousness, wickedness, deceit, lasciviousness, an evil eye, blasphemy, pride, foolishness: All

these evil things come from within, and defile the man.
(Mark 7:21-23 KJV)

The other tree, rooted in the Spirit of God and fed by the "Streams of Living Water" is a "Tree of Life" bearing fruits of the Spirit -
But the fruit of the Spirit is love, joy, peace, longsuffering, gentleness, goodness, faith, Meekness, temperance: against such there is no law.
(Galatians 5:22-23 KJV)

Note: Genesis chapter two not only mentions these two trees as having been placed in the Garden. It also mentions a river that flowed out into the world.

And out of the ground made the LORD God to grow every tree that is pleasant to the sight, and good for food; the tree of life also in the midst of the garden, and the tree of knowledge of good and evil. And a river went out of Eden to water the garden, and from thence it was parted, and became into four heads. The name of the first is...
(Genesis 2:9-11 KJV)

In our case a River of Life.

Just like Adam and Eve in the garden, we have a choice to eat from the Tree of the Knowledge of Good and Evil ruling as god of our own life and destiny based on the "serpent's" wisdom. Or, we can choose to eat from the Tree of Life sourced in the Spirit of God with an agreeable mind "renewed" by the Word of God.

You decide daily and in each circumstance which tree is going to sustain you. Which fruit you are going to eat? Ultimately sourcing the fruit of your lips - life or death. (*Matt 7:16-20*)

...All That is in the World.

Lust of the flesh (she/Eve saw that the fruit of the tree was good for food)
Lust of the eyes (and pleasing to the eye)
Pride of life (and also desirable for gaining wisdom)

Satan personalized these temptations when he approached Jesus in the wilderness...
Flesh - stones to bread for hunger.
Eyes - showed and offered the kingdoms of the world.
Pride - cast yourself from the pinnacle of the temple and the angels will catch you. I'm certain many would see this and His fame would spread.

Since then, Satan has had over 2,000 years to fine-tune his message. Especially in the Westernized world. They are all rooted in these same three areas with the focus that we will become like God. We are in control. Of course, this ends up with Satan ultimately becoming our god as we embrace his "doctrine".

Follow your heart - You be you - Live YOUR truth - Love the one you're with - Believe in yourself - You deserve a break today - If it feels good do it.

We are bombarded with these messages via social media, television commercials, and movies (How many movies have you seen where the lead actor and actress have a magic moment and end up in bed? It is presented as natural and approved.)

They (the seeds) on the rock are they, which, when they hear, receive the word with joy; and these have no root, which for a while believe, and in time of temptation fall away. And that which fell among thorns are they, which, when they have heard, go forth, and are choked with cares and riches and pleasures of this life, and bring no fruit to perfection. (Luke 8:13-14 KJV)

Wherefore seeing we also are compassed about with so great a cloud of witnesses, let us lay aside every weight, and the sin which doth so easily beset us, and let us run with patience the race that is set before us, Looking unto Jesus the author and finisher of our faith; who for the joy that was set before him endured the cross, despising the shame, and is set down at the right hand of the throne of God. (Hebrews 12:1-2 KJV)

2 Peter 3:5 says *"the earth was formed out of water by water."* As such, in birth, we are "born of water".

Jesus was born of water through Mary and blood by the power of the Holy Spirit as the new Adam... The first fruit of many who by faith live by the power of His blood.

Through new birth, as we are placed in the Spirit of God, we are born of the Spirit.

"...unless they are born of water and the Spirit..." (John 3)
This is he that came by water and blood, even Jesus Christ; not by water only, but by water and blood. (1 John 5:6 KJV)

Looking back at the "First Roots" coming from the world, Jesus needed to be born into the Jewish culture. A culture that would instill God's Law into him from birth overriding the "wisdom of this world". A culture prepared for *"such a time as this". (Esther 4:14)*
His input from the world would be the Word of God in alignment with His spirit.

A Question on the Geneology of Jesus

The lineage of Jesus is given in Luke Chapter 3 and Matthew Chapter 1. They both end up with Joseph although one line descends from David through Solomon while the other passes down from David through another son, Nathan. It can be confusing as Matthew 1 lists from Abraham to Joseph while Mary's line in Luke begins with Jesus and goes backward in time to Adam and ultimately to God.
" the son of Enos, the son of Seth, the son of Adam, the son of God.."
(Luke 3:38 ESV)
This is the lineage through which the promised "Son of Man" who would crush the serpent's head would derive.

I have placed a chart on the following page showing both lineages progressing from David to Jesus. Since the lineage from Adam to David is the same in both cases I have placed that in the left column.

Different translations show a variance in the spelling of names. To avoid confusion I have placed the KJV in parentheses.

The Two Lineages Compared

To avoid confusion names in parentheses are from KJV

Creation to David	Luke 3 - Mary's Lineage	Matthew 1 - Joseph's Lineage	
God	David	David	
Adam	**Nathan**	**Solomon**	
Seth	Mattatha	Rehoboam (Roboam)	
Enosh	Menna (Menan)	Abijah (Abia)	
Kenan	Melea	Asa	
Mahalalel	Eliakim	Jehoshaphat (Josaphat)	
Jared	Jonam (Jonan)	Jehoram (Joram)	
Enoch	Joseph	Uzziah (Ozias)	
Methuselah	Judah	Jotham (Joatham)	
Lamech	Simeon	Ahaz (Achaz)	
Noah	Levi	Hezekiah (Ezekias)	
Shem	Matthat	Manasseh (Manasses)	
Arphaxad	Jorim	Amon	
Cainan	Eliezer	Josiah (Josias)	
Shelah	Joshua (Jose)	NOT MENTIONED IN LINEAGE	Jehoiakim birth name Eliakim - renamed by Pharoah Neco
Eber	Er	Jeconiah (Jechonias) - Coniah	
Peleg	Elmadam (Elmodam)	Shealtiel (Salathiel)	
Reu	Cosam	Zerubbabel (Zorobabel)	
Serug	Addi	Abihud (Abiud)	
Nahor	Melki (Melchi)	Eliakim	
Terah	Neri	Azor	
Abraham	Shealtiel (Salathiel)	Zadok (Sadoc)	
Isaac	Zerubbabel (Zorobabel)	Akim (Achim)	
Jacob	Rhesa	Elihud (Eliud)	
Judah	Joanan (Joanna)	Eleazar	
Perez	Joda (Juda)	Matthan	
Hezron	Josek (Joseph)	Jacob	
Ram	Semein (Semei)	Joseph husband of Mary	Named as legal father
Amminadab	Mattathias	Mother of Jesus	
Nahshon	Maath	Jesus	
Salmon	Naggai (Nagge)		
Boaz	Esli		
Obed	Nahum (Naum)		
Jesse	Amos		
David	Mattathias		
	Joseph		
	Jannai (Janna)		
	Melki (Melchi)		
	Levi		
	Matthat		
	Heli		
	Mary	The text names Joseph as legal father	
	Jesus		

If you follow the history of the kings of Judah and Israel you will find five good and thirty-three evil kings. God had finally had enough. Especially after Josiah who *"...did that which was right in the sight of the Lord, and walked in all the way of David his father, and turned not aside to the right hand or to the left." (2 Kings 22:2 KJV)*

Son - Evil King (Jehoash)
Grandson - Evil King (Jehoiakim)
Great Grandson - Evil King (Jeconiah/Coniah)

Jehoiakim

Jehoiakim's original name was Eliakim but Pharoah Neco changed his name to Jehoiakim. This was after Josiah went against Egypt and was killed. Jehoaz (Shallum) became king after Josiah but he "did evil in the sight of the Lord" so Pharaohnechoh took him prisoner and placed Jehoiakim as king.

Jehoahaz was twenty and three years old when he began to reign; and he reigned three months in Jerusalem. And his mother's name was Hamutal, the daughter of Jeremiah of Libnah. And he did that which was evil in the sight of the Lord, according to all that his fathers had done. And Pharaohnechoh put him in bands at Riblah in the land of Hamath, that he might not reign in Jerusalem; and put the land to a tribute of an hundred talents of silver, and a talent of gold. And Pharaohnechoh made Eliakim the (second) *son of Josiah king in the room of Josiah his father, and turned his name to Jehoiakim, and took*

Jehoahaz away: and he came to Egypt, and died there.
(2 Kings 23:31-34 KJV).

God had many times prophesied His judgment against wicked kings. To end the lineage of David from the throne. It was now coming to pass.

Thus says the LORD: "Execute judgment and righteousness, and deliver the plundered out of the hand of the oppressor. Do no wrong and do no violence to the stranger, the fatherless, or the widow, nor shed innocent blood in this place. For if you indeed do this thing, then shall enter the gates of this house, riding on horses and in chariots, accompanied by servants and people, kings who sit on the throne of David. But if you will not hear 1these words, I swear by Myself," says the LORD, "that this house shall become a desolation."
(Jeremiah 22:3-5 KJV)

During the reign of Jehoiakim Jeremiah received word from God and had Baruch the scribe write it down and read it in public allowing Jehoiakim to repent.

And it came to pass in the fourth year of Jehoiakim the son of Josiah king of Judah, that this word came unto Jeremiah from the Lord, saying, Take thee a roll of a book, and write therein all the words that I have spoken unto thee against Israel, and against Judah, and against all the nations, from the day I spake unto thee, from the days of Josiah, even unto this day. It may be that the house of Judah will hear all the evil which I purpose to do unto them; that they may return every man from his evil way; that I may forgive their iniquity and their sin. (Jeremiah 36:1-3 KJV)

King Jehoiakim became upset by this. He did not repent. Rather, he cut Jeremiah's scroll to pieces and burned it. *(Jeremiah 36:22-25 KJV)* God told Jeremiah to write a duplicate scroll and send it to Jehoiakim along with this message.

And thou shalt say to Jehoiakim king of Judah, Thus saith the Lord; Thou hast burned this roll, saying, Why hast thou written therein, saying, The king of Babylon shall certainly come and destroy this land, and shall cause to cease from thence man and beast? Therefore thus saith the Lord of Jehoiakim king of Judah; He shall have none to sit upon the throne of David: and his dead body shall be cast out in the day to the heat, and in the night to the frost. And I will punish him and his seed and his servants for their iniquity; and I will bring upon them, and upon the inhabitants of Jerusalem, and upon the men of Judah, all the evil that I have pronounced against them; but they hearkened not. (Jeremmiah 36:30-31 KJV)

You will notice in the genealogy from Matthew 1 Jehoiakim is missing. The genealogy goes from Josiah to Jeconiah (Conia) to Shealtiel (Salathiel). This took quite a bit of research. I believe Matthew purposedly left him out because of the above curse placed on him.

Coniah Cursed and Bypassed

The next curse in the line was against Coniah/Jechoniah/Jehoiachin. I bet the mailman was confused. God cursed Jechoniah (Coniah) because he did not repent. He continued to do evil.

Is this man Coniah a despised and shattered pot, a jar that no one wants? Why are he and his descendants hurled out and cast into a land they do not know? O land, land, land, hear the word of the LORD! This is what the LORD says: "Enroll this man as childless, a man who will not prosper in his lifetime. None of his descendants will prosper to sit on the throne of David or to rule again in Judah." (Jeremiah 22:28-30 Berean Standard Bible)

King James says *"Write ye this man childless."*. A better translation is *"write this man off as childless." (ISV)*. Coniah had children, but the throne was taken from him and given to his Uncle Zedekiah. Zedekiah was appointed king by Nebuchadnezzar king of Babylon. This would be another reason Joseph could not be Jesus' real father. God had Jeremiah prophesy that no one from his lineage would sit upon the throne of David. Zedekiah was the last of the lineage of the kings of Judah.

Every seven years all Hebrew slaves were to be set free *(Exodus 21:2)* but, the people were not doing this. Upon being appointed king, Zedekiah made a covenant with the people of Judah to free their Hebrew slaves and not hold any fellow Hebrews in bondage. As a result, Zedekiah was promised a peaceful death.

Thus saith the Lord, the God of Israel; Go and speak to Zedekiah king of Judah, and tell him, Thus saith the Lord; Behold, I will give this city into the hand of the king of Babylon, and he shall burn it with fire: And thou shalt not escape out of his hand, but shalt surely be taken, and delivered into his hand; and thine eyes shall behold the eyes of the king of Babylon, and he shall speak with thee mouth to mouth, and thou shalt go to Babylon. Yet hear the word of the Lord, O Zedekiah king of Judah; Thus saith the Lord of thee, Thou shalt not die by the sword: But thou shalt die in peace: (Jeremiah 34:2-5 KJV)

Zedekiah and the people reneged on their promise and took back the slaves so God took back His promise of a peaceful death.

"I will deliver Zedekiah king of Judah and his officials into the hands of their enemies who want to kill them, to the army of the king of Babylon, which has withdrawn from you. I am going to give the order, declares the Lord, and I will bring them back to this city. They will fight against it, take it and burn it down. And I will lay waste the towns of Judah so no one can live there." (Jeremiah 34:21-22 KJV)

Zedekiah ruled for a while but rebelled against the king of Babylon. He was captured and taken to Babylon and put in prison. "*There at Riblah the king of Babylon killed the sons of Zedekiah before his eyes; he also killed all the officials of Judah. Then he put out Zedekiah's eyes, bound him with bronze shackles and took him to Babylon, where he put him in prison till the day of his death." (Jeremiah 52:10-11)*

Then, as a final blow, Zedekiah's sons were killed before his eyes before he was blinded. The physical line of royalty through the line of David has now been cut off. Zedekiah was the last of Judah's kings.

I want to confirm that this is the correct lineage by referencing 1 Chronicles:

*And the sons of **Josiah** were, the firstborn Johanan, the second **Jehoiakim**, the third Zedekiah, the fourth Shallum. And the sons of Jehoiakim: **Jeconiah** his son, Zedekiah his son. And the sons of Jeconiah; Assir, **Salathiel** his son, Malchiram also, and Pedaiah, and Shenazar, Jecamiah, Hoshama, and Nedabiah. And the sons of Pedaiah were, **Zerubbabel**, and Shimei: and the sons of Zerubbabel; Meshullam, and Hananiah, and Shelomith their sister:* (1Chronicles 3:15-19)

Josiah - Jehoiakim (not mentioned in Matthew 1 lineage) - Jeconia (Coniah) - Shealtiel (Salathiel) - Zerubbabel

By the way, God in His mercy restored Zerubbabel into His good graces. *(Zechariah 4)*. (see also Haggai, Ezra, Nehemiah). But, the throne was never restored either physically or spiritually. The next and final King of the Jews from the line of David is Jesus son of Mary descended through David's son, Nathan.

COVENANTS FULFILLED: 159

- JESUS FULFILLED ALL CONDITIONAL COVENANTS 160
  - *Noahic Covenant - The Rainbow* 160
  - *Abrahamic Covenant - Circumcision* 162
  - *Covenant with Israel - The Ten Commandments* 163
  - *Lord of the Sabbath* 163
- JESUS WAS MORE THAN A PROPHET OR TEACHER 167
  - *Jesus Forgave Sin* 167
  - *Jesus Accepted Worship* 167
  - *Jesus Was Known as the Son of God* 168
  - *Jesus Confirms His Messiahship* 168
- "SON OF MAN" VS. "SON OF MAN" 169
  - *Son of Man* 169
  - *The Serpent* 170
- THE TEMPTATION OF CHRIST VICTORIOUS 170
- PARALLELS 173
- THE SUBSTITUTE LAMB 174
  - *First Adam - Second Adam (Sin in - Sin Out)* 178
  - *A Spiritual Progeny* 179

Covenants Fulfilled

"The days are coming, declares the Lord, when I will make a new covenant with the people of Israel and with the people of Judah. It will not be like the covenant I made with their ancestors when I took them by the hand to lead them out of Egypt, because they did not remain faithful to my covenant, and I turned away from them, declares the Lord.

This is the covenant I will establish with the people of Israel after that time, declares the Lord. I will put my laws in their minds and write them on their hearts. I will be their God, and they will be my people. No longer will they teach their neighbor, or say to one another, 'Know the Lord,' because they will all know me, from the least of them to the greatest.

For I will forgive their wickedness and will remember their sins no more."

By calling this covenant "new," he has made the first one obsolete; and what is obsolete and outdated will soon disappear.
(Hebrews 8:8-13 NIV)

How much more shall the blood of Christ, who through the eternal Spirit offered himself without spot to God, purge your conscience from dead works to serve the living God? And for this cause he is the mediator of the new testament, that by means of death, for the redemption of the transgressions that were under the first testament,

they which are called might receive the promise of eternal inheritance. For where a testament is, there must also of necessity be the death of the testator. For a testament is of force after men are dead: otherwise it is of no strength at all while the testator liveth.
(Hebrews 9:14-17 KJV)

And he took bread, and gave thanks, and brake it, and gave unto them, saying, This is my body which is given for you: this do in remembrance of me. Likewise also the cup after supper, saying, This cup is the new testament in my blood, which is shed for you. (Luke 22:19-20 KJV)

What is this new covenant that Jesus is speaking of? And, what qualifies Him to give it? After all, the Jews had been following the old covenant for thousands of years. And, which covenant is Jesus replacing?

Jesus Fulfilled All Conditional Covenants

The Bible speaks of four main covenants that God made with man. Five if you count His promise to Eve in the Garden of Eden. Jesus met the requirements for every conditional covenant.

"Do not think I have come to get rid of what is written in the Law or in the Prophets. I have not come to do this. Instead, I have come to fulfill what is written (Matthew 5:17)

Noahic Covenant - The Rainbow

God tells Noah to multiply and fill the earth.
And you, be ye fruitful, and multiply; bring forth abundantly in the

earth, and multiply therein. And God spake unto Noah, and to his sons with him, saying, And I, behold, I establish my covenant with you, and with your seed after you; (Genesis 9:7-9 KJV)

God promised Noah that even though man is corrupt and stiff-necked He will not destroy the earth like He did with the flood and gives him a sign to mark the covenant. The sign of the promise is the rainbow.

And God said, This is the token of the covenant which I make between me and you and every living creature that is with you, for perpetual generations: I do set my bow in the cloud, and it shall be for a token of a covenant between me and the earth. And it shall come to pass, when I bring a cloud over the earth, that the bow shall be seen in the cloud: And I will remember my covenant, which is between me and you and every living creature of all flesh; and the waters shall no more become a flood to destroy all flesh. (Genesis 9:12-15 KJV)

It is interesting that, as in the Garden, God commissioned the descendants of Noah to spread out over the earth.

And God blessed Noah and his sons, and said unto them, Be fruitful, and multiply, and replenish the earth. (Genesis 9:1 KJV)

Only to have that command defied four generations later by Nimrod who founded the infamous Babel where God had to forcibly disperse mankind by confusing their tongues.

Go to, let us go down, and there confound their language, that they may not understand one another's speech. So the Lord scattered them abroad from thence upon the face of all the earth: (Genesis 11:7-8 KJV)

Noah was to encourage his descendants to spread across the earth; Jesus renewed this covenant telling His disciples to *"Go into all the world and preach the gospel to all creation." (Mark 16:15)* *"...you will be my witnesses in Jerusalem and in all Judea and Samaria, and to the end of the earth." (Acts 1:8b ESV)*

Abrahamic Covenant - Circumcision

God chooses Abraham and promises him a family. He promises to bless Abraham and make him into a great nation through his progeny that would flourish and become a blessing to the whole world.

And in thy seed shall all the nations of the earth be blessed; because thou hast obeyed my voice. (Genesis 22:18 KJV)

In return, Abraham is called to trust - to believe.

And he brought him forth abroad, and said, Look now toward heaven, and tell the stars, if thou be able to number them: and he said unto him, So shall thy seed be. And he believed in the Lord, and he counted it to him for righteousness. (Genesis 15:5-6 KJV)

Whereas in the covenant with Noah God gave us the sign of the rainbow. The outward manifestation of this covenant was the act of circumcision on the part of Abraham and his descendants.

This is my covenant, which ye shall keep, between me and you and thy seed after thee; Every man child among you shall be circumcised. And ye shall circumcise the flesh of your foreskin; and it shall be a token of the covenant betwixt me and you. And he that is eight days old shall be circumcised among you, every man child in your generations, he that is born in the house, or bought with money of any stranger, which is not of thy seed. (Genesis 17:10-12)

Jesus fulfilled the Abrahamic Covenant. As a Jewish male, Jesus was circumcised.

Covenant with Israel - The Ten Commandments

On Mount Horeb, God made a covenant with Moses and the entire nation of Israel to follow His law and gave ten commandments. He followed up with a system of rituals, festivals, codes of ethics, and procedures for sacrifices to properly worship Him and called them to a life of holiness. *(Leviticus and Deuteronomy)*

The Sabbath was given as the sign of this covenant.

Speak thou also unto the children of Israel, saying, Verily my sabbaths ye shall keep: for it is a sign between me and you throughout your generations; that ye may know that I am the LORD that doth sanctify you. (Exodus 31:13 KJV)

Jesus not only followed the Ten Commandments. He raised them to a higher level. Love your neighbor as yourselves. Love your enemy. If you have looked at a woman with lust you have committed adultery. If you hate your brother you have committed murder.

Lord of the Sabbath

Jesus kept the Sabbath. Jesus fulfilled the Sabbath. Jesus declared Himself as the Lord of the Sabbath.

But I say unto you, That in this place is one greater than the temple.

But if ye had known what this meaneth, I will have mercy, and not sacrifice, ye would not have condemned the guiltless. For the Son of man is Lord even of the sabbath day. (Matthew 12:6-8 KJV)

Davidic Covenant - The Throne

God promised an heir to David. One that would come through his loins and reign forever.

*And thine house and thy kingdom shall be established forever before thee: thy throne shall be established forever. (2 Samuel 7:16 KJV)
And there shall come forth a rod out of the stem of Jesse, and a Branch shall grow out of his roots: And the spirit of the Lord shall rest upon him, the spirit of wisdom and understanding, the spirit of counsel and might, the spirit of knowledge and of the fear of the Lord; And shall make him of quick understanding in the fear of the Lord: and he shall not judge after the sight of his eyes, neither reprove after the hearing of his ears: But with righteousness shall he judge the poor, and reprove with equity for the meek of the earth: and he shall smite the earth: with the rod of his mouth, and with the breath of his lips shall he slay the wicked. And righteousness shall be the girdle of his loins, and faithfulness the girdle of his reins. (Isaiah 11:1-5 KJV)
Behold, the days come, saith the Lord, that I will raise unto David a righteous Branch, and a King shall reign and prosper, and shall execute judgment and justice in the earth. (Jeremiah 23:5 KJV)*

Jesus is the *rod out of the stem of Jesse* and *righteous Branch*.

For unto us a child is born, unto us a son is given: and the government

shall be upon his shoulder: and his name shall be called Wonderful, Counsellor, The mighty God, The everlasting Father, The Prince of Peace. Of the increase of his government and peace there shall be no end, upon the throne of David, and upon his kingdom, to order it, and to establish it with judgment and with justice from henceforth even forever. The zeal of the Lord of hosts will perform this.
(Isaiah 9:6-7 KJV)

Confirmation was given to Joseph:

But while he thought on these things, behold, the angel of the Lord appeared unto him in a dream, saying, Joseph, thou son of David, fear not to take unto thee Mary thy wife: for that which is conceived in her is of the Holy Ghost. And she shall bring forth a son, and thou shalt call his name Jesus: for he shall save his people from their sins. Now all this was done, that it might be fulfilled which was spoken of the Lord by the prophet, saying, Behold, a virgin shall be with child, and shall bring forth a son, and they shall call his name Emmanuel, which being interpreted is, God with us. (Matthew 18:20-23 KJV)

Confirmation was given to Mary:

And the angel said unto her, Fear not, Mary: for thou hast found favour with God. And, behold, thou shalt conceive in thy womb, and bring forth a son, and shalt call his name Jesus. He shall be great, and shall be called the Son of the Highest: and the Lord God shall give unto him the throne of his father David: (Luke 1:30-32 KJV)

Only a few verses later Mary went to visit her cousin Elizabeth who was pregnant with John the Baptist *(v. 39-55)* "*when Elisabeth heard the salutation of Mary, the babe leaped in her womb; and Elisabeth was filled with the Holy Ghost:"* It is interesting to note that the first recognition of the Messiah was by a six-month-old fetus. Hmmm.

Confirmation was given to the shepherds:
And there were in the same country shepherds abiding in the field, keeping watch over their flock by night. And, lo, the angel of the Lord came upon them, and the glory of the Lord shone round about them: and they were sore afraid. And the angel said unto them, Fear not: for, behold, I bring you good tidings of great joy, which shall be to all people. For unto you is born this day in the city of David a Saviour, which is Christ the Lord.(Luke 2:8-11 KJV)

Jesus was born of the line of David physically through His mother, Mary, and legally through Joseph. (see **Bloodline**)
Hath not the scripture said, That Christ cometh of the seed of David, and out of the town of Bethlehem, where David was? (John 7:42 KJV)

It was well-known among the Jews that Jesus was a descendant of David. This may have been compounded by the fact that both Joseph and Mary were descended from David. Mary through Nathan and Joseph through Solomon.
And all the people were amazed, and said, Is not this the son of David? (Matthew 12:23 KJV)
And the multitudes that went before, and that followed, cried, saying, Hosanna to the son of David: Blessed is he that cometh in the name of the Lord; Hosanna in the highest. (Matthew 21:9 KJV)

And, behold, a woman of Canaan came out of the same coasts, and cried unto him, saying, Have mercy on me, O Lord, thou son of David; my daughter is grievously vexed with a devil. (Matthew 15:22 KJV)
Then they came to Jericho. As Jesus and his disciples, together with a large crowd, were leaving the city, a blind man, Bartimaeus (which means "son of Timaeus"), was sitting by the roadside begging. When he heard that it was Jesus of Nazareth, he began to shout, "Jesus, Son of David, have mercy on me!" (Mark 10:46)
More examples: *(Mark 10:46-52)(Matthew 20:30) (Luke 18:38-41)*

Jesus Was More Than a Prophet or Teacher

Jesus Forgave Sin

When Jesus saw their faith, he said to the paralyzed man, "Son, your sins are forgiven." Now some teachers of the law were sitting there, thinking to themselves, "Why does this fellow talk like that? He's blaspheming! Who can forgive sins but God alone?" (Mark 2:5-7)
Then Jesus said to her, "Your sins are forgiven." (Luke 7:48)

Jesus Accepted Worship

And as they went to tell his disciples, behold, Jesus met them, saying, All hail. And they came and held him by the feet, and worshipped him. (Matthew 28:9 KJV)
And when he was come out of the ship, immediately there met him out of the tombs a man with an unclean spirit, Who had his dwelling among the tombs; and no man could bind him, no, not with chains: Because that he had been often bound with fetters and chains, and the

chains had been plucked asunder by him, and the fetters broken in pieces: neither could any man tame him. And always, night and day, he was in the mountains, and in the tombs, crying, and cutting himself with stones. But when he saw Jesus afar off, he ran and worshipped him, (Mark 5:2-6 KJV)

Jesus Was Known as the Son of God

The disciples knew it when they were on the boat during the storm and saw Jesus walking on the water.

And immediately Jesus stretched forth his hand, and caught him, and said unto him, O thou of little faith, wherefore didst thou doubt? And when they were come into the ship, the wind ceased. Then they that were in the ship came and worshipped him, saying, Of a truth thou art the Son of God. (Matthew 14:31-33 KJV)

Demons recognized Jesus as the Son of God.

And unclean spirits, when they saw him, fell down before him, and cried, saying, Thou art the Son of God. And he straitly charged them that they should not make him known.
 (Mark 3:11-12 KJV)

Jesus Confirms His Messiahship

*Again the high priest asked him, "Are you the **Messiah**, the Son of the Blessed One?" "**I am**," said Jesus. "And you will see the **Son of Man** sitting at the right hand of the Mighty One and coming on the clouds of heaven." (Mark 14:61-62)*

Simon Peter answered, "You are the Messiah, the Son of the living

God." Jesus replied, "Blessed are you, Simon son of Jonah, for this was not revealed to you by flesh and blood, but by my Father in heaven. (Matthew 16:16)

"son of man" vs. "Son of Man"

Son of Man

Let's take a look at the term "son of man'. Jesus made more references to Himself as the Son of Man than as the Messiah. The phrase "son of man" occurs 87 times in the New Testament (83 times in the four Gospels) and 103 times in the Old Testament. This is a Hebrew phrase referring to a descendant of Adam and Eve. A human.

How then can man be justified with God? or how can he be clean that is <u>born of a woman</u>? Behold even to the moon, and it shineth not; yea, the stars are not pure in his sight. How much less man, that is a worm? and the <u>son of man</u>, which is a worm? (Job 25:4-6 KJV)

And it came to pass, when men began to multiply on the face of the earth, and daughters were born unto them, That the sons of God saw the <u>daughters of men</u> (Genesis 6:1-2 KJV)

The heaven, even the heavens, are the Lord's: but the earth hath he given to the <u>children of men</u>. (Psalm 115:16 KJV)

The phrase "son of man" is used 93 times in the book of Ezekiel.

And he said unto me, <u>son of man</u>, stand upon thy feet, and I will speak unto thee.(Ezekiel 2:1 KJV)

The term Son of Man as Messianic is first seen in the book of Daniel.
I saw in the night visions, and, behold, one like the Son of man came

with the clouds of heaven, and came to the Ancient of days, and they brought him near before him. And there was given him dominion, and glory, and a kingdom, that all people, nations, and languages, should serve him: his dominion is an everlasting dominion, which shall not pass away, and his kingdom that which shall not be destroyed. (Daniel 7:13-14 KJV)

This Son of Man is referred to as the Most High in verses 18 and 27 of the same chapter.

The Serpent

Immediately after the fall, God declared to the serpent a seed (singular) from the woman would:
bruise thy head, and thou shalt bruise his heel. (Genesis 3:15 KJV)
Some translations say crush his head.
Of all the sons and daughters of men that had been born since the creation of the world, Jesus was declaring Himself as the one that would defeat the serpent. The deceiver. Satan.

The Temptation of Christ Victorious

The temptations Satan used when he tempted Jesus in the wilderness were legitimate. *(Hebrews 4:15)* Jesus had put down His flesh, considering it as dead at His baptism. He was still a man. A human.

But, he no longer considered himself obligated to the flesh.
So then, brothers, we are debtors, not to the flesh, to live according to the flesh. (Romans 8:12 ESV)

Jesus refused to pick up the divine nature He had set aside.

Who, being in very nature God, did not consider equality with God something to be used to his own advantage; rather, he made himself nothing by taking the very nature of a servant, being made in human likeness. And being found in appearance as a man, he humbled himself by becoming obedient to death—even death on a cross!
(Philippians 2:6-8 KJV)

He was determined to live as a man filled and led by the Spirit of God and trusting in the written Word of God. This is the same way we are encouraged to live as Christians today. Jesus is the author and finisher of our faith. *(Hebrews 12:2)*

Lust of the Flesh

The tempter came to him and said, "If you are the Son of God, tell these stones to become bread." Jesus answered, "It is written: 'Man shall not live on bread alone, but on every word that comes from the mouth of God.'[(Matthew 4:3-4 KJV)

Jesus was hungry and could have turned the stones into bread. After all, He later fed the 5,000 and the 7,000 with a few loaves of bread and some fish. By not succumbing to the desires of the flesh but by "feeding" from the Word *(John 4:32)* He was able to present Himself as the "Bread of Life".

Pride of Life

Jesus had responded to the first temptation with scripture so Satan decided to add Scripture to his next temptation.

Then the devil took him to the holy city and had him stand on the

highest point of the temple. "If you are the Son of God," he said, "throw yourself down. For it is written: "'He will command his angels concerning you, and they will lift you up in their hands, so that you will not strike your foot against a stone.'" Jesus answered him, "It is also written: 'Do not put the Lord your God to the test.'
(Matthew 4:5-7 KJV)

The temple area was a busy place with many people coming and going. I'm certain this would be seen by many and His fame would quickly spread. Jesus knew He could have called angels to rescue Him *(Matthew 26:53)*. Once again, Jesus was determined to follow the Father's plan and live according to the Word.

Lust of the Eyes

Again, the devil took him to a very high mountain and showed him all the kingdoms of the world and their splendor. "All this I will give you," he said, "if you will bow down and worship me." Jesus said to him, "Away from me, Satan! For it is written: 'Worship the Lord your God, and serve him only.' (Matthew 4: 8-10 KJV)

Jesus, as the Son of Man was prophesied to receive sovereignty and authority over all nations. *(Daniel 7:13-14).*

He could have bypassed all the trauma and torture by submitting. Instead, He "set His face like flint" *(Isaiah 50:7- Luke 9:51)* determined to follow through and fulfill His destiny according to God's will. *(Luke 22:42).* Jesus was one with the Father and He was determined to keep that unity. To remain one with the Father and continue with the "mystery", the plan of salvation. He wasn't only going to fulfill the role of "Son of Man" and rule with all authority. He planned to conquer Satan, death, and sin, and provide freedom to all who believed in him and accepted Him as Lord.

"The Spirit of the Lord is upon me, for he has anointed me to bring Good News to the poor. He has sent me to proclaim that captives will be released, that the blind will see, that the oppressed will be set free, (Luke 4:18 NLT)

Then the devil left him, and angels came and attended him. (Matthew 4:11 KJV)

Jesus began His ministry.

Parallels

God had promised Abraham: a seed. *(Genesis 15:5-6)* Then He told Abraham to sacrifice the firstborn of that seed, Isaac. *(Genesis 22:2)* I am certain that Abraham agonized over this but decided to trust God and take Isaac with him up Mount Moriah. He believed that God could, if necessary, bring Isaac back from the dead to fulfill His promise that the seed would come through Isaac.

By faith Abraham, when he was tried, offered up Isaac: and he that had received the promises offered up his only begotten son, Of whom it was said, That in Isaac shall thy seed be called: Accounting that God was able to raise him up, even from the dead; from whence also he received him in a figure. (Hebrew 11:17-19 KJV)

On the way, Isaac asked where is the lamb for the burnt offering?

Abraham responded *"My son, God will provide <u>himself</u> a lamb for a burnt offering" (Genesis 22: 8 KJV)*

God intervened and provided a ram as a sacrificial substitute for Isaac, the first of Abraham's promised progeny, stating,

By myself have I sworn, saith the Lord, for because thou hast done this thing, and hast not withheld thy son, thine only son: That in blessing I will bless thee, and in multiplying I will multiply thy seed as the stars of the heaven, and as the sand which is upon the sea shore; and thy seed shall possess the gate of his enemies; And in thy seed shall all the nations of the earth be blessed; because thou hast obeyed my voice. (Genesis 22:16-18 KJV)

And the scripture was fulfilled which saith, Abraham believed God, and it was imputed unto him for righteousness: and he was called the Friend of God. (James 2:23 KJV)

The Substitute Lamb

Jesus knew who He was from a very young age. *"Why did you seek Me? Did you not know that I must be about My Father's business?" (Luke 2:49)* He was twelve. Like the ram God provided as a substitute for Isaac Jesus knew that He was to be that substitute. This time for the entire world. *(John 3:16)*

Even as the <u>Son of man</u> came not to be ministered unto, but to minister, and to give his life a ransom for many. (Matthew 20:28 KJV)

Like Abraham, Jesus believed that God was able to raise Him the sacrificial Lamb from the dead.

And as they came down from the mountain (of transfiguration), *Jesus charged them, saying, Tell the vision to no man, until the Son of man be risen again from the dead. (Matthew 17:9 KJV)*

As Isaac had carried the wood for the sacrifice *(Genesis 22:6)* Jesus carried His cross up to Golgotha to be sacrificed *(John 19:17)*.

As previously stated in "**A Mind for Battle**" Solomon built that first temple in the same location as Abraham's altar, Mount Moriah *(2 Chronicles 3:1)*. It has since come to be known as Mount Zion. Most scholars believe this to be where Jesus was crucified, Golgotha - the place of the skull. The Latin word for skull is calvaria. The same location where God provided a ram in place of Isaac revealing Himself as Jehova Jireh, God will provide. *(Genesis 22:14)*

> This evening we are looking at Mount Moriah, Golgotha, and Calvary. Where is Golgotha or the Place of the skull located today? Golgotha is located just outside the walls of Jerusalem, not more than 700 m from the spot where King Solomon built the first Jewish Temple. According to Jewish tradition, Solomon built the temple on Mount Moriah, commemorating the exact spot where Abraham stretched out Isaac upon the altar of sacrifice (Genesis 22: 1-19). Mount Moriah, the Temple of Solomon, the place of Isaac's sacrifice, and Golgotha — are all the same place.

All mark the place where God bound himself to fulfill the promises of the Abraham ic covenant.

The crucifixion of Jesus took place in that same "region of Moriah" where over 2000 years before Abraham had stood prepared to offer to God his only son, his innocent son, at God's command. But this time as Jesus was led to the Cross carrying the wood upon which he would be offered, there was no ram caught in the bushes to take his place. The ancient prophecy was also a promise. God told Abraham that someday " in the mountain of the Lord — it will be provided". And now it was provided, in the person of Jesus Christ. He gave Himself for me.

(https://dtbm.org/moriah-and-golgotha-2/)

In the final days leading to His death, Jesus revealed more and more of His destiny.

Identity:

When Jesus came into the coasts of Caesarea Philippi, he asked his disciples, saying, Whom do men say that I the Son of man am? (Matthew 16:13 KJV)

Purpose:

For the Son of man is come to save that which was lost. (Matthew 18:11 KJV)

Betrayal:

And while they abode in Galilee, Jesus said unto them, The Son of man shall be betrayed into the hands of men: (Matthew 17:22 KJV)

Behold, we go up to Jerusalem; and the <u>Son of man</u> shall be betrayed unto the chief priests and unto the scribes, and they shall condemn him to death, (Matthew 20:18 KJV)

Suffering:

But I say unto you, That Elias is come already, and they knew him not, but have done unto him whatsoever they listed. Likewise shall also the <u>Son of man</u> suffer of them. (Matthew 17:12 KJV)

Death:

Ye know that after two days is the feast of the passover, and the <u>Son of man</u> is betrayed to be crucified. (Matthew 26:2 KJV)

Resurrection:

For as Jonas was three days and three nights in the whale's belly; so shall the <u>Son of man</u> be three days and three nights in the heart of the earth. (Matthew 12:40 KJV)

When they came together in Galilee, he said to them, "The <u>Son of Man</u> is going to be delivered into the hands of men. They will kill him, and on the third day he will be raised to life." And the disciples were filled with grief. (Matthew 17:22-23 KJV)

Glorification and Return:

For the <u>Son of man</u> shall come in the glory of his Father with his angels, and then he shall reward every man according to his works. Verily I say unto you, There be some standing here, which shall not taste of death, till they see the <u>Son of man</u> coming in his kingdom. (Matthew 16:27-28 KJV)

When the <u>Son of man</u> shall come in his glory, and all the holy angels with him, then shall he sit upon the throne of his glory: (Matthew 25:31 KJV)

Adam and Eve, Noah, Abraham, and Israel were all promised countless descendants and told to subdue and fill the land/earth.

First Adam - Second Adam (Sin in - Sin Out)

Adam disobeyed. He took the fruit from Eve and ate. He wasn't even tempted or deceived. The bloodline of mankind became infected with the sin of self-determination. Separated from God. Continuing with each generation until today.

Therefore, just as sin entered the world through one man, and death through sin, and in this way death came to all people, because all sinned—To be sure, sin was in the world before the law was given, but sin is not charged against anyone's account where there is no law. Nevertheless, death reigned from the time of Adam to the time of Moses, even over those who did not sin by breaking a command, as did Adam, who is a pattern of the one to come. (Romans 5:12-14 KJV)

By faith in the New Covenant offered by Jesus through his fulfillment of the Old Covenant and the shedding of his blood sin has been removed and we have been given a new spiritual bloodline by the Spirit of God.

But the gift is not like the trespass. For if the many died by the trespass of the one man, how much more did God's grace and the gift that came by the grace of the one man, Jesus Christ, overflow to the many!

Nor can the gift of God be compared with the result of one man's sin: The judgment followed one sin and brought condemnation, but the gift followed many trespasses and brought justification. For if, by the trespass of the one man, death reigned through that one man, how much more will those who receive God's abundant provision of grace and of the gift of righteousness reign in life through the one man, Jesus Christ! Consequently, just as one trespass resulted in condemnation for all people, so also one righteous act resulted in justification and life for all people. For just as through the disobedience of the one man the many were made sinners, so also through the obedience of the one man the many will be made righteous. (Romans 5: 15-19 KJV)

A Spiritual Progeny

We are born via the Holy Spirit into a new type of being. Recreated after the image of Christ. The First-Born. The New Adam.

So it is written: "The first man Adam became a living being"(Genesis 2:7); the last Adam, a life-giving spirit. The spiritual did not come first, but the natural, and after that the spiritual. ⁴⁷ The first man was of the dust of the earth; the second man is of heaven. As was the earthly man, so are those who are of the earth; and as is the heavenly man, so also are those who are of heaven. And just as we have borne the image of the earthly man, so shall we bear the image of the heavenly man. (1 Corinthians 15:45-49 KJV)

Now you, brothers and sisters, like Isaac, are children of promise. At that time the son born according to the flesh persecuted the son born by the power of the Spirit. It is the same now. (Galatians 4:28-29 KJV)

Dear friends, now we are children of God, and what we will be has not yet been made known. But we know that when Christ appears, we shall be like him, for we shall see him as he is.
(1 John 3:2 KJV)

If you belong to Christ, then you are Abraham's seed, and heirs according to the promise. (Galatians 3:29 KJV)

He is also head of the body, the church; and He is the beginning, the firstborn from the dead, so that He Himself will come to have first place in everything. (Colossians 1:18 KJV)

The Spirit you received does not make you slaves, so that you live in fear again; rather, the Spirit you received brought about your adoption to sonship. And by him we cry, "Abba, Father."
(Romans 8:15 KJV)

BETTER COVENANT? 183

- IN THE FAITH 183
  - Walking With God - a Letter to Lori 183
- I WILL MAGNIFY 184
- PERSONAL SHORTCOMINGS 185
  - Regarding the Spirit vs. the Flesh: 186
  - "I Can Do All Things Through Christ..." 187
  - Resting in the Storm 188
  - Examine Yourselves 189
  - A Different Law 189
  - Code of Behavior 190
  - An Unchanging Law 191
  - Love is Fulfillment of the Law 192
- LEST I BE DISQUALIFIED 192
  - God's Righteousness - Not Ours 197
- EYE FOR AN EYE VS A BETTER WAY 198

Better Covenant?

In The Faith

Walking With God - a Letter to Lori

I have only the best hopes and beliefs for you and will pray for God's guidance to rule strongly in your heart for every decision you make and that you will be able to walk easily in that guidance; not second-guessing, but believing that for every step you take - from that step to the next God is always able to work for the best in your life and has the love, compassion, wisdom, and power to complete the work He has begun in you.

Whatever "mistakes from the past" plague your mind, true or not, God can guide you as you put your trust, not in your ability to hear or not stumble; but in the fact that you are holding His hand. As you hold His hand in your walk, His grip will keep you from falling headlong. If you don't let go of His hand, you can be assured He will never let go of yours. Keep your trust and faith strong and constant based on His grace, love, and faithfulness. Don't allow Satan, the accuser of the brethren, to draw your focus on your failings.

What you allow as your focus is what will be "magnified" in your life. It can turn a "mote" into a plank and obscure your vision. Focus on "magnifying" the Lord and His character and attributes.

I Will Magnify

O magnify the Lord with me, and let us exalt his name together. (Psalm 34:3)
What or who are you magnifying in your sight?

Hold your thumb out in front of you with your arm extended. How much of your view does it block? Now, close one eye and bring your thumb up until it touches the eyelash on your open eye. It's the same thumb, but look how much this new perspective affects your view.

The closer we focus or "magnify" things; the more they dominate our perspective.
A tiny *"mote"* in our eye can become a log. *(Matthew 7:3-5)*

You have a choice - to focus on your failures and the failures of others. To "magnify" negatives? Or, to seek out God's mercy, grace, and intervention in our lives and the lives of others.

Finally, brothers and sisters, whatever is true, whatever is noble, whatever is right, whatever is pure, whatever is lovely, whatever is admirable--if anything is excellent or praiseworthy--think about such things. (Philippians 4:8)

Personal Shortcomings

We sometimes get so caught up in our shortcomings, failed efforts, and struggles with personal demons that we are afraid to step out in faith. Why would God bless me or answer my prayers? Look at me. I'm a mess. We fear sharing our faith with others will place us in a hypocritical status. We Christians have had that label thrown at us for so long that we accept it as truth.

Is the soldier who faces his fears and continues in battle a coward?

If a heroin addict says heroin is bad does that make his statement untrue? If he has trouble escaping and staying out of addiction; does that invalidate the truth that heroin is bad and make him a hypocrite?

One of the basic tenets of Scripture is that we are in a fallen state and are born with a sinful nature. We struggle daily with everything from sloth to anger, addiction, fear, etc. All these things manifest through different venues. But we all struggle.

Christianity teaches that our answer is a personal relationship with God through Jesus' sacrifice on the cross.

The point is that the message is not based on our success but on Christ's success. We are all "working out our salvation through fear and trembling" *(Philippians 2:12)* (read it in context). A quick tip: you get stronger by lifting weights...

Don't let your shortcomings inhibit you from sharing your faith or from approaching the *"Throne of Grace"* with confidence because that confidence is based on God's mercy and Christ's success and that is Good News.

For he is our peace, who hath made both one, and hath broken down the middle wall of partition between us; (Ephesians 2:14 KJV)

This is where the New Covenant comes in and why it is the "Better Covenant". Because to walk in faith we need to walk with a clear conscience.

Let us therefore come boldly [with confidence NIV] *unto the throne of grace, that we may obtain mercy, and find grace to help in time of need. (Hebrews 4:16 KJV)*

Regarding the Spirit vs. the Flesh:

The battle is not choosing to be good or trying not to be bad. No matter how well-intentioned, unless we are trusting in God's grace we will be fighting the battle in our strength, seeking our righteousness, and coming under the law. The paradigm is to look toward Jesus, the Author and Finisher of our faith.

"My people have committed two sins: They have forsaken me, the sping of living water, and have dug their own cisterns, broken cisterns that cannot hold water." (Jeremiah 2:13)

As we pursue intimacy with Him the supernaturally natural response will be fruits of the Spirit, plucked from the tree of life growing in the "garden of our heart".

He has promised we will *"hear His voice"* that He will *"light our path"* He will *"hold our hand so we don't stumble"* He will *"make our paths straight"* and *"take every obstacle out of the way of My people"* He will *"work all things together for the good"*.

Seek "His righteousness" and "all these things will be added unto you." Enter His rest

"I Can Do All Things Through Christ..."

We hear this phrase used out of context so often. It has almost become a cliche for a "Christianized" version of the "Law of Attraction". "If I can psyche my mustard seed up to 51% positive and 49% negative I can make it happen."

Paul begins this context as *"I know both how to be abased, and I know how to abound: every where and in all things I am instructed both to be full and to be hungry, both to abound and to suffer need." Philippians 4:12 KJV)* Then he says, *"I can do all things through Christ which strengtheneth me." (v 13 KJV)*

I am not belittling faith or the concept of the mustard seed. I am concerned with our approach. We can plant. We can water. But it is God who gives the growth. No matter how hard we try to make that seed grow. No matter how fervently we water. It is the Spirit of God who empowers and brings that tiny seed into maturity. Where you place that seed is important. That hope. That trust needs to be placed in the provision and hope of Christ's work on the cross. The love and care for you that He initiated and completed on your behalf. Not on how hard you can psyche your faith.

Resting in the Storm

Jesus rested in the storm. If you are not at rest you are not in faith and you are working out the problem in the futility of your mind. Take that energy, that focus, and use it to enter into His rest.

For <u>we who have believed enter that rest</u>, as he has said, "As I swore in my anger, 'They will never enter my rest!'" And yet God's works were accomplished from the foundation of the world. For he has spoken somewhere about the seventh day in this way: "And God rested on the seventh day from all his works," (Hebrews 4:3-4) Consequently a Sabbath rest remains for the people of God. For the one who enters God's rest has also rested from his works, just as God did from his own works. (Hebrews 4:9-10)

If the storm is too violent to lay in the boat stand up and watch the storm with Jesus.
Wherefore take unto you the whole armour of God, that ye may be able to withstand in the evil day, and having done all, to stand. (Ephesians 6:13 KJV)
Let Him hold you in peace. Knowing that no matter how great the tempest - *"Greater is He that is in you..." (1 John 4:4 KJV)*

Examine Yourselves

For to be sure, he was crucified in weakness, yet he lives by God's power. Likewise, we are weak in him, yet by God's power we will live with him in our dealing with you. Examine yourselves to see whether you are in the faith; test yourselves. Do you not realize that Christ Jesus is in you—unless, of course, you fail the test? And I trust that you will discover that we have not failed the test.
(2 Corinthians 13:4-6)

May the God of hope fill you with all joy and peace as you trust in him, so that you may overflow with hope by the power of the Holy Spirit. (Romans 15:13)

A Different Law

I grew up in the church. I was raised on a series of Do's and Dont's. Don't smoke, drink, cuss, or chew. Or, run around with those who do. Don't gamble, play cards, play pool, drink alcoholic beverages,... If you were raised in the church, you know the drill. The funny thing is none of these were absolutes. As time passed and pool tables became more affordable people began putting them in their homes. Suddenly, playing pool was acceptable. My cousins and I would go to a Baptist camp in the summer where the boys and girls had to swim at different times. They were not allowed to swim together. As I traveled more and more I saw that in some areas men and women swam together but at some places, the women had to wear shirts over their bathing suits while they did not at other locations. These were all church-sponsored. While growing up, if I needed to use the restroom I was to refer to it as

"I have to go potty" or "poop." I had cousins, raised in the church, who would say "Take a crap", or "Pee'. When I heard one of my cousins tell his father he need to "Piss" I expected a severe reprimand. But, there was none. It didn't make sense. Why was a word wrong for one family and okay for another? We were all church-going Christians.

Code of Behavior

We were being raised on a varying code of behavior. It varied by age, by location, and by clan. There were no absolutes. When you are young you look to your parents for guidance. As you get older and your environment widens you begin to be introduced to other authorities - peers, teachers, and age restrictions are removed. The "laws" change. You begin to see behavior as malleable. The rules apply according to your environment. According to your peers. According to your current authority. This only reinforces the tendency to do "what is right in our own minds". We are being good by our standards. By the mores of our current environment. We have been raised under the law in the age of grace and, as we have seen, laws change. Laws have become relevant in our eyes to what is happening at the moment. Example: Marijuana used to be illegal; but, is now being legalized in varied degrees in many states. Marijuana was not made illegal until the Marihuana Tax Act in 1937. That was struck down in 1969 by the Supreme Court. 1970 - Controlled Substance Act. And so on...

(https://en.wikipedia.org/wiki/Timeline_of_cannabis_laws_in_the_United_States)

An Unchanging Law

On one of my recent travels, I saw a sign in front of a church - "Do the Works of Christ" That's a great message. But, what exactly are the works of Christ?

Go to church twice a week. Tithe. Don't smoke, drink, cuss, or...
It is for freedom that Christ has set us free. Stand firm, then, and do not let yourselves be burdened again by a yoke of slavery. Mark my words! I, Paul, tell you that if you let yourselves be circumcised, Christ will be of no value to you at all. Again I declare to every man who lets himself be circumcised that he is obligated to obey the whole law. You who are trying to be justified by the law have been alienated from Christ; you have fallen away from grace. (Galatians 5:1-4)

Circumcision in and of itself was not the issue. "False teachers" were bringing the new Christians back under the law. Placing them back under the yoke of covenants that had been fulfilled. This would be like making payments on a debt that no longer existed. That had been paid in full. These people were being pulled from grace back into works. The faith struggle here is to trust in the work that Jesus did on the cross. Basing your behavior on living a life pleasing to Him rather than to appease the law.

What best motivates your behavior in a relationship? Fear or love? Are you afraid of displeasing the other and facing consequences? Or, are you driven by a desire to please and reap the benefits of a close personal relationship?

Love is Fulfillment of the Law

"A new command I give you: Love one another. As I have loved you, so you must love one another. By this everyone will know that you are my disciples, if you love one another."
(John 13:34)

Let no debt remain outstanding, except the continuing debt to love one another, for whoever loves others has fulfilled the law. The commandments, "You shall not commit adultery," "You shall not murder," "You shall not steal," "You shall not covet," and whatever other command there may be, are summed up in this one command: "Love your neighbor as yourself." Love does no harm to a neighbor. Therefore love is the fulfillment of the law. (Romans 13:8-10)

So, what are the works of God? What are the works of Christ?
Then they asked him, "What must we do to do the works God requires?" Jesus answered, "The work of God is this: to believe in the one he has sent." (John 6:28-40 KJV)

Lest I Be Disqualified

No, I strike a blow to my body and make it my slave so that after I have preached to others, I myself will not be disqualified for the prize. (1 Corinthians 9:27 KJV)

Paul wrote a majority of the books of the New Testament. He was the first to bring the Gospel to the Gentiles. He set up churches in Galatia,

Philippi, Thessalonica, Corinth, and Ephesus. According to his own words:

I have worked much harder, been in prison more frequently, been flogged more severely, and been exposed to death again and again. Five times I received from the Jews the forty lashes minus one. Three times I was beaten with rods, once I was pelted with stones, three times I was shipwrecked, I spent a night and a day in the open sea, I have been constantly on the move. I have been in danger from rivers, in danger from bandits, in danger from my fellow Jews, in danger from Gentiles; in danger in the city, in danger in the country, in danger at sea; and in danger from false believers. I have labored and toiled and have often gone without sleep; I have known hunger and thirst and have often gone without food; I have been cold and naked.
(2 Corinthians 11:23-27 KJV)

That is quite a resume.

For we are the circumcision, which worship God in the spirit, and rejoice in Christ Jesus, and have no confidence in the flesh. Though I might also have confidence in the flesh. If any other man thinketh that he hath whereof he might trust in the flesh, I more: Circumcised the eighth day, of the stock of Israel, of the tribe of Benjamin, an Hebrew of the Hebrews; as touching the law, a Pharisee; Concerning zeal, persecuting the church; touching the righteousness which is in the law, blameless. But what things were gain to me, those I counted loss for Christ. Yea doubtless, and I count all things but loss for the excellency of the knowledge of Christ Jesus my Lord: for whom I have suffered the loss of all things, and do count them but dung, that I may win Christ, And be found in him, not having mine own righteousness, which is of the law, but that which is through the faith of Christ, the righteousness which is of God by faith: That I may know him, and the power of his resurrection, and the fellowship of his sufferings, being made conformable unto his death;(Philippians 3:3-10 KJV)

How could Paul possibly be concerned with disqualification from the race?

The biggest issue early Christians struggled with was letting go of the law and trusting in grace. They thought they still needed to add something to God's provision to complete their salvation. There were, in fact, many teachers who came in teaching the newly converted Gentiles adherence to Jewish Law to complete their salvation.

You foolish Galatians! Who has bewitched you? Before your very eyes Jesus Christ was clearly portrayed as crucified. I would like to learn just one thing from you: Did you receive the Spirit by the works of the law, or by believing what you heard? Are you so foolish? <u>After beginning by means of the Spirit, are you now trying to finish by means of the flesh?</u> Have you experienced so much in vain—if it really was in vain? So again I ask,<u> does God give you his Spirit and work miracles among you by the works of the law, or by your believing what you heard?</u> So also Abraham "believed God, and it was credited to him as righteousness."

Understand, then, that those who have faith are children of Abraham.

Scripture foresaw that God would justify the Gentiles by faith, and announced the gospel in advance to Abraham: "All nations will be blessed through you." So those who rely on faith are blessed along with Abraham, the man of faith. (Galatians 3:1-9 KJV)

According to the New Covenant, that missing element was faith. Trusting that Christ's provision was sufficient. Resting in the final words of the Prince of Peace as He consummated a new covenant - this Better Covenant - with these words "It is finished."

I can list many scriptures such as 1 Timothy 6:21, where people for various reasons have departed from the faith. They were being seduced by "false teachings" such as the need to be circumcised as a completion to their salvation, to observe certain holidays, and to abstain from certain foods after God had approved all foods.
(Acts 10:9-16, Acts 15:20, Acts 21:25)
These "legalists" were preaching a different Christ.
In rebuttal to these teachings Paul states:
I repeat: Let no one take me for a fool. But if you do, then tolerate me just as you would a fool, so that I may do a little boasting. In this self-confident boasting I am not talking as the Lord would, but as a fool. Since many are boasting in the way the world does, I too will boast. You gladly put up with fools since you are so wise! In fact, you even put up with anyone who enslaves you or exploits you or takes advantage of you or puts on airs or slaps you in the face. To my shame I admit that we were too weak for that! Whatever anyone else dares to

boast about—I am speaking as a fool—I also dare to boast about. Are they Hebrews? So am I. Are they Israelites? So am I. Are they Abraham's descendants? So am I. Are they servants of Christ? (I am out of my mind to talk like this.) I am more.
(2 Corinthians 11:16-23 KJV)

Paul is so adamant about this distinction as to whose works are sufficient for salvation - Christ's or ours - that he points out that if anyone could make it by their works it would be him. Yet, even he cannot win the battle against sin.

I do not understand what I do. For what I want to do I do not do, but what I hate I do. And if I do what I do not want to do, I agree that the law is good. As it is, it is no longer I myself who do it, but it is sin living in me. For I know that good itself does not dwell in me, that is, in my sinful nature. [Phil] *For I have the desire to do what is good, but I cannot carry it out. For I do not do the good I want to do, but the evil I do not want to do—this I keep on doing. Now if I do what I do not want to do, it is no longer I who do it, but it is sin living in me that does it. So I find this law at work: Although I want to do good, evil is right there with me. For in my inner being, I delight in God's law* [Shep]*; but I see another law at work in me, waging war against the law of my mind and making me a prisoner of the law of sin at work within me. What a wretched man I am! Who will rescue me from this body that is subject to death? Thanks be to God, who delivers me through Jesus Christ our Lord! So then, I myself in my mind am a*

196

slave to God's law, but in my sinful nature a slave to the law of sin. (Romans 7:15-25 KJV)

Hap is caught in the middle. Even if he could psyche the determination and was able to live the rest of his life without sin, the law would have already been broken in the past. He is already dead in trespasses.
If you live under the law and break one law you have broken them all and fall short of salvation. For whosoever shall keep the whole law, and yet offend in one point, he is guilty of all. (James 2:10 KJV)
For it is by grace you have been saved, through faith—and this is not from yourselves, it is the gift of God—not by works, so that no one can boast. (Ephesians 2:8-9 KJV)

This is our only hope. The only way to have peace.
Therefore, since we have been justified through faith, we have peace with God through our Lord Jesus Christ, through whom we have gained access by faith into this grace in which we now stand. And we boast in the hope of the glory of God.(Romans 5:1-2 NIV)

God's Righteousness - Not Ours

Now to the one who works, wages are not credited as a gift but as an obligation. However, to the one who does not work but trusts God who justifies the ungodly, their faith is credited as righteousness. David says the same thing when he speaks of the blessedness of the one to whom God credits righteousness apart from works: "Blessed are those whose transgressions are forgiven, whose sins are covered. Blessed is

the one whose sin the Lord will never count against them."
(Romans 4:4-8)

But seek ye first the kingdom of God, and <u>his righteousness</u>; and all these things shall be added unto you. (Matt 6:33)

Eye for an Eye vs A Better Way

Jesus' command to *"Love your neighbor as yourself..." (Mark 12:31)wa*is not a call to develop a love of ourselves. It was a call to *"Do unto others as you would have them do to you." (Matt 7:12 - Luke 6:31)* In the Old Testament, vengeance was getting out of hand (read Genesis 34 - the rape of Dinah). Everyone was doing what was right in his own eyes. (*Judges 21:25*)

The concept of "an eye for an eye" was promulgated to bring a legal balance or stay to the overreactions of the offended toward the offender.

The establishment of "Cities of Refuge" was established to protect those involved with accidental manslaughter and provide them with a haven until provided an opportunity for a fair trial. To extend to others the same grace and mercy you would want for yourself is one of the highest forms of consideration we can give to others.

...forgive our trespasses as we forgive them that trespass against us (Matthew 6:12 NMB)
Therefore, if you are offering your gift at the altar and remember that

your brother has something against you...go and be reconciled...
(Matt 5:23-24)
"forgive your brother seventy times seven" (Matt 18:21-22)
the parable of the unforgiving servant *(Matt 18:23-35)*
Etc.

Let no debt remain outstanding, except the continuing debt to love one another, for whoever loves others has fulfilled the law. The commandments, "You shall not commit adultery," "You shall not murder," "You shall not steal," "You shall not covet," and whatever other command there may be, are summed up in this one command: "Love your neighbor as yourself." Love does no harm to a neighbor. Therefore love is the fulfillment of the law. (Romans 13:8-10)

VOICES: 201

- Where Did That Thought Come From? 201
  - *Wax on - Wax Off* *202*
- "Feed Me" 202
- Buffet or Buffet 203
- Can We Hear Evil Spirits? 204
- Simeon the Sorcerer Tried to Buy the Holy Spirit - Acts 8 210
- Practicing God's Voice 213
- Practicing His Presence 215
- My Sheep Hear My Voice 217
- Interactions 219
- McDonald's 221

Voices

Where Did That Thought Come From?

A song triggers a memory. Is it a good memory or bad? Your mind goes down a rabbit hole. A thought comes in out of nowhere during your prayer time. It is not relevant to your studies. Another rabbit hole.

In "**As We Are One - Phil, Shep, and Hap**" we talked about our flesh as a person - "Phil". He is one person of our trinity. His temperament is very different from "Hap" or "Shep". Being flesh he is extremely influenced by physical stimuli - taste, smell, touch, hearing, and sight. Phil interacts directly with the physical world. This can be good. This can be BAD.

As we drive we depend on Phil to keep things smooth. Negotiating curves, swerves, and stop signs. Hap is free to listen to the radio, navigate directions, hold a conversation with another passenger or passengers, call on the phone, text - Oops - that's a No-No. He only needs to jump in when that renegade rabbit runs across the road or if there is a flat tire. The car next to us swerves and Hap jumps in. They synchronously handle the situation without a glitch. These guys have worked together for years. They are a team. Depending on the level of your mind renewal Shep might jump in with a quick prayer.

Through hours of training in martial arts, gymnastics, archery, and even bricklaying behaviors become indoctrinated in our bodies/flesh to the point of instinct. Unfortunately, there is a potential downside to this. If the "training' is contrary to the Word of God we can have serious issues.

Going back to our lunch at the park - Phil wanted all the food. He did not want to give any food away and had to be convinced by Hap to share.

"Feed Me"

Phil is a person. He has a temperament. He has a voice. And, he wants to be the main star of the show. He wants it his way.

How many times have you been watching TV with a bag of potato chips in front of you? You determine you have eaten enough and fold the bag shut. A few minutes later you catch yourself with a mouthful of chips and a hand reaching back into the bag for more. Wait a minute. I said, "No more chips tonight!" You move the chips farther away. Eventually, you have to get up and put the chips back in the pantry because some mysterious force is causing you to unconsciously eat them. This is Phil. I wonder how much of what we term as subconscious can be attributed to Phil.

Jesus is the Word Incarnate. As a part of the Holy Trinity, Jesus came in the flesh. While here, Jesus had a will of His own.

Father, if thou be willing, remove this cup from me: nevertheless not my will, but thine, be done. (Luke 22:42 KJV)

As we are created in the image of God our flesh - Phil - has a mind of his own. He is self-indulging, and self-gratifying, and he wants those chips.

Hap and Phil synchronize well. They have had years of practice. They have also spent years colluding to get what they want. If not careful they can go off course down the path of self-serve moving toward hedonism and depravity.

We have got to break that type of comradery.

Buffet or Buffet

I therefore so run, not as uncertainly; so fight I, not as one that beateth the air: But I keep under my body, and bring it into subjection: lest that by any means, when I have preached to others, I myself should be a castaway. (1 Corinthians 9:26-27 KJV)

In other versions, such as the ASV the word buffet is used.

"but I buffet my body, and bring it into bondage:"

(noun) *Buffet*: a counter for refreshments (I went back to the *buffet* for a second helping)

(verb) *Buffet*: to drive, force, move, or attack by or as if by repeated blows (schools being *buffeted* by budget cuts)

(Merriam-Webster Dictionary)

Phil has a voice. Hap has a voice. We have Shep speaking in the background. Pre New Birth Shep is mostly dormant. Only a "conscience". After he has been empowered through New Birth he will have a stronger voice. As you become more attentive to the Holy Spirit and your mind is renewed to the Word the louder that voice will be.

"You deserve a break today." "If it feels good do it." "Love the one you are with." So many voices. Voices coming from the world system. Voices of past hurts and future misgivings. They can be deafening.

Spending too much time pondering how someone has hurt us is not helpful. As Pastor Tim Ritzel would say, "Sitting there in the Mulligrubs". Feeling sorry for ourselves allows resentment to build into bitterness. Just one word from someone can evoke an immediate response. Usually a regretful one. The fruit of verbal battles fought in your mind with an imaginary foe.

Like the old cartoon. An angel sitting on one shoulder and a demon sitting on the other. Is it Me? Is it THEM? It doesn't have to be a demon speaking. Whatever the source it is a starting point for futile and negative arguments in your head.

Can We Hear Evil Spirits?

Suggestions may come in from another source. An outside supernatural source.

I was driving in Biscayne Park, near North Miami Beach. As I approached a stop sign, "Run it!" jumped into my head. It wasn't an audible voice, but it was so sharp and so present that it startled me. I had to think quickly, "No, no, I'm not going to do that." I stopped. But, it was almost like someone in the backseat had yelled, "Go for it, Hit it." That is how strong the impulse was.

I continued through the intersection. As I looked back in the rearview mirror the car behind me ran the stop sign and crashed into a police car as it was entering the intersection. I thought, "Wow! If I had responded to that voice I would have run a stop sign right in front of a police car." I wondered if that lady had been hit with that same impulse and responded leading to her crashing into the Police car. What if there was an entity behind that voice? An evil spirit. And if it wasn't a spirit, then who? Or, what? Was his job assignment just to sit there and say, "Run that sign." If so, just how far up and down the totem pole does this go?

In the introduction and in "**A Spiritual Legacy**" at the end of the book, I mention that my maternal grandmother was an orphan. I am told her father, my great-grandfather committed suicide. It was during the Great Depression. If I am getting the story correct, his wife died from measles. When he found out he went down to the basement, sat down in a chair, and slashed his throat with a straight razor. Was this premeditated? Did a voice jump into his head like at the stop sign? He reacted and ended his life. However it happened, I'm sure he got caught up in the voices. Voices of despair, hopelessness, and more.

Dean Sherman has written an excellent book entitled "Spiritual Warfare". I highly recommend reading it. In the book Dean talks about *"... principalities, against powers, against the rulers of the darkness of this world, against spiritual wickedness in high places."*
(Ephesians 6:12)

He breaks it down down into categories. Regions of authority and geographic areas. Spirits are assigned over cities, states, and countries. At the top, you have beings such as the Prince of Persia and the Prince of Greece from the book of Daniel. They are regimented to the lowest level. You have spirits over political systems, families, corporations, etc. They work in opposition to proper authority. Fighting against marriages, families, and communities with a purpose to steal, kill, and destroy. *(John 10:10)*

Have you ever been on a mountaintop? Galveston, Tennessee, Lookout Mountain. You stand at the overlook and this impulse says "Jump!" "Wouldn't that be fun? Just jump." You are driving down the road and an impulse hits you. "Swerve and hit that car." "Swerve and hit that tree." I don't know. Maybe I'm the only person that that ever happens to.

In Matthew Chapter Sixteen, Jesus asked His disciples who they thought He was. Simon Peter answered He is the Christ (Messiah), the Son of the living God. In response, Jesus began to explain to them that He was going to be killed and raised again on the third day. Peter rebuked Him saying *"Be it far from thee, Lord: this shall not be unto* *thee. But he turned, and said unto Peter, <u>Get thee behind me, Satan</u>: thou art an offence unto me: for thou savourest not the things that be of God, but those that be of men. (Matthew 16:22-23 KJV)*

We hear of lying spirits and doctrines of spirits in both the Old and New Testaments.

*Beloved, believe not every spirit, but try the spirits whether they are of God: because many false prophets are gone out into the world.
(1 John 4:1 KJV)*

Now the Spirit speaketh expressly, that in the latter times some shall depart from the faith, giving heed to seducing spirits, and doctrines of devils; (1 Timothy 4:1 KJV)

Where and how do these doctrines, these teachings enter the minds of these teachers?

God might allow this as a test.

If a prophet, or one who foretells by dreams, appears among you and announces to you a sign or wonder, and if the sign or wonder spoken of takes place, and the prophet says, "Let us follow other gods" (gods you have not known) "and let us worship them," you must not listen to the words of that prophet or dreamer. The Lord your God is testing you to find out whether you love him with all your heart and with all your soul. (Deuteronomy 13:1-3)

...Or use this to move forward with His plan as with the downfall of the wicked Ahab King of Israel.

And he said, Hear thou therefore the word of the Lord: I saw the Lord sitting on his throne, and all the host of heaven standing by him on his right hand and on his left. And the Lord said, Who shall persuade Ahab, that he may go up and fall at Ramothgilead? And one said on this manner, and another said on that manner. And there came forth a spirit, and stood before the Lord, and said, I will persuade him. And the Lord said unto him, Wherewith? And he said, I will go forth, and I will be a lying spirit in the mouth of all his prophets. And he said, Thou shalt persuade him, and prevail also: go forth, and do so. Now therefore, behold, the Lord hath put a lying spirit in the mouth of all these thy prophets, and the Lord hath spoken evil concerning thee. (1 Kings 22:19-23 KJV)

Some people have seared their "conscience" *(1 Timothy 4:1-2)* giving themselves over to the realm of the flesh and are, therefore completely open to these teachings. This "wisdom of the world" was formulated by the "father of all lies". *(John 8:44)* Of these the Lord says *This is what the Lord Almighty says: "Do not listen to what the prophets are prophesying to you; they fill you with false hopes. They speak visions from their own minds, not from the mouth of the Lord. (Jeremiah 23:16)*

We have been created as triune beings. Our flesh, mind, and spirit are designed to interact with each other. Just as the flesh has a greater connection with the physical realm, the spirit is close to the spiritual and the mind with the mental or metaphysical realm. All three of these realms are bombarded with active and diverse voices calling out lies and deception from the one who was a liar from the beginning - Satan. This is why we need to determine that our source of truth comes from the Word of God. The Bible. Guided by the Holy Spirit of God. Anything that disagrees with that is to be taken as false no matter how much it tickles the ears. We have been given a teacher to lead us into all truth - the Holy Spirit. We have been placed in Him and He is in us. We need to learn His language and listen to the Teacher.

Okay, at what point is it an evil spirit? At what point is it us? It is a moot point.

My friend Randy Cutrell and I spent about a year going back and forth on eternal security. It was not an everyday thing. But during our daily reading, we would see a verse that seemed to either support or refute the general concept of eternal security. If you're part of the family, you're always part of the family. Then Paul speaks about some of leaving the faith. It is better for them if they've never been involved.

We finally came to the point that if you're in an active relationship with God through Christ it doesn't matter. The only time a question like that is relevant is if you're goofing off or want to live in sin. At that point, you had better do something about the relationship. You may never have come into a legitimate relationship with Christ. If two people get drunk and take marriage vows in Las Vegas. They sign the papers. They are "technically" married but, are they in a marriage? If a "fire and brimstone" evangelist comes to town and scares you to the point where you come to the altar, on the 23rd repetition of "Just as I

am" then you go and live your life as you wish thinking you have received salvation are you now saved? Are you born again?
"Examine yourselves, whether ye be in the faith;" (2 Corinthians 13:5)

Look at the different voices - so many voices calling out. Voices from TV commercials, radio, various mentors, Hap, Phil, demons, and more. What it comes down to is this:

For though we walk in the flesh, we do not war after the flesh: (For the weapons of our warfare are not carnal, but mighty through God to the pulling down of strong holds;) Casting down imaginations, and every high thing that exalteth itself against the knowledge of God, and bringing into captivity every thought to the obedience of Christ;
(2 Corinthians 10:3-5 KJV)

As those thoughts come in, just stop and think, is this a blessing or a curse? Is this positive or negative? Is this thought in obedience to Christ? Because there is only one voice that matters. That is the voice of Christ - the Word of God.

Finally, brethren, whatsoever things are true, whatsoever things are honest, whatsoever things are just, whatsoever things are pure, whatsoever things are lovely, whatsoever things are of good report; if there be any virtue, and if there be any praise, think on these things.
(Philippians 4:8 KJV)

Simeon the Sorcerer Tried to Buy the Holy Spirit - Acts 8

So many, in the church, are being induced into a type of witchcraft; where the Word of God is used as an "incantation" to generate power or income. A weapon or charm to be thrown at a situation. A "holy hand grenade", so to speak.

Jesus claimed in John 5:39 *"You search the Scriptures because you think that in them you have eternal life; and it is they that bear witness about me..."*

"As for everyone who comes to me and hears my words and puts them into practice, I will show you what they are like. They are like a man building a house, who dug down deep and laid the foundation on rock. When a flood came, the torrent struck that house but could not shake it, because it was well built. But the one who hears my words and does not put them into practice is like a man who built a house on the ground without a foundation. The moment the torrent struck that house, it collapsed and its destruction was complete." (Luke 6:47-49)

The wise man built his house on the rock (relationship with Jesus - the Foundation Stone). The foolish man built his house on sand (various verses and teachings - small pieces of "The Rock). Our relationship and prayer life are not to be based on this or that verse pulled out to be used as a promise. They are based on our relationship with the "Promised One". Jesus is the author and finisher of our faith. He is the Word of God. Am I seeking a relationship; or trying to manipulate the hand of God?

The same thing goes for our relationship with the Lord Holy Spirit. So many "teachers" present an idea of the Holy Spirit as a hovering cloud of power for us to tap into for ecstatic thrills during worship or to plug into as a source of supernatural power.

In that case, we are being turned into spiritual sycophants. Seeking a connection to His power rather than Him. The Holy Spirit is just as much a person as is the Lord Christ or the Lord God.

Our purpose in life is not only to share the Gospel. God can do that through His angels and with dreams and visions. He wants to accomplish this in a partnership with us. We are called to live a holy life; and, to know Him. All of Him. Father, Son, and Holy Spirit. And to become one as Jesus was one with Him *(John 17:21)*.

As we become more and more involved in our relationship with Him; the result is increased holiness or separation from that which is not congruent to Him. When you are in love with someone, your thoughts and actions are drawn to them moving more and more in line with their personality and priorities. The natural response to this is to speak of that relationship and share their attributes with others. As our love and relationship grow; the desire to praise that person to others also grows. A desire to "proclaim their loveliness to the world", to the nations.

"Here is my servant, whom I uphold, my chosen one in whom I delight; I will put my Spirit on him, and he will bring justice to the nations. (Isaiah 42:1 NIV)

As we spend more and more time with a person; their perfume, their aroma will begin to cling to us. Their behavior will become more and more ingrained in ours. The same goes with the Holy Spirit. People will notice and either be drawn toward or pushed away from the aroma we carry with us as we go about our daily business.
(2 Corinthians 2:15-17)
We need to seek God for intimacy and love of who He is; rather than what He can do for us. All of the rest is a by-product of that relationship.

Practicing God's Voice

When I first began to practice hearing God's voice, I decided if I am in a relationship with God, if He is my father why shouldn't we be able to converse? I believe He hears me. I should be able to hear Him. Not just some tug at my heart. Why not an actual conversation? I did not expect to hear an audible voice; but, it should be tangible. More than a vague feeling.
As I began directing my faith in this manner, I remember one particular instance when I asked him, "Why is it when you talk to me, you always say, 'My son'?" "Why don't you ever call me Jon?" In a conversation with a friend or one of my siblings, it would be weird for them to call me "my friend" or "my brother". They just say "Jon". I was curious because people would stand up in the church and say, "My children." "My son". "My daughter." I felt like they were trying to sound religious and it bothered me. I wasn't expecting the response

that I got at all, which was "Everyone calls you Jon, but only your father calls you son."

It was in the 1980s. I was working in Colima, El Salvador helping build a village for "desplazados" (displaced people). A group of families had lost their homes in the guerrilla fighting. Around sixty people - men, women, and children had moved into an abandoned sugar mill. They were living in hoppers, bins, closets, anywhere they could find some sort of privacy. The government wanted to begin using the mill again so they teamed up with Para Vida Ministries and donated a large parcel of land for the construction of a small community. This consisted of quite a few homes, a church, two wells, and a medical center. The entire time we were there we could hear mortar fire in the distance. I was warned not to wander too far from the area as I might get kidnapped by the guerrillas. One night as I lay in my hammock at the motel where we were staying I saw soldiers running past my window. A while later there was gunfire and explosions not too far away. The next morning I learned that some communist soldiers had tried to blow up a bridge. The same one we crossed every day in our back and forth to the work project.

During the few breaks in our work, I had a few opportunities to sightsee. On one occasion, I was sitting up on a cliff looking out at the beauty of the jungle below. I could see for miles. Just taking it all in I said, "God, this is beautiful. This is so beautiful. What a beautiful creation you've made." Again there came an unexpected response. "No, this is terrible. I wish you could have seen the creation I made before the fall. What you see is filled with sin, disease, and death. It is not my original creation."

These are a few of many confirmations that I was speaking to and heard from someone with a very different viewpoint than mine.

Practicing His Presence

In the Luke Chapter Ten, Jesus is visiting the home of His friend Lazarus. Lazarus' sisters Mary and Martha were there. While Martha was going around preparing things for the meal. Doing this and that. Mary just sat down at Jesus' feet. Martha complained to Jesus and said, "Why don't you tell her to get up and help me?" His response?

Martha, Martha, thou art careful and troubled about many things: But one thing is needful: and Mary hath chosen that good part, which shall not be taken away from her. (Luke 10:41-42 KJV)

All kinds of things need attention, but Mary chose the better thing. In other words, while I'm here, sit. Sit at my feet and listen to me. Don't worry about all that busy work.

...do not worry about tomorrow, for tomorrow will worry about itself. Each day has enough trouble of its own. (Matthew 6:34 NIV)

I remember a time just after my divorce from Debbie. I was going to get my car worked on. Our daughter, Jamie wanted to go with me. I told her. "It's going to be boring. It's going to be a hot day. We will just be sitting around waiting while they work on my car. We're not going to go out and get ice cream or do anything fun." Jamie was twelve years old. She said, "I don't care. I just want to be with you." It touched my heart so much that she didn't care what we did. She just wanted to be with me.

I was so pleased I decided afterward to take her for ice cream. She ate only part of her cone saying she was saving the rest for her younger brother Chon. I told her to finish it and we would get more to take to him. I decided then and there I wanted to be more like her.

I was very involved with my "rescue church" Abundant Love Fellowship in Cahokia, Illinois. Youth leader, worship team, hospital ministry, church newspaper editor, children's church - my time was so tied up that I began to feel stressed. I looked at my schedule and determined that Wednesday night would be my time out with the Lord. I wouldn't plan anything. Just hang. We might go for a walk. Go someplace private where I would play my trombone for Him. It became one of the most important times in my life.

I wanted to live that Kent Henry song:

> When I look into Your holiness
> When I gaze into Your loveliness
> Your loveliness
> When all things that surround become shadows
> In the light of You

When I've found the joy of reaching Your heart
When my will becomes enthroned in Your love
When all things that surround become shadows
In the light of You
I worship You I worship You
I worship You worship You
The reason I live is to worship You

While reading in one of my journals from India I was reminded of how I would practice being in the presence of Jesus. I would sit and just spend time with him several times during the day, especially in the mornings, I would set my alarm clock for 10 or 15 minutes, depending on what was going on that day, and pretend that nothing existed except Him and me. Nothing mattered except our relationship. I would not worry about the film team, not worry about bills, not worry about anything like that. Just focus on my time with Him. Just enjoy being with Jesus.

My Sheep Hear My Voice

I was a co-youth leader at Abundant Love Fellowship in Cahokia, Illinois for a few years before my full-time involvement in Missions. I say co-leader. My partner, Stacee "Sumler" Evans was the driving force behind the Youth program. Always fresh with ideas and a heart to disciple. I led worship and shared in teaching.

My sheep hear my voice, and I know them, and they follow me: (John 10:27 KJV)

I wanted to make a point of hearing the voice of the Shepard. After reading the above scripture I had the group stand in a circle. I had them take turns standing in the middle blindfolded. I told them that there were voices in the room that they were more familiar with - friends/family. But, I wanted them to filter out those voices and listen to mine. I would stand in one place and tell them to come to me while the others were doing the same. I wouldn't raise my voice. They needed to filter out the other voices and find me. This went well. Afterwords, I told them., "Many voices are calling out to us in the world today. Many familiar. Some not. They call to us. Tempting us. Some cause fear and try to get us to hide or run from our position of rest and trust in God.

"Be sober, be vigilant; because your adversary the devil, as a roaring lion, walketh about, seeking whom he may devour:"(1 Peter 5:8)

There is only one voice that we can always trust. That is the voice of the Shepard. We need to practice hearing that voice. It will always agree with the scripture. The more time we spend reading the scripture the better will be our ability to hear and understand that voice.

So then faith cometh by hearing, and hearing by the word of God. (Romans 10:17)

Interactions

I had an opportunity to go to the Dominican Republic (January 1986) with a Youth With a Mission team led by my cousin Terry Keith and his wife, Donna. I wanted to be more available for missions so I sold my car and bought a motorcycle. The transition gave me much better mileage and cheaper insurance.

I spent quite a bit of time in prayer about the change. I kept hearing stories about the dangers of motorcycles. People would say, "You better watch out. You're tempting God. Blah, blah, blah." I was invited to a church softball game. Something I am usually not interested in but I decided to go. This is where I first met Jim Waltmann, President of Alouette Cosmetics Illinois who I later worked for in that company. Another great story.

At the game, someone offered me some Bazooka Bubblegum. The kind with the comic inside the wrapper. I don't normally chew gum. Chewing gum gives me a TMJ headache. I wanted to be nice so I said yes. I opened it, put the gum in my mouth, and read the cartoon. Something I "never" do is read the fortunes. Any type of fortune. I enjoy the cartoon but avoid the fortune at the bottom. It's not necessarily bad but is just one or two steps away from fortune-telling. My thinking is to avoid all those kinds of things. For some reason, I read it.

I had been asking God if I should get the motorcycle or not. Am I tempting you? Will you protect me? It made sense to me. Save money on gas. Save money on insurance. I read the fortune and it said, "Angels are watching over you." I've never seen anything like that before or since. It's not like I chew a lot of Bazooka bubble gum. I carried that little cartoon in my wallet for years until I lost my wallet. I said, "Okay. I'm taking this as a yes on the motorcycle and you'll protect me."

I bought the motorcycle. Mary Johnson, one of the girls in my youth group, (the one who wrote the song I used to open **Chapter 18: New Habits**) bought my car on the condition that I teach her how to drive a stick shift. It's kind of funny that the guy I bought the motorcycle from taught me how to ride a motorcycle. And I taught the girl who bought my car how to drive a stick shift. I left the day after Christmas because it was starting to get cold. I only had enough money to get to Florida but I figured if God was sending me He would provide just like He had always done before.

I drove straight down Hwy-55 occasionally hitting patches of ice. Pretty scary ride. But, "angels were watching over me". I reached Metarie and spent New Year's Eve with some friends. They went to bed at nine. I was used to staying up and celebrating New Year's Eve and didn't know what to do. They had some wine so I took some bread, and at midnight for New Year's, I took communion. I sat there and prayed from 1 Corinthians 11:26 "*For as often as you eat this bread and drink this cup, you proclaim the Lord's death till He comes*" and committed myself to God.

The next day I headed out for Orlando, Florida. While in Orlando waiting to go on the outreach to the Dominican Republic my brother-in-law, Bruce Lasota, was doing a new project called Reflect-Address. He gave me some really good training in sales and sent me out as a salesman. This is how I made money for the trip to the Dominican Republic.

The Dominican Republic was the first time I ever wore a clown outfit. On the first night of the performance, while performing some clown skits the electricity went out. Everything stopped. My brother R. Dale and I were used to doing funny finger tricks and jokes and playing around so we jumped out front and did our stuff. Most of it was improvised on the spot. This drew quite a crowd. Once we had a good crowd the power came back on and we were able to do the performances that we were trained to do.

There was a man in the crowd who had a national television show. He saw us and invited the team to come on and perform our Skits on national TV.

McDonald's

Upon returning to the United States, I had an offer to go to the Texas/Mexico border to help build a feeding center in McAllen, Texas, and worship and children's ministry in Reynosa, Mexico. I was headed West on I-10 on my motorcycle. It was late in the night and very cold.

I stopped in at a McDonald's to grab a couple of burgers. Some to eat there and some to take on the road so I wouldn't have to stop again until I got to Texas. I saw an elderly couple sitting at a booth talking to each other and felt strong in my heart that I should go tell them "Jesus loves you and cares about you."

A very simple message. So simple I'm thinking this is such a "CLICHE", "bumper sticker" -"Jesus loves you." message. I ignored it. I got on my bike and started riding off. But, I could not stop that feeling, the tug at my heart saying I should have spoken to them. It reached the point where about 20 minutes out I turned around and went back to McDonald's. I told God, "Okay, If they're still there, I will tell them." They were still there sitting in the same booth. I walked up to them and said, "Pardon me, I don't mean to interrupt what you're doing, but I'm feeling very strongly to tell you that God loves you and he cares about you.

They both started crying. They looked at me and said, "We have so many things going on in our lives. So many issues right now, that we came here to talk. We were just asking 'Is there really a God? Does God really care? Is He really interested in us?' We prayed and were asking God for an answer. We just got our answer. Thank you." I determined then and there not to judge what God might inspire.

I never say "Thus says the Lord." I share what I think God is prompting me to share. I ask the person I am speaking with to put it on the shelf. To allow God to confirm it. But, many times the person will respond with "You just confirmed something I was praying about." or "Someone gave me that same word this morning." I am not a prophet.

But, I believe we need to be sensitive to God's voice and His desire to meet needs with the right word or gift at the right time. I share these things because living a life focused on the Spirit of God should normalize this in our lives. Living as one with yourself and with God isn't a big psyche. As my friend Randy Cutrell always said, "It's supernaturally natural."

He also used to say, "An apple tree doesn't have to strain to produce an apple. It doesn't strain and pop out an apple. It sinks its roots deep into the soil drinking in water, taking in nutrients, and in the season it produces apples."

Now, I'm speaking of the Garden of Eden in our hearts. God told Adam and Eve to be caretakers. We are called to be caretakers of our personal Garden of Eden. The garden of our hearts.

Above all else, guard your heart, for everything you do flows from it. (Proverbs 4:23 NLT)

If we feed from the Tree of Life we will produce the proper fruit in each season. Fruit and gifts of the Holy Spirit - love, joy, peace, patience, kindness, goodness, faithfulness, gentleness and self-control, knowledge, tongues, prophecy, interpretation, healing, miracles. Whatever is needed to serve God's purpose at that time.

But the fruit of the Spirit is love, joy, peace, patience, kindness, goodness, faithfulness, gentleness, self-control; against such things there is no law. (Galatians 5:22-23 ESV)

AWESOME VOICE: 225

- VOICE OF GOD: DIRECT OR ECHOES? 226
  - Law of Attraction (L.O.A.) 226
  - 51% Positive vs. 49% Negative 228
  - Law of vibration vs. law of attraction.. 228
  - Christ Consciousness.. 232
  - Angels of Light 233
- SOUND SPECTRUM 234
  - God's Voice: the Ultimate White Noise 234
- GOD IS PURE LIGHT (1 JOHN 1:5 TPT) 235
  - Incantation? 237
  - Word of Faith.. 239
  - Positive Confession 239

Awesome Voice

How can God be separate from the universe if the universe includes all that there is, hence the "uni" part? Where did God get the "matter" to build with? Outside of himself? How? If He created it all? From what? Out of what? His thoughts and then it became the universe? How? Are we just in God's imagination then?

I'm not arguing. I just want to know because I really did appreciate what you said about God creating the Universe and that would make God a consciousness separate from all that there is. Supposedly God is in everything nothing exists that doesn't come from God. How does that part work? What was there before God said let there be light? Just God's consciousness?

I remade my class after u said that God CREATED the universe (for me God is consciousness) and okay then the universe is the "physical" part that came after God created it. I did like and appreciate that distinction.

V. Winter

A close friend who is strongly into L.O.A. (Law of Attraction) and teaches it sent me these questions. She is a former Rastafarian who accepted Christ but has been pulled into a belief system that attempts to use the vibrations of the universe to accomplish their will. They see God and the universe as the same.

There is one voice above all others. The Original Voice. And, the Voice of all Origins. How we approach this voice is crucial.

Voice of God: Direct or Echoes?

Law of Attraction (L.O.A.)

> Proponents say the law of attraction is supported by theories from quantum physics that suggest this "law" has an energetic and vibrational element.
>
> "It's the principle that 'like attracts like.' What we put out into the universe, we receive back, because everything, even thoughts and feelings, carry a vibration," says Emma Halley, a spiritual wellness coach.
>
> "By believing that we've already achieved [our desires], we put a matching frequency and vibration out into the universe that will, in turn, attract it to us."
>
> (https://www.healthline.com/health/how-to-use-the-law-of-attraction-without-suppressing-your-emotions#the-science)

Let's take a look at the forming and maintenance of the universe. Point number one: God is separate from the universe. God existed before the universe and created the universe from nothing except His wisdom and the words of His mouth. Genesis Chapter One starts, *"In the beginning God..."* then goes through a series of statements *"and then God said"* (verses 3, 6, 9, 11, 14, 20, 24, and 26). Each time "God said" something was created or established.

As we have already seen, Jesus is the total expression of the Godhead relative to the physical realm. He did not become manifest at creation. He was preexistent with God before the creation.

In the beginning was the Word, and the Word was with God, and the Word was God. The same was in the beginning with God. All things were made by him; and without him was not any thing made that was made. (John 1:1-3 KJV)

For by him were all things created, that are in heaven, and that are in earth, visible and invisible, whether they be thrones, or dominions, or principalities, or powers: all things were created by him, and for him: And he is before all things, and by him all things consist. (Colossians 1:16-17 KJV)

The NIV in verse seven says *"He is before all things, and in him all things hold together."*

...but in these last days, he has spoken to us by his Son, whom he appointed heir of all things, and through whom also he made the universe. The Son is the radiance of God's glory and the exact representation of his being, sustaining (upholding) all things by his powerful word. (Hebrews 1:2-3)

Can you imagine a God so powerful that, even in its fallen state, the universe is still held together by His voice, by His spoken words? All things are held together by the power of His voice. A voice encompassing but not limited to the entire known spectrum of frequency and energy.

This same God has come to you in a personal relationship through Jesus Christ. He holds your hand and walks with you as both the "Great I Am" and "Abba (Daddy) Father.
The steps of a good man are ordered by the Lord: and he delighteth in his way. Though he fall, he shall not be utterly cast down: for the Lord upholdeth him with his hand.(Psalm 37:23-24 KJV)

51% Positive vs. 49% Negative

There are many variations of this positive thinking process but they all seem to follow the same formula. Faith or hope is only achieved if the positive outweighs the negative. It is reached through the manipulation of God, gods, or the universe via our thought process and speech. We have already taken a quick look at the Law of Attraction. According to many of its followers, a higher law needs to be understood for the L.O.A. work work effectively. This is the Law of Vibrations.

Law of vibration vs. law of attraction.

> You might be wondering, how is this law (vibration) different from the law of attraction? It's a good question, as they are similar—and can even work together.
> As Kaiser explains, "The law of vibration is the first law that must happen before the law of attraction; in creating that vibration within yourself, you invoke the law of vibration deliberately, and only then can the law of

attraction happen."

The law of vibration is about matching the specific frequency of what you're looking for, and the law of attraction takes this idea a bit further by allowing you to "create [the frequency] within yourself by any means, like visualization, meditation, or affirmations," she adds.

At the end of the day, whenever we're manifesting, we do need to work with these two laws so we can both attract and vibrate at the same level as what we want. "What you align with vibrationally is easier to attract," Richardson notes.

https://www.mindbodygreen.com/articles/law-of-vibration

These "laws" are just as much a part of creation as the sun, moon, stars, constellations, idols, or anything else we might place our faith in other than the true God and Creator of the universe.

This would be a form of worshipping the creation vs worshipping the Creator. A demonically inspired delusion from the god of this world. Leading away from the true creator towards "You are God and you can control your destiny."

This would encompass the same three temptations he used against Eve and attempted to use against Jesus.

ALL THAT IS IN THE WORLD

It looks good - Lust of the Eyes.

It will satisfy an Appetite (natural or unnatural) - Lust of the Flesh.

I did it myself / **"I am God"** - Pride of Life.

I sometimes wonder if the "Positive Thinking" and "Law of Attraction" aren't somehow tapping into the echoes of God's voice. The energy/vibrations that are continually sustaining creation instead of the source - His Word.

I believe many people adhere to a Christianized version of the law of attraction. I believe that some of this may be possible. But what we're doing is manipulating the resonance of God's voice. The same voice that organized and created the universe and now holds it together in His power. It is an attempt to manipulate the power of those sound waves, the frequencies of God's voice that are holding everything together. Vibrations extend from Brownian movement to light waves, radio waves, and more. And, this is only what we have been able to discover. I am sure God's voice goes well beyond this.

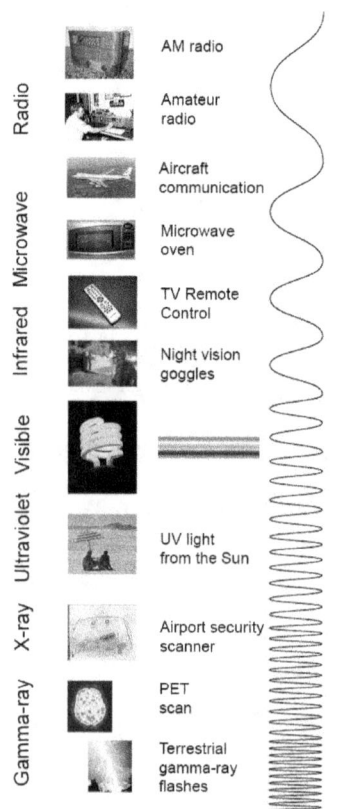

Imagine how we form words and ideas in our limited vocal range. We sing music and create moods and harmonies. And the frequencies of our voices are only a fraction of the range within our hearing.

IMAGE: EM_spectrum_full.jpg
source:(https://imagine.gsfc.nasa.gov/science/toolbox/emspectrum1.html

Those frequencies beyond our hearing run the gamut from sub-harmonic to, increasingly, radio waves, Very High and Ultra High (VFH UFH), microwaves, X-rays, Gamma Waves, and Light Waves. The frequencies go up and up until they reach the level of energy that holds the components of atoms and molecules together. Could this be one of the reasons that God confused the languages at Babel and removed the original Adamic language?

And the whole earth was of one language, and of one speech. (Genesis 11:1 KJV)

And the Lord said, Behold, the people is one, and they have all one language; and this they begin to do: and now nothing will be restrained from them, which they have imagined to do. Go to, let us go down, and there confound their language, that they may not understand one another's speech. (Genesis 11:6-7 KJV)

This could explain why we have so many references in witchcraft and New Age teachings to ancient incantations and books of knowledge, I.E. the Necronomicon, occult symbols, runes, etc. Possibly brought in by spirit guides, avatars, and, "Angels of Light". Words of power from the original language of creation? This is only conjecture; but, worth consideration in this instance.

Christ Consciousness

The philosophy of Christ Consciousness is based upon the belief that Jesus was a god, but not God. He can be looked to as an inspiration, and His spiritual status is something we can all achieve. The idea is that human beings spend their lifetime evolving toward the level of Spirit. This Spirit level is the New Age concept of god. It is an intangible cosmic... something... that we can all tap into. There are two main ways that Jesus is understood in this capacity. The most common belief is that Jesus was a man of flesh, born as you and I were, who was able through diligent study and focus to achieve the highest state of Spirit, and thus was able to manipulate natural laws to perform miracles. These folks will be quick to say that Jesus was not wrong to call Himself God, because anyone who achieves such a high state of spiritual enlightenment has tapped into the god-source, and is, in fact, god.

The other concept is that Jesus was an ascended master. That he was sent to Earth to act as a guide, along with other ascended masters throughout time, including Buddha, Krishna, Mohammed, et al. These ascended masters came here for the purpose of teaching mere mortals how to transcend our humanity, break the mortal coil, and become like them through a process of ascension, which once again means that we must reach the pinnacle of Spirit. Both philosophies lead to the same end.

from: https://christianobserver.net/having-the-mind-of-christ-christ-consciousness-whats-the-difference/#:~:text=The%20philosophy%20of%20Christ%20Consciousness%20is%20based%20upon,level%20is%20the%20New%20Age%20concept%20of%20god.

Angels of Light

Don't be fooled. All this talk of higher beings, ETs, spirit guides - they exist; but, they are not benign nor do they care about your well-being. They appear in various forms according to your appeal to deceive and lead you away from the real Truth.

And no marvel; for Satan himself is transformed into an angel of light. Therefore it is no great thing if his ministers also be transformed as the ministers of righteousness; whose end shall be according to their works. (2 Corinthians 11:14-15 KJV)

But I fear, lest by any means, as the serpent beguiled Eve through his subtilty, so your minds should be corrupted from the simplicity that is in Christ. (2 Corinthians 11:3 KJV)

For there shall arise false Christs, and false prophets, and shall shew great signs and wonders; insomuch that, if it were possible, they shall deceive the very elect. (Matthew 24:24 KJV)

In whom the god of this world hath blinded the minds of them which believe not, lest the light of the glorious gospel of Christ, who is the image of God, should shine unto them. (2 Corinthians 4:4 KJV)

"Law of Attraction", "Power of Positive Thinking", "Universal Consciousness", and "Christ Consciousness".

Whether we term the universe as "god" or "forces"- these are all just various manifestations of "Self-Godness" in which our thoughts attempt to either direct the "universe" or control the flow of "its power" to serve our purpose and desires.

Sound Spectrum

Our spoken vocal range will have a fundamental frequency from 85 to 155 Hz for a male and from 165 to 255 Hz. for an adult female. Our range of hearing runs from about 20 to 2,000 Hz.

God's Voice: the Ultimate White Noise

> White noise, in music, the effect of the complete range of audible sound-wave frequencies heard simultaneously, analogous to white light, which contains all the frequencies of the light spectrum. The sound of cymbals and snare drums has white-noise characteristics. Electronically synthesized white noise can be filtered so as to produce combinations of frequencies not obtainable on traditional musical instruments; or the white noise itself may be used as an element of music. White noise is aperiodic sound (that is, its wave pattern is not repetitive) and consists of equal intensities of all frequencies of the

audible spectrum.

from: https://www.britannica.com/art/white-noise-music

...and I saw the glory of the God of Israel coming from the east. His voice was like the roar of rushing waters, (Ezekiel 43:2)

I can only imagine what it must have been like for the Nation of Israel to stand before Mount Sinai and hear God speak from the top of the mountain.

And all the people saw the thunderings, and the lightnings, and the noise of the trumpet, and the mountain smoking: and when the people saw it, they removed, and stood afar off. And they said unto Moses, Speak thou with us, and we will hear: but let not God speak with us, lest we die. (Exodus 20:18-19 KJV)

The voice of Your thunder was in the whirlwind; The lightnings lit up the world; The earth trembled and shook. (Psalm 104:7)

God is Pure Light (1 John 1:5 TPT)

Visible light is only .0035 percent of the entire known electromagnetic spectrum. The United States is approximately 3,000 miles wide. If the entire electromagnetic spectrum was laid out across the US our spectrum of visible light would be 10.5 miles wide.

This then is the message which we have heard of him, and declare unto you, that God is light, and in him is no darkness at all. (1 John 1:5 KJV)

But ye are a chosen generation, a royal priesthood, an holy nation, a peculiar people; that ye should shew forth the praises of him who hath called you out of darkness into his marvellous light; (1 Peter 2:9 KJV) Every good gift and every perfect gift is from above, and cometh down from the Father of lights, with whom is no variableness, neither shadow of turning. (James 1:17 KJV)

We have recently discovered how to produce pure light. Light with no ambiance. This was done initially through the use of a LASER. We now have what is called cross-polarized light. This is done with two polarized filters at right angles to each other. They have taken extremely thin slices of various precious stones for microscopic purposes and shone this pure light through them. These stones break down into two categories - anisotropic and isotropic. Anisotropic jewels in pure light, no matter their original color turn into all the rainbow colors and present fantastic patterns. Other precious stones, Isotropic lose all their color and go pure black like a lump of coal. Among these are diamonds, rubies, and garnets.

(from:https://www.youtube.com/watch?v=JhC6iPuh4XM - To see these in color go to 3:33 on the timeline.)

God names twelve precious stones in the New Jerusalem. They are anisotropic. These stones are Jasper (quartz), Sapphire, Chalcedony, Emerald, Sardonyx, Sardius (Carnelian), Chrysolite (Peridot), Beryl (Aquamarine), Topaz, Chrysoprasus, Jacinth (Zircon), and Amethyst. *(Revelation 21:19-20)*

This was written over two thousand years ago. Science has just learned this.

Incantation?

Many, in the church, are being induced into a form of witchcraft where the Word of God is used as an incantation or formula to generate power. A weapon or charm to be thrown at a situation. A "Holy Hand Grenade", so to speak.

Years ago, a friend of mine had a close family member go through a near-death experience where they had been mugged. This person's faith was almost destroyed. "But, I prayed Psalm 91 every day over my family." I want to be careful how I say this. All Scripture is God-breathed. All Scripture is His Word. But, the promises are not to be spoken out as having power in and of themselves. This would relegate them to the level of incantations, closely bordering on witchcraft. The power of the Word flows from the Spirit of God within us via our relationship with Christ based on His righteousness and not on self-generated faith and our "many repetitions".

But when ye pray, use not vain repetitions, as the heathen do: for they think that they shall be heard for their much speaking.
(Matthew 6:7 KJV)

Jesus stated, *"You search the Scriptures because you think that in them you have eternal life, and it is they that bear witness about me..."*
(John 5:39)

The wise man built his house on the rock (relationship with Jesus). The foolish man built his house on sand (various verses - small pieces of the Rock). Are we basing our trust on our relationship with Christ or just speaking Scripture?

"My people have committed two sins: They have forsaken me, the spring of living water, and have dug their own cisterns, broken cisterns that cannot hold water." (Jeremiah 2:13)

Jesus is the author and finisher of our faith. He is the Word of God. Am I seeking a relationship and putting my trust in a personal, loving relationship with HIM or am I trying to manipulate the hand of God to meet my goals?

Our hearts/souls/minds are to be sourced by our spirit, empowered and directed by the Spirit of God. Our mind must be in agreement with our spirit which is rooted and aligned with God via the Spirit of God. The flow continues through our flesh/body into the physical realm as we act or speak. As Jesus said, If you have seen me you have seen the Father. I do and speak what the Father says; we, in a similar pattern, display the "Mind of Christ" by acting as one - spirit, mind, and flesh in line with the Spirit and Word of God.

How, then do we achieve the necessary faith?

We read our Bibles. As we read our minds become familiar with the Word, renewed, and can match up with what the Spirit of God is speaking.

So then faith cometh by hearing, and hearing by the word of God. (Romans 10:17 KJV)

We hear the Word through our senses and mind so we can hear the Word from the Spirit.

Word of Faith

Many Word of Faith teachers use phrases such as "little gods" to describe believers. Kenneth Hagin wrote that God had created humans "in the same class of being that he is himself," and reasoned that if humans are made in God's image, they are "in God's class", and thereby 'gods'. Prosperity theology (sometimes referred to as the prosperity gospel, the health and wealth gospel, the gospel of success, or seed faith) [A] is a religious belief among some Charismatic Christians that financial blessing and physical well-being are always the will of God for them, and that faith, positive speech, and donations to religious causes will increase one's material wealth. Wikipedia"

Positive Confession

Positive confession is the practice of saying aloud what you want to happen with the expectation that God will make it a reality. It's popular among prosperity gospel adherents who claim that words have spiritual power and that, if we speak aloud the right words with the right faith, we can gain riches and health, bind Satan, and accomplish anything we want. To confess positively is to speak words that we believe or want to believe, thus making them reality. This is opposed to negative confession, which is to acknowledge hardships, poverty, and illness and thus (supposedly) accept them and refuse the ease, wealth, and health God has planned for us.

There are several things wrong with this philosophy. The most dangerous is the belief that words have a kind of spiritual, magical power that we can use to get what we want. The practice borrows not from biblical truths, but from a new-age concept called the "law of attraction." It teaches that "like attracts like"—a positive statement or thought will draw a positive reaction. Everything is imbued with God's presence and power—not "God" as the omnipresent Creator, but "god" in a Hindu/pantheistic way. The net result is the idea that our words hold the power to force God to give us what we want—a heretical belief. Additionally, the results attributed to positive confession are powered by the faith of the individual. This leads to the old belief that illness and poverty are a type of punishment for sin (in this case, lack of faith). John 9:1-3 and the entire book of Job refutes this soundly.(https://www.gotquestions.org/positive-confession.html)

We waste a lot of time trying to get our righteousness going. Trying to get up to par. To get good enough to expect answers to prayer. This is where the New Covenant comes in because it is based on the righteousness of Jesus. Once again, the Scripture says *"Seek first the kingdom of God and His righteousness"* not our righteousness.

What then shall we say that Abraham, our forefather according to the flesh, discovered in this matter? If Abraham was justified by works, he had something to boast about—but not before God. What does Scripture say? "Abraham believed God, and it was credited to him as righteousness."

Now to the one who works, wages are not credited as a gift but as an obligation. However, to the one who does not work but trusts God who justifies the ungodly, their faith is credited as righteousness. David says the same thing when he speaks of the blessedness of the one to whom God credits righteousness apart from works: ***(Romans 4:1-6)***

A MIND FOR BATTLE: 243

- A New Mindset 243
  - He Trains My Hands for Battle 243
  - Rest in His Voice 244
- High Places 245
  - 30, 60, 100-Fold 247
- Flesh, Eyes, Pride - Warfare 249
  - Lust of the Eyes 250
  - Spiritual Pride - The Pride of Life 251
  - Lust of the Flesh 251
- "Why could we not cast him out?" 256
- More on Fasting - Empty Phil 259
  - Regarding the FAT 261
- Talents 262
  - Your "Talent of Time" 262
  - The Talent of You 264
- Battle Strategies 265
  - Loose Lips Sink Ships 265
  - The Spirit Helps Us to Pray. 266
  - The Motor on the Bus Makes the Wheels Go Round 267
  - Koshkai 270

A Mind for Battle

A New Mindset

It is God who arms me with strength and keeps my way secure. He makes my feet like the feet of a deer; he causes me to stand on the heights. He trains my hands for battle; my arms can bend a bow of bronze. You make your saving help my shield, and your right hand sustains me; your help has made me great. (Psalm 18:32-35 NIV)

He Trains My Hands for Battle

You were born on a battlefield. You have been a target since conception. There is only one path to victory in this battle. With Jesus Christ as your head and the leadership of the Holy Spirit, you can have victory. It is a necessity to train our minds in the language of the Spirit of God and be attentive to His voice. We must recognize certain strategies used in battle by both the enemy and God.

Voices from many sources are calling for our attention and devotion. Some are familiar. They have been with us since childhood or since experiencing a trauma. Some speak fear. Others speak of desire. They appeal to our appetites, our pride, and our insecurities. Past remembrances and future possibilities are a constant. A song, a smell, a word - any one of these can be an opening to a rabbit hole. Or, a gauntlet in the face, challenging us to a dual.

We are in a war. A war of ideas, of thoughts, of dreams. We need to wear our helmet of salvation as more than ceremonial. It is there to protect our mind against anything that rises against the knowledge of Christ and His accomplished work in us through His blood on the cross.

Rest in His Voice

Be alert and of sober mind. Your enemy the devil prowls around like a roaring lion looking for someone to devour. (1 Peter 5:8 KJV)

A rabbit lies safe at the side of the road. All is quiet. Suddenly the ground begins to tremble. The shaking quickly increases. A rumbling noise and a bright light assault the rabbit's senses. What is this? Fear takes over. "I need to escape. I need to run. " There is a clearing in front of him. He runs like his life depends on it. Unfortunately, the clearing is a road. The sound and light are those of a truck. He is struck by the vehicle as he runs across the most unobstructed path in sight. His life depended on it. It depended on his decision to run or remain in his place of security, his sanctuary.

We need to train our minds to remain in our position of rest. Our Hightower, our Sanctuary, our Cleft in the Rock.

A soldier crouches in his foxhole surrounded by sounds of gunfire, explosions, and cries of wounded men. His mind is screaming for him to run. To leave the safety of the foxhole, exposing himself to injury. He remains in its protection. It takes discipline but his mind has been trained. A command comes to attack. Now, his mind is screaming to stay.

His mind has also been trained to respond to the voice of his commander. Likewise, as Christians, we need to heed the voice of our commander, the Prince of Peace and the victorious Lord of Lords.

> An old hymn from my childhood comes to mind. "Rock of Ages, cleft for me, Let me hide myself in Thee;"

We need to train our minds for battle.

High Places

There are many references in the Old Testament to 'high places'. Places of worship that remained after the Canaanites were driven out. Dedicated to idol worship they would include an altar or object of focus such as a pillar of stone or wood or a carved representation of a god, goddess, animal even a constellation. Various false gods were worshipped at these high places including Molech and Baal. After the conquest of Canaan, because the Israelites associated the divine presence with elevated places (e.g., Mount Sinai), they began using these abandoned altars for worship or built new ones. Unfortunately, in many cases, they also incorporated artifacts left by the Canaanites into their rituals developing a bastardized version of worship to the true God.

Then the angel of the Lord came to Gilgal to Bochim, and said: I led you up from Egypt and brought you to the land of which I swore to your fathers; and I said, I will never break my covenant with you. And you shall make no covenant with the inhabitants of this land; you shall tear down their altars. But you have not obeyed my voice. Why have you done this? Therefore I also said, I will not drive them out before you; but they shall be thorns in your side, and their gods shall be a snare to you (Judges 2:1-3)

Some high places were built to honor God. Joshua set up stone pillars after crossing the Jordan *(Joshua 4:20)*. Abram built altars to the Lord at Shechem and Hebron *(Genesis 12:6-8)*.

He built another altar to the LORD, who had appeared to him at the great tree of Moreh in Shechem saying, *"Unto thy seed I will give this land." (Genesis 12:6-7 KJV)*. Jacob set up a stone pillar to the Lord at Bethel *(Genesis 28:18-19)*.

Regardless of their focus, once the temple was built all the high places became off-limits for worship. Israel was given one "high place" to worship and sacrifice. That place was the temple at Jerusalem. An interesting note: Solomon built the temple on Mount Moriah *(2 Chronicles 3:1)* at the same location as the altar Abraham built to sacrifice his son, Isaac *(Genesis 22:1-2)* and where David offered himself to stop the angel from destroying Jerusalem after he took a census of the people of Israel. *(1 Chronicles 21:1-29 & 22:1)*

It has since come to be known as Mount Zion. Most scholars believe this to be where Jesus was crucified, Golgotha - the place of the skull. The Latin word for skull is calvaria. God provided a ram in place of Isaac revealing Himself as Jehova Jireh, God will provide.

(Genesis 22:14) God offered Jesus as a substitute for the entire world. *(John 3:16)*

30, 60, 100-Fold

The Bible describes Israel and Judah's kings as being evil or good. How they dealt with the high places has a great part in the defining. Ahaz was probably the most evil of all the kings. He built high places in every city in Judah.

Of all the kings of Israel and Judah, these kings were considered good by the Lord. They did what was right in God's eyes. Except for one thing.

Joash - *Jehoash did what was right in the sight of the Lord all the days in which Jehoiada the priest instructed him. But the high places were not taken away; the people still sacrificed and burned incense on the high places. (2 Kings 12:2-3 KJV)*

Amaziah - *And he did what was right in the sight of the Lord, yet not like his father David; he did everything as his father Joash had done. However the [a]high places were not taken away, and the people still sacrificed and burned incense on the high places.*
(2 Kings 14:3-4 KJV)

Azariah - *"And he did that which was right in the sight of the Lord, according to all that his father Amaziah had done; Save that the high places were not removed: the people sacrificed and burnt incense still on the high places." (2 Kings 15:3-4 KJV)*

Asa - *"Although he did not remove the high places, Asa's heart was*

fully committed to the LORD all his life." (1 Kings 15:14)
They did not remove the high places.

Only two kings, Hezekiah *(2 Kings 18:4)* and Josiah *(2 Kings 23:19)* followed God's ways while going the extra step and removing the high places.

Several years ago, I stopped in to see my pastor, Tim Ritzel while visiting in the St. Louis area. As always, he gave me lots of encouragement and advice. Pastor Tim offered me a challenge, "Jon, don't sell yourself short. Don't sell God short. Don't settle for 30 or 60%. Go for 100-fold."

Jesus spoke the Parable of the Sower, saying. *"A farmer went out to sow his seed. As he was scattering the seed, some fell along the path, and the birds came and ate it up. Some fell on rocky places, where it did not have much soil. It sprang up quickly, because the soil was shallow. But when the sun came up, the plants were scorched, and they withered because they had no root. Other seed fell among thorns, which grew up and choked the plants. Still other seed fell on good soil, where it produced a crop—a hundred, sixty or thirty times what was sown. Whoever has ears, let them hear." (Matthew 13:3-9)*

"Jon. Don't settle for 30 or 60%. Go for 100-fold."
Hezekiah and Josiah went the extra step. They removed the high places.

What cares or distractions in our lives inhibit us from doing the 100-fold? I am going to term these distractions as "High Places". Things that interfere or distract us from going the extra step with God. I don't want my epitaph to say, "Jon was a good Christian. He lived a good life. But, he didn't remove the high places in his life. Therefore he never achieved 100%. He settled for 30 or 60 or less." More than that, when I come face to face with Jesus I want to hear Him say "Well done, my good and faithful servant."

In this context, what might your high places be?

Flesh, Eyes, Pride - Warfare

In the "Sermon on the Mount", *(Matthew 6)* Jesus spoke of three things - Giving, prayer, and fasting I believe these can be used as points of warfare against the world's system of thought. "For *all that is in the world, the lust of the flesh, and the lust of the eyes, and the pride of life, is not of the Father, but is of the world." (1 John 2:16-17 KJV)*

Eve and Jesus were both tempted in these three areas.
And when the woman saw that the tree was good for food **(lust of the flesh)** *and that it was pleasant to the eyes* **(lust of the eyes)**, *and a tree to be desired to make one wise* **(pride of life***), she took some and ate it, she took of the fruit thereof, and did eat, and gave also unto her husband with her, and he did eat. (Genesis 3:6 KJV).*

Immediately following His water baptism Jesus was led into the wilderness by the Spirit where He entered a prolonged fast.
After fasting for forty days and forty nights, He was hungry. The

tempter came to him and said, *"If you are the Son of God, tell these stones to become bread."* (v. 2-3) -**Lust of the flesh.**

Then the devil took him to the holy city and had him stand on the highest point of the temple.

"If you are the Son of God," he said, *"throw yourself down. For it is written: "'He will command his angels concerning you, and they will lift you up in their hands, so that you will not strike your foot against a stone.'"* (v. 5-6) - **Pride of life**

Again, the devil took him to a very high mountain and showed him all the kingdoms of the world and their splendor. *"All this I will give you,"* he said, *"if you will bow down and worship me."* (v. 8-9) - **Lust of the eyes.**

Jesus did not succumb to temptation. Eve did. We will cover both of these in more depth in other areas of the book.

Matthew Chapter Six: *"When you give."* (v2) *"When you pray."* (v5) *"When you fast."* (v16).

Lust of the Eyes

I want. I want. Gimme, gimme, gimme. Greed. When you tithe, when you give, you are going against that desire to acquire. The inward spiral of, "I want, I need, Gimme, Gimme," becomes an outflow of blessing to others.

'Now this was the sin of your sister Sodom: She and her daughters were arrogant, overfed, and unconcerned; they did not help the poor and needy. They were haughty and did detestable things before me."

(Ezekiel 16:49-50) The selfish inward spiral of greed led to self-indulgence and *"every evil work" (James 3:16)* eventually leading to perversion while ignoring the poor and needy.

Giving is a weapon of warfare, against the lust of the eyes.

Spiritual Pride - The Pride of Life

"For God knows that when you eat from it your eyes will be opened, and you will be like God, knowing good and evil." (Genesis 3:5)
Prayer, in this case, would be placing ourselves in a position where God is God and we are not. We are stating, "You are Lord. I will not do what is right in my mind. I want to do what was right in Your mind." Thy will be done.

Prayer is a weapon of warfare against the pride of life.

Lust of the Flesh

Fasting is a weapon of warfare against the lust of the flesh. The appetites of the flesh.

Jesus said, *"When you fast."* Not if you fast, but when you fast. This is where we set aside physical appetites for spiritual appetites. In *Luke 5:39*, Jesus adds *"No one after drinking the old wine immediately desires the new.* I would like for us to look at fasting not only in a physical context but also apply it to the soul. The old wine is the spirit of this world. The desires, the fulfillment, the draw of this world. The new wine is the Spirit of God. It is nourishment from the Spirit fulfilling an appetite, a longing for the Kingdom of God. We are called to be new wineskins filled with new wine. Filled with the Holy Spirit.

The old wineskin is the nature of the flesh. When we are born of the Spirit we become a "new creation" with a new nature. The new wineskin is the nature of this "new creation".

We often have trouble finding the desire to spend time in the Word. To spend time in prayer. We just don't have the appetite. Or, we become distracted.

You make a big meal of HotPockets. Not that HotPockets are bad. A friend stops by and invites you for steak and lobster. "Sorry, I'm full." After a few occurrences like this, you might think to yourself, "Maybe I should save part of my appetite in case my friend shows up and invites me to a restaurant for some nice food." You set aside some appetite for something better. In the same way, we tend to glut our souls with the "wine of this world".

Examples:
You come home from work, sit down, and turn on the TV.
"PawnStars" takes over the rest of the evening. It's interesting. "Wow, a Civil War bayonet. A 200-year-old pistol. I didn't know that. Here's a coin from Ancient Rome." This all comes with a complete history of the items. FASCINATING.
"Wow, a show about wild animals rescued in the jungle, nursed back to health, and released again into the wild. Will they survive?"
"Let's watch Jeopardy."
Let's not forget the Hallmark Channel and various soap operas where you can glut your soul on the emotions and drama of fictitious

characters. Multiple movie genres seek to fill an area of our life with excitement, supernatural, emotion, and wonderment. They are seeking to fill an area in our soul that should be filled with the new wine of the Holy Spirit.

We passively allow our minds to be filled with information that has nothing pertaining to eternal life and godliness.

It's a distraction. *All things are lawful for me, but not all things are helpful. (1 Corinthians 6:12 ESV)*

You had planned to spend time in the Word but now it's bedtime. You are tired. Your mind is full. "I'll try again tomorrow." You lost that window of time.

"No one, after drinking the old wine immediately desires the new."

What have you done for the Kingdom? What have you produced spiritually in your life over the past few hours? What part of this was eternal?" I'm not looking to blame or attack anyone. I struggle with distractions, too.

I have been reading my journals from India - 1986-87. Something in my second journal caught my attention yesterday.

> Wednesday - July 29, 1987
>
> I'm practicing the presence of Jesus. I don't pray. I don't work. I don't repent, make plans, or ask questions. I refuse all these. I simply exist with Him. I speak of my love and commitment to Him. I relax and just exist in His presence. Five, ten, or fifteen minutes at a time. I don't worry or

wonder. Nothing in the world matters except that I am with Jesus.

I say, practice. My mind is not still all that time. It still wants to wander. But, it is learning to shut up. This is not transcendental meditation. I am not emptying my mind; I am spending time with Jesus.

I need to get back to this.

As Jesus and his disciples were on their way, he came to a village where a woman named Martha opened her home to him. She had a sister called Mary, who sat at the Lord's feet listening to what he said. But Martha was distracted by all the preparations that had to be made. She came to him and asked, "Lord, don't you care that my sister has left me to do the work by myself? Tell her to help me!"
"Martha, Martha," the Lord answered, ***"you are worried and upset about many things, but few things are needed—or indeed only one. Mary has chosen what is better****, and it will not be taken away from her." (Luke 20:38-42)*

We all have high places. Think of them as comfort food for the soul. You're tired or frustrated. You had a rough day and need to veg out. Kick back. Relax. It is good and necessary to relax after a stressful day. While her sister Martha spent her time busy, flustered, and distracted, Mary did just that. She relaxed. But, in her relaxation, she "chose what is better". For her R&R she chose the highest place. The presence of Jesus.

YouTube has a lot of high places for me. Many are good - Answers in Genesis, One for Israel, Is Genesis History, Facts Matter, Bible Project, political news, and more. "Don't settle for 30%." I love communicating with my friends on Facebook. "He didn't produce 100-fold." I am not saying these are bad. But, they can detour us from our path to the "Temple" for the "New Wine".

I stopped listening to the radio in my car in 2018. No news. No music. I wanted to leave my ears, my thoughts, and my hearing attentive to the Lord's voice. I got the idea when I would drive my niece, Alex, to work or school while my sister was out of town. I would see something en route and comment. Alex would pull out her earbuds and say, "What?". By this time we had already passed it. Moment missed.

I don't want God to say something to me and I need to pull the "earbuds" out of my thought process and say, "What?" Or, worse yet, not hear His voice at all. I want to be ready for Him to speak at all times. Be attentive toward His voice. I want to be one of the wise bridesmaids from *Matthew 25* who kept their lamps filled with oil versus the foolish ones.

> On February 9, 1958, Pastor David Wilkerson made the transformational decision to sell his television. He only used to watch it for a couple of hours at the end of each day to wind down, but felt God was asking him to give that time to him instead. Wilkerson put the TV up for sale,

saying the deal was off if it didn't sell within the first half hour, but at minute 29, it was sold!

Slowly, the pastor learned how to spend that length of time in prayer. It didn't come easily, and at first he would often find himself stuck after quite a short while. But gradually he became more and more acclimatized to his special nightly times with the Lord.

He grew more attuned to God's voice.

It was during that precious season of self-sacrifice that God put it on his heart to go to serve among the gangs of New York – a task not for the faint-hearted back in the 1950s! As a result, hundreds of gang members, addicts, and prostitutes came to know the Lord through his ministry, and "Teen Challenge" was born, helping many more thousands all across the world to find freedom in the Messiah.

https://www.oneforisrael.org/bible-based-teaching-from-israel/why-does-fasting-work/

"Why could we not cast him out?"

Upon Jesus, John, and Peter's return from the mountain after experiencing Jesus' transfiguration the other disciples had been unsuccessfully attempting to cast out a demon. After Jesus rebuked the devil and it departed from the boy the disciples asked a great question

"Why could not we cast him out?"

Jesus' response? *"Because of your unbelief: for verily I say unto you, If ye have faith as a grain of mustard seed, ye shall say unto this mountain, Remove hence to yonder place; and it shall remove, and nothing shall be impossible unto you. Howbeit this kind goeth not out but by prayer and fasting. (Matthew 17:19-21 KJV)*

Not too long before this Jesus had sent out the twelve disciples with a command to "proclaim this message: *'And as ye go, preach, saying, The kingdom of heaven is at hand. Heal the sick, cleanse the lepers, raise the dead, cast out devils: (Matthew 10:7-8 KJV)*

Jesus later sent another group of seventy with the same message. *And the seventy returned again with joy, saying, Lord, even the devils are subject unto us through thy name. (Luke 10:17 KJV)*

I am certain that the twelve came back from their mission with the same elation as the seventy. *"even the devils are subject unto us through thy name"*.

I can imagine the scene before Jesus showed up. One disciple steps forward and commands the demon to leave. Nothing happens. No response. Another tells him to step aside, "This is how it's done." No response. Or, maybe an adverse one as the demon manifests more. One by one the disciples take turns each pushing harder than the last. They are becoming bewildered. "It worked so well when we were sent out." "Maybe I should put oil on his head this time and lay hands on him." I'll stop here as this is just conjecture. But, the fact is it didn't work and

Jesus named prayer and fasting as the key. I would like to make an observation.

I think the disciples may have stepped into the situation with a bit of spiritual pride. "No problem. Been there. Done that. Watch and be amazed."

Prayer, as a weapon of warfare, is a positioning of oneself in the proper order with God. *Submit yourselves therefore to God. Resist the devil, and he will flee from you. (James 4:7 KJV)*

Fasting places your physical appetites on hold while directing your hunger toward the spirit.

The disciples returned from the city having gone to buy meat and found Jesus speaking with a Samaritan woman. When they offered Him food He responded "I have meat to eat that ye know not of. Therefore said the disciples one to another, Hath any man brought him ought to eat? Jesus saith unto them, My meat is to do the will of him that sent me, and to finish his work. (John 4:32-34 KJV)

In this case, through prayer and fasting the disciples would have approached the demon in proper alignment and submission to God with the focus of demonstrating that the Kingdom of God was at hand to destroy the works of the devil *(1 John 3:8)* and to glorify God. Not for self-aggrandizement.

More on Fasting - Empty Phil

My first extended fast lasted 30 days. I was single and renting a room at my friend Randy Cutrell's house. Randy shared with me that he felt led to go on an extended fast but wasn't sure if he would be able to maintain it for 30 days. I told him I would fast alongside him. We could be each other's encouragement. We committed to the fast. On the second day of the fast, I came home from work to the smell of BROWNIES. Randy's wife, Laurie, is an amazing cook and she suddenly became even more amazing as the brownies called unto me desiring to be devoured. I couldn't cave so soon. I needed a rationale to deal with this new nemesis. I believe the Lord gave me the following as a physical example of a spiritual principle.

Tastewise
Take one bite of a brownie. Enjoy the rich flavor. (Hypothetically. I didn't take a bite. That would have ended the fast prematurely) Now, take another bite. Where did the wonderful flavor of that first bite go? It was buried in the flavor of the second bite. And it was not even a new flavor. Same flavor. Each bite only replaces the previous one. No matter how slowly I eat the brownie is eventually consumed. Time to brush my teeth. Now my mouth tastes like toothpaste. No more brownie taste. All gone. I have a Crest-flavored mouth. I go to sleep. I wake up. Where is that delicious brownie taste? Where is the minty taste of the toothpaste? Gone. Gone. My mouth tasted like a monkey slept in it. Like the bottom of a birdcage.

Physical Benefit

How has this benefitted my body? Let's switch to something a bit more healthy. A BLT on toasted rye bread. During the night my body processed and assimilated the nutrients it determined were beneficial. In the process of digestion, my body has allocated various elements of the sandwich to building muscle, energy for my cells, excess stored as fat, and more. It has taken the unneeded parts and other waste products and sent them down the line to be eliminated. But not all. Some of it has become a part of my physical body. Muscle tissue - fat (we'll talk about that later).

Eventually, I die. My body goes into the ground and becomes food for worms. What a great contribution to eternity.

Spiritual Benefit - Feasting on the Word

Let's say we set aside physical food for the spiritual.

In **Baptized - Tree of Life** we looked at the Word of God as food.
"Come, all you who are thirsty, come to the waters; and you who have no money, come, buy and eat! Come, buy wine and milk without money and without cost. Why spend money on what is not bread, and your labor on what does not satisfy? Listen, listen to me, and eat what is good, and you will delight in the richest of fare." (Isaiah 55:1-2)

Our body knows how to assimilate food, taking in the needed nutrients and bypassing the rest. In the same way, our spiritual body assimilates the Word. Strengthening us spiritually. Every Word from the mouth of God is valid and carries His grace for spiritual life.

Regarding the FAT

I have often been asked if it would be wrong to fast to lose weight. Would God honor this as a spiritual fast? I believe any time we set aside our physical appetite for a spiritual purpose God will honor that. If in doubt? Move toward your faith. A fast doesn't need to be severe. It should be according to the leading of the Spirit.

"I ate no pleasant bread, neither came flesh nor wine in my mouth, neither did I anoint myself at all, till three whole weeks were fulfilled." (Daniel 10:3 KJV)

Regarding a fast to lose weight. Let me just say this.

As we read Leviticus we see many different types of sacrifices assigned by God along with the proper ritual. We have a sin offering, a peace offering, the trespass offering. We even have a sacrifice offering given in case someone sinned without knowing it. In most of these cases, the fat is removed from the entrails and burned as a *"pleasing aroma to the Lord" (Leviticus 4:3)*

The sacrifice was performed by a priest in the temple.

Your body is a temple *(1 Corinthians 6:19-20)*

You are the priest of that temple *(1 Peter 2:9)*

As stewards of our bodies/temples, we want them to be clean and healthy. We are told to *"present your bodies a living sacrifice, holy, acceptable unto God, which is your reasonable service." (Romans 12:1 KJV)*

I'll let you take it from there.

Talents

Your "Talent of Time"

In *Matthew 25:14-30* Jesus spoke a parable about talents. The master gave five talents to one servant, two to another, and one to another. Then, Jesus gave the master's response as to how they invested those talents. In the parable the talents were money. Because of how we use the word talent in the English language we see it as a special ability. We tend to look at this parable and think some people have talent and others do not. "This person is a talented actor, singer, or football player and needs to use their platform or talent to promote God. I don't have that talent so I'm off the hook." Not so fast.

Considering talents as abilities let's extend these to the Body of Christ. Abilities or the gifts of ministry given by the Holy Spirit for working in the church are *"first of all apostles, second prophets, third teachers, then miracles, then gifts of healing, of helping, of guidance, and of different kinds of tongues"*. *(1 Corinthians 12:28)*

I used to teach drama while working full-time with YWAM Miami and Orlando. I would teach youth groups at various churches and work with groups passing through on their way to mission venues in the Caribbean and Central America. Often members of the "cast" would feel completely out of place in a drama. "I'm not an actor" they would say. "I have never been on stage. How can I properly present the Gospel Message to a group of strangers in a foreign country?"

The first thing I would tell them is you are created in the image of the Creator. Therefore, it is in your nature to be creative. You might have the ability to make wealth, a gift of organization, or bring peace into a situation between friends during a conflict. Right now I am asking you to channel your innate creativity into this drama.

When Moses asked God who was he to speak to Pharoah God said *"I will be with you." (Exodus 3:12)* Then, Moses asked what if they don't believe he was sent by God? God answered, *"What is in your hand?"* It was a staff. God told him to throw it down and it became a snake. *(Exodus 4:1-3)*

There was no power in that staff to become a snake. Moses certainly didn't have the power to change the staff into a snake. He was so startled he ran away from it. Don't be afraid to use your abilities for God. He will be with you and He will supply the power, the grace needed for the job.

"Not by power or by might, but by my Spirit..." (Zechariah 4:6)

There is one "talent" that each of us has in common and in equal amounts. The talent of "time". Every one of us is given a 24-hour day. Jesus challenges us to *"do the works of Him who has sent Me while it is day." (John 9:4)* Everyone has 24 hours in a day, seven days a week. So the question is, how are you spending your time? What are you doing with your time? I'm not saying you need to go into the mission field or become a Sunday School Teacher. But, are you wasting it in front of the TV? Are you wasting it partying? How are you using your "Talent of Time"?

The Talent of You

When Satan tempted Jesus in the wilderness he began the first two temptations with the phrase *"If you are the Son of God." (Matthew 4)* Jesus knew who He was and responded accordingly. We need to stand in faith realizing that "in Christ" we are *"more than conquerors through Him who loved us." (Romans 8:37)* We are sons and daughters of God.

"Yes, I am a child of God. But, I lost my temper this morning with my kids." "I have a bad habit I cannot break." I - I -I! No, it needs to be Him - Him - Him. We stand in God's grace provided through the complete success of Jesus' life, death on the cross, and His resurrection.

Now that we have that issue out of the way.

Each of you has a gift, a talent - more than that - a heart that needs presentation to the world. Not only for your sake; but for the sake of others. For the Kingdom of God. You are a unique creation carrying a special light to shine in the lives of many. To experience a true life of fulfillment the unique quality of who you are needs to flow unrestricted by fear and distraction. You are a light that needs to shine. The best talent you can invest in the Kingdom of God is You.

Battle Strategies

Loose Lips Sink Ships

I believe your prayer language is unique to your spirit. You are using it to communicate with God. *For he that speaketh in an unknown tongue speaketh not unto men, but unto God: for no man understandeth him; howbeit in the spirit he speaketh mysteries. (1 Corinthians 14:2 KJV)* Unless God is speaking through you to someone else, like when I was in El Salvador or during the deliverance session with Maury, what you're speaking is not necessarily an earthly language. *"Though I speak with the tongues of men and of angels,"*
(1 Corinthians 13:1 KJV)
Regarding control of the tongue, the Holy Spirit might be guiding us in strategic prayer as we speak by faith.

One reason praying in tongues is strategic in prayer battle is because the enemy cannot understand what we are praying. During the war special codes were used in communications so that the enemy couldn't understand the plans. If I pray in an unknown tongue, God understands, because God originated that tongue. God knows what we need and what is best for us. It might be best if my mind doesn't understand what I am praying. Maybe it's something I don't want. I might fight against that prayer. Fight against it thinking "In no way could this be God". The fact is we don't know what to pray for. We know what we want and, in our limited thinking, how we think God should approach a situation. We are encouraged to bring our petitions before God. *(Philippians 4:6)* But, only God knows His plan. *For my thoughts are not your thoughts, neither are your ways my ways, saith the Lord. For as the heavens are higher than the earth, so are my ways higher than your ways, and my thoughts than your thoughts. (Isaiah 55:8-9 KJV)*

The Spirit Helps Us to Pray.

Likewise, the Spirit also helpeth our infirmities: for we know not what we should pray for as we ought: but the Spirit itself maketh intercession for us with groanings which cannot be uttered. (Romans 8:26-27 KJV)

The word translated as infirmities is "asthensia" in Greek. It can also be translated as weakness and is used in the singular form. So, if we remain with the word infirmity (singular) what infirmity would that be? Let's look at the context. The Spirit helps our infirmity/weakness by making intercession for us with groanings that cannot be uttered because <u>we don't know what to pray for</u>. Our weakness or limitation is our lack of knowledge or understanding. God has no limitations. The Holy Spirit and God the Father speak the same language. Our minds cannot comprehend or fathom the mysteries of the Spirit's working in our spirit. But, by faith, we can allow the Spirit of God to communicate our needs by proxy directly to God. For this communication to manifest into the physical realm it must pass through our flesh. Believe in your heart and confess with your mouth (*Romans 10:9*). Demonstrate your faith by your works (*James 2:18*).

Your confession is one of the three main points of contact between the Kingdom of Heaven you carry inside you and the world.

For he that speaketh in an unknown tongue speaketh not unto men, but unto God: "for no man understandeth him; howbeit in the spirit he speaketh mysteries." (1 Corinthians 14:2 KJV)

We can pray perfect prayer directly from the Spirit of God to the Father God speaking His will into the physical world. When I drive with the radio off I pray in the spirit and with the understanding.

Regarding spiritual warfare, the enemy also has no way of knowing what is being prayed. No matter how he tries to decode it. Therefore, he is unable to set up barriers or contest the plan.

But if we have an idea of what it is and speak it out -the enemy now knows. Many times while on the mission field, or at home we would pray as a group and make plans for the next day only to have the plans change at the last minute and find the "New Plan" worked out so well and so much better that it seemed to be "How can I say it?" PLANNED.

Let me share a few stories from my father's book "A History of Missions".

https://www.amazon.com/History-Missions-ends-Earth/dp/1495992349

The Motor on the Bus Makes the Wheels Go Round

Once again Ruth (Lockhart) is preparing to lead a team into Panama. In our prayer-release time, we all sensed something special about the approaching outreach. As we were praying, Terry Keith received a word of the Lord to be shared with Ruth. Basically, the message was, "Ruth, if you trust me on this outreach I will bless you. I want you at all times to be prepared for ministry and to trust me to make whatever provision is necessary for its accomplishment." With great excitement and anticipation, we released the team to proceed to the airport, wondering what all those special words might mean.

As a good team leader, Ruth had made all the necessary preparations for ministry and transportation. The first day proceeded well until the team was on their way back to their lodging. The bus blew a head gasket and became instantly unavailable for use. God had said, "Trust Me!" Frantic calls indicated that because of special events taking place in the area, no buses were available for rent. That evening Ruth attended a meeting in which she was seated right next to the secretary of the new President who had just replaced Noriega. In the course of the conversation, Ruth mentioned the transportation problem she was facing on behalf of the team. The secretary volunteered the fact that the President had two buses and could only use one at a time. Providentially, transportation was now available for the next day's ministry which took place without a problem. As Ruth and her team were relaxing at the end of the day she received an emergency call from the President's secretary. The bus the President had been using blew a head gasket and he would now need the bus being used by the team. Of course, this left the team without transportation for the following day which was fully scheduled for ministry.

Ruth and her team went immediately to prayer. One young man asked if he could make a call to his home in Hollywood, Florida. Interestingly enough, he attended the Episcopal church pastored by the priest mentioned earlier. He knew that a house-church group was meeting in his home that evening and he wanted to enlist their help, in prayer, about the problem they were facing in Panama. Because a significant amount of time was necessary to apply make-up and put on costumes for the program presentation, Ruth instructed the team members to come to breakfast the next morning prepared for ministry. I am sure there were those in the group who wondered why they should get ready for ministry when they had no transportation to get them to the ministry location. However, they obeyed their instructions.

In His special word to Ruth before the outreach, the Lord had said, essentially, "You do what you can do and trust Me to do what I can do." As the team was eating breakfast the next morning, one of them shouted that he saw a bus in the driveway. Ruth quickly commissioned one of the young men to run out and see if they could rent it for the day. The team member came back, walking in a daze. He said that before he could ask the bus driver anything, the driver said to him, "Is this the Youth With A Mission team that needs a bus?"

It seems that someone in the house church meeting in Florida knew someone in Panama who had a bus. "RUTH, YOU DO WHAT YOU CAN DO AND LEAVE THE REST UP TO ME!"

Koshkai

The story I want to share now has been documented by the Episcopalian Church. They printed the story on the front page of their international newsletter several years ago. There is a small but very strong underground Church in Iran. Several years ago two young Iranian Christians were praying in the capital. They sensed that God was speaking to them and asking that they translate a portion of the Gospel of John into the Koshkai language.

The Koshkai are a people group that lives in the southeastern section of Iran. They are known in mission circles as the farthest people in the world from the Gospel. Out of a list of ten thousand people groups who do not have the Gospel, number one on the list is the Koshkai. They are very difficult to reach because of where they live and they are very difficult to reach because they are hardened against anything outside the Muslim religion. They won't even listen to anything about another religion. They are a people very, very far from the Gospel.

The young men translated the requested portion of Scripture and had many copies made. With their stacks of literature, they drove to Koshkai territory and began passing out the scripture portions in a Koshkai village. The people immediately began to rip the booklets to shreds and said, "We don't know what these booklets are, but we will kill you if you don't leave our village." They went to another village that responded in the same way.

The young believers started to drive back home. As you might imagine, they were very sad and felt they had somehow failed to hear God properly or had somehow done something very wrong. At any rate, they were wondering why God would let them get involved in the project in the first place if He knew what a failure it might become.

While they were on their way home, however, some very interesting things were taking place in one Koshkai village. It was Friday evening and the villagers had gathered in their mosque to listen to their Imam. As the Muslim pastor was reading from the Koran, all the passages he read that evening spoke of Jesus. Actually, Jesus is mentioned more times in the Koran than Mohammed.

As he was reading, the pastor looked up and said, "Jesus is mentioned everywhere in the Koran, but I know nothing about Him." He asked the people gathered if any of them knew anything about Jesus. Of course, none of them did. The pastor then said, "Well, Jesus is mentioned so often in the Koran that Allah must want us to know about Him. Let's Pray!" So they prayed, "Allah, please tell us who Jesus is." They closed the service and everyone went home. One of the men who had been in the service went home and went to bed. Jesus came to him in a dream and said, "Go to the bridge at 3:00 a.m. There will be two men there who can give you information about Jesus."

Now let's go back to our two young men who are driving home so discouraged. As they approach the middle of a bridge near a Koshkai village, their jeep dies. They got out, looked under the hood, and checked every possible problem spot they could think of but found nothing wrong. Every system seemed to be O.K. but nothing was working.

Suddenly, they heard a sound and in the moonlight, they saw a Koshkai man running down the mountain and onto the bridge in his pajamas. With no introduction, the man simply said, "I came to get the information about Jesus." The two men gave him all the literature they had. He then turned around and ran back up the hill. In amazement, they turned the key once again in the ignition. At this point, they were not even surprised when the engine roared to life and they made their way home without further incident.

They had a plan. God had more of a plan.

The men had planned to distribute a portion of the Gospel of John throughout the area. As the plan seemed to be failing and the men became more and more bewildered I'm certain the powers of darkness were brimming with elation. Their plan was unfolding only to be ambushed by God's bigger plan. A timely dream, the walk to the bridge, the stalled jeep, and the information about Jesus. We have an Awesome God.

CARRY THE KINGDOM: 275

A "Garden of Eden" in Your Heart 275
    Seek First, the Kingdom of God.. 275
    The Kingdom of Light.. 275
    Two Trees 277
    Is God Your GPS or Your "Pillar of Cloud/Fire"?... 278
    Paradigm 280
    To The Ends of the Earth.. 283
    Mission-Minded.. 285

Carry the Kingdom

A "Garden of Eden" in Your Heart

Seek First, the Kingdom of God.

I think many of us as Christians understand the need and have a desire to seek the Kingdom of God. But the tendency is to seek our kingdom, to build our lifestyle and environment to fit what we want, what we desire.

These desires are greatly influenced and derived through our "world roots" tapped into the wisdom of this world as we are bombarded daily with commercials presenting "The Lifestyle"- canoeing, beer & barbecue, vacation resorts, as the normal desirable life. Everyone in those commercials is having a great time.

I am not saying there is anything wrong with these things. But, they should not be our goal. The Bible says to seek God's Kingdom. Not our own. To do what is right in His mind. Not what is right in our mind. This is why it is so important to renew our minds. To train our minds to align with Scripture. We have been placed in God's kingdom and His kingdom has been placed in us.

The Kingdom of Light

"I am the light of the world. Whoever follows me will never walk in darkness, but will have the light of life" (John 8:12)

You are all children of the light and children of the day. We do not belong to the night or to the darkness. (I Thessalonians 5:5)

We are no longer children of the darkness. We are now children of light called to carry His light to the nations.

I am the Lord; I have called you in righteousness; I will take you by the hand and keep you; I will give you as a covenant for the people, a light for the nations (Isaiah 42:6 ESV)

God does not live in houses made by human hands *(Acts 7:48)*

He lives in us. We are His temple.

Do you not know that you are God's temple and that God's Spirit dwells in you?(1 Corinthians 3:16 ESV)

We are the priests of our temples. *(1 Peter 2:9)*.

We are ambassadors. *(2 Corinthians 5:20)*

As Christians, everywhere we go we carry within us the presence of God. **We carry His Kingdom of Light in our walk throughout the kingdom of darkness.** As disciples, we are to abide in the Word. Abide in Jesus. As ambassadors, we are to carry the Kingdom of God to the ends of the earth.

For this is what the Lord has commanded us: "'I have made you a light for the Gentiles, that you may bring salvation to the ends of the earth." (Acts 13:47 ESV)

We are literally "traveling temples". This is why Paul refers to our bodies as tabernacles. *(2 Corinthians 5:1)*

Two Trees

We carry two trees in the gardens of our hearts. A "Tree of Life" rooted in the Spirit of God and a "Tree of the Knowledge of Good and Evil" rooted in the spirit of the world. I would venture that this "Garden of Eden" and our bodies being a "temple of the Holy Spirit" are the same.

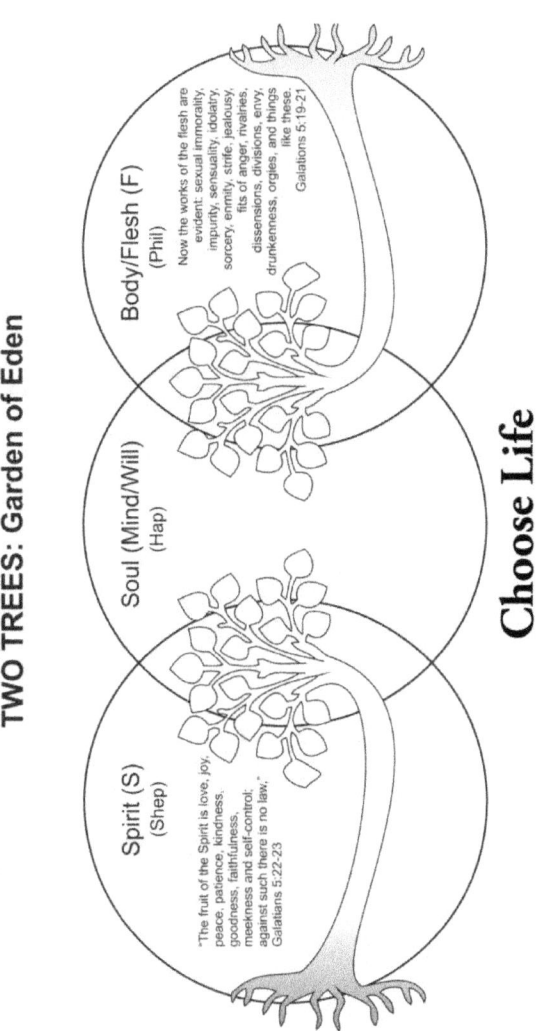

God told Adam and Eve to be fruitful and multiply. He commissioned them to extend the garden to the entire world (*Genesis 1:28*). This is the same garden where God would walk in the cool of the day (*Genesis 3:8*) and commune with Adam and Eve.

Just as God told Adam and Eve to extend the Garden to the whole earth Jesus commissioned the disciples to carry the Kingdom to the ends of the earth. The same commission but with an added dimension. We are carrying the Spirit of God. We are carrying the "Light of the World". As the Nation of Israel carried the Tabernacle, filled with the glory of the Lord (*Exodus 40:35*) we carry the Kingdom of God.

"Neither shall they say, Lo here! or, lo there! for, behold, the kingdom of God is within you." (Luke 17:21)

Is God Your GPS or Your "Pillar of Cloud/Fire"?

What is the difference between using God as our GPS versus our pillar of fire/cloud?

"...He will direct your path" (Proverbs 3:6)

"Thy Word Is a Lamp Unto My Feet and Light Unto My Path" (Psalm 119:105

We want God to guide our lives, but, so often we determine our direction and then ask Him to bless it.

If we're not careful we will base our steps on what is right in our mind. For example: The "American Dream" while appealing can be a potential sidetrack to fulfilling God's purpose in our lives. Does this make it sinful? No.

"All things are lawful for me, but all things are not expedient: all

things are lawful for me, but all things edify not.
(1 Corinthians 10:23 KJV)

We need to trust that God wants the best for us and can bring it about in our lives if we follow His leading regardless of how circumstances appear. Only then can we do our best for Him.

But other (seed) *fell into good ground, and brought forth fruit, some an hundredfold, some sixtyfold, some thirtyfold. (Matthew 13:8 KJV)*
Our goal is "*an hundredfold*".

Although we seek God and spend time in His word; we are still greatly influenced by the media, friends, books, et anon. So many of our goals can be polluted by the "wisdom of this world".

One of my earliest memories of my Uncle Cliff (Howard Clifton) was walking out in a wooded area near a river or lake. As we walked I would see a flower or butterfly and wander off the path to investigate. He would wait patiently for me to return and we would continue on our journey. He was a very patient and loving man. He never scolded me for wandering off and would often walk over and help me explore. Especially if it looked like I might be getting near a troubling area. We would wander following my wonder. Fortunately, this was a casual walk. Unfortunately, the path we are on is fraught with spiritual perils and pitfalls. Frivolous paths that lead to potential destruction in our lives and the lives of others. The eternal destinies of many of these others depend on us turning neither to the right nor the left (*Deuteronomy 28:14*)

They depend on us to *"run the course"*. God depends on us to *"run the course"*. The Spirit of God - the Word - is a lamp to our feet and a light to our path.

Paradigm

Our paradigm is to see God as our pillar of fire. Our pillar of light. He lays out our itinerary. While we may, at times, seem to be wandering in the wilderness like Israel God sees the big picture. He may be using that momentary side-track to teach us something or to bring us alongside someone else to be an encouragement.

Driving my car, I had an incident where I could not figure out why the truck in front of me was not moving. The light turned green. It's green - go! Then, I realized the driver was waiting for a person in a wheelchair to finish crossing the intersection. My perspective didn't allow me to see that person. I remember once when Chon was very young and learning about traffic lights. We were stopped at a red light. The light turned green. I continued to wait. Chon said, "Dad, the light is green. You are supposed to go." I said, "Tell that to the car in front of me." It wasn't moving. He said, "Oh!"

The GPS on our phone or car dashboard informs us of traffic changes and detours, helping our journey. I can see how we can easily see God's lead as being similar to a GPS. The difference is who is planning the destination and route.

In our paradigm, we place the Spirit of God as our destination travel planner and decision-maker. *"Thy will be done".*

When God was leading Israel through the wilderness they would camp where He rested.

When the pillar moved they would follow. In the wilderness, God led Israel by pillar of cloud by day and fire by night. When the pillar moved they moved with it.

What if God moved on but they decided they liked where they were and stayed? There would be no provision. The same thing would occur if they moved out on their own. God is our provision. God makes our path. He makes the roads even and supplies our needs.

This word from Pastor Tim Ritzel is so appropriate.

> "So letting your sinful nature control your mind leads to death. But letting the Spirit control your mind leads to life and peace." …Rom 8:6
>
> We have a choice in our future. We either let this world's logic, which is all about me control us, or we choose to follow the Holy Spirit.
>
> Choose to let God help your thoughts. Refuse to let pain or the reasoning of this world lead you to a life of destruction. Stop trying to figure it out; choose to walk in faith, love, and forgiveness.
>
> (from one of his "Thought for the Day" - Facebook posts)

Is God initiating and guiding "our path"? Are we following God's leading?

I cannot emphasize enough when we determine our path we are relegating God to the position of being our spiritual GPS. "Lord, this is my destination. This is what I want. Make my path straight. Provide my needs. Get me there."

The part of us that wants to lead, that follows earthly wisdom is the part that wars against the spirit. What we are saying by doing this is that we don't trust God with our lives. We are wiser and can do better. God cares about our well-being more than we can imagine and is continually working on our behalf.

And we know that all things work together for good to them that love God, to them who are the called according to his purpose. (Romans 8:28 KJV)

For I know the plans I have for you, declares the Lord, plans for welfare and not for evil, to give you a future and a hope. (Jeremiah 29:11 ESV)

If you then, who are evil, know how to give good gifts to your children, how much more will your Father who is in heaven give good things to those who ask him! (Matthew 7:11 ESV)

Trust in the Lord with all thine heart; and lean not unto thine own understanding. In all thy ways acknowledge him, and he shall direct thy paths. (Proverbs 3:5-6 KJV)

God is the "light to my path..."
He will point out and illuminate the direction you are to take.
God is a "lamp to my feet..."
He will show you where and when to take the next step.
He will point you in <u>His</u> next direction for your life.

For it is God which worketh in you both to will and to do of his good pleasure. (Philippians 2:13 KJV)

You may wonder why it is taking so long to get to your goal. You have prayed, waited, and received confirmation. Why so long? Maybe you are just not ready physically, emotionally, or spiritually.
And it came to pass, when Pharaoh had let the people go, that God led them not through the way of the land of the Philistines, although that was near; for God said, Lest peradventure the people repent when they see war, and they return to Egypt: (Exodus 13:17 KJV)

Maybe, God is still in the process of preparing the path.
And we know that all things work together for good to them that love God, to them who are the called according to his purpose.
(Romans 8:28)
Being confident of this very thing, that he which hath begun a good work in you will perform it until the day of Jesus Christ:
(Philippians 1:6 KJV)

On your part, be ready and willing - instant in season and out of season - to trust and respond to His voice. To step out in faith trusting that you hear His voice. Knowing that He will not allow you to fall headlong because He is holding your hand (*Psalm 37:24*).

To The Ends of the Earth
Also I heard the voice of the Lord, saying, Whom shall I send, and who will go for us? Then said I, Here am I; send me. (Isaiah 6:8 KJV)

Does this mean you need to go out on the mission field? Sell everything you have and move to the Amazon? Maybe. Don't panic, this is usually the exception. But, God just may lead you to work at Amazon.

Several years back, I had the pleasure to work with a missions organization called T.C.C.I. (Teams Commissioned for Christ International - TCCI.org). We put a video together based on the song "Please Don't Send Me to Africa" by Scott Wesley Brown. In the video, I find myself concerned that God might send me to Africa. I offer to serve in all types of other areas for the church in the video as an alternative. Just don't ask me to go to Africa. While humerous. There is a point to be made. Many of us are afraid to fully commit to God because of our fear of what He might ask us to do. All of the alternatives suggested in the video are legitimate positions of service in church ministry and we should be willing to help in those areas if asked or if the opportunity arises. They don't need to be lifetime commitments.

For everything there is a season and a time - (Ecclesiastes 3:1)
You can find several links to this video by searching "Please Don't Send Me to Africa - TCCI" on YouTube.

If God does call you to go on the mission field He will give you the grace and the desire to do exactly that. You will want to do nothing else. God will give you the desires of your heart. We like to interpret that as giving us what we want. But, in God's perfect plan, we want Him to place His desires for us into our hearts so we desire His will.

Mission-Minded

There are mission fields and then there are mission fields. The world is filled with them.

Then saith he unto his disciples, The harvest truly is plenteous, but the labourers are few; Pray ye therefore the Lord of the harvest, that he will send forth labourers into his harvest. (Matthew 9:37-38 KJV)

Your mission of the moment could be to take a few minutes to pray for someone during your busy day or, to call someone you haven't spoken to for a long time and let them know you are thinking about them. To help someone at the grocery store. To be a light at your workplace. You don't need to preach. Live in such a way that someone experiencing a difficult situation would be drawn to you for possible answers to their dilemma. As my friend Rob Zimmerman pointed out - "Focus on being sensitive to God's leading that He might draw your attention to them and ask how they are doing. An open-ended question demonstrating concern and a possible opening to share hope."

But sanctify the Lord God in your hearts: and be ready always to give an answer to every man that asketh you a reason of the hope that is in you with meekness and fear: (1 Peter 3:15 KJV)

Let your speech be always with grace, seasoned with salt, that ye may know how ye ought to answer every man. (Colossians 4:6 KJV)

Don't overthink it. God loves you and cares for you. Ask for His will. Trust him. Believe that He wants the best for you and wants to use His kingdom that is in you to touch the world, the Mission Field.

POINTS OF KINGDOM CONTACT: 289

- Hands - Feet - Mouth 289
- **HANDS** 292
  - Hands Evoke Emotion 292
  - "Uppy?" 293
  - Laying On of Hands 294
  - Our Hands Need to be Clean 295
- **FEET** 298
  - Our Spiritual Walk 298
  - A "Seasonal Walk" 300
  - Carry the Good News 302
  - Rest In Peace (Hebrews 4:10) 303
  - Are You In the Faith? 305
- **MOUTH** 305
  - With My Understanding 306
  - Adversary vs. Advocate 307
  - My Demons Know Your Demons 309
  - Blessings or Curses 312
  - With My Spirit 316
  - More Than All of You (1 Corinthians 14:18) 319

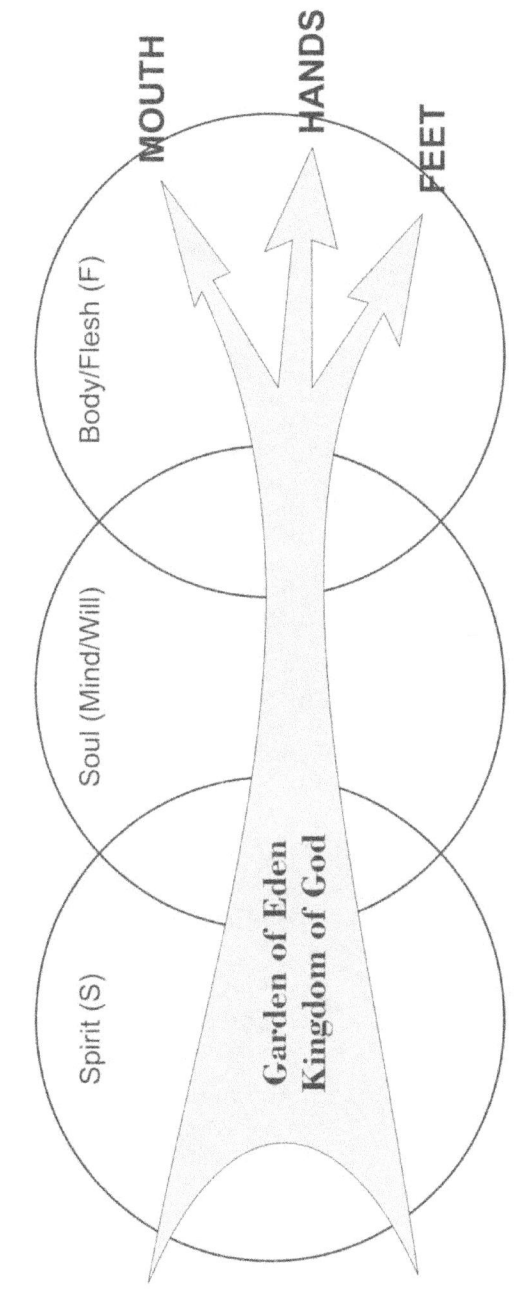

Points of Kingdom Contact

Jesus instructed us to pray *"Thy Kingdom come. Thy will be done."* The Kingdom has come. It is in you. You carry it wherever you go. What are you doing with it? You want the Kingdom of God manifested in your life but what about in the lives of others?

We have five main sources of input from the world - smell, touch, taste, sight, and hearing. How do we express or manifest ourselves outwardly to the world? How does the Kingdom within us connect to the world without? From the beginning, God planned to work alongside and through humanity. After creating the world He built a beautiful garden – Eden, and placed Adam and Eve in it as caretakers. They and their offspring were to populate the earth, care for, and expand the garden. Here are some examples of how God has worked through humanity to accomplish His will.

Hands - Feet - Mouth

HANDS

When God parted the Red Sea He used Moses' outstretched hand. *Then Moses stretched out his hand over the sea; and the Lord caused the sea to go back by a strong east wind all that night, and made the sea into dry land, and the waters were divided. (Exodus 14:21 NKJV)*

FEET

God could have repeated this when Israel crossed the Jordan River by using Joshua's hand as He had used Moses' outstretched hand to part the Red Sea forty years earlier But, He wanted to expand His faith base. Although the older generation had died out during the wandering years the priests would have been witnesses to the Red Sea parting. Now, it was their turn to "literally" step out in faith. The water was at flood stage this time of year so it had to be a bit daunting to walk out into the river carrying the ark. The priests obeyed. They stepped in and the water upstream stood in a heap while the water downstream continued to flow exposing dry land.

and as those who bore the ark came to the Jordan, and the <u>feet</u> of the priests who bore the ark dipped in the edge of the water (for the Jordan overflows all its banks during the whole time of harvest), that the waters which came down from upstream stood still, and rose in a heap very far away (Joshua 3:15-16 NKJV)

MOUTH

In *Exodus 19:6* God had proclaimed His desire to make Israel a kingdom of priests. It was now time for everyone to become involved in the process. It is one thing to watch someone else pray and see an answer to that prayer. It is another to be a part of the process. Upon command the Children of Israel opened their mouths and shouted. "And the walls came tumbling down."

So the people shouted when the priests blew the trumpets. And it happened when the people heard the sound of the trumpet, and <u>the people shouted with a great shout</u>, that the wall fell down flat. Then the people went up into the city, every man straight before him, and they took the city. (Joshua 6:20 NKJV)

The entire nation had become involved in the supernatural process of God's intervention on their behalf.

None of these things - Moses' hand, the priest's feet, or the voices of the Children of Israel had the power to accomplish these feats. God could just as easily have performed any of these acts without their "help". One of the greatest displays of God's wisdom, power, and imagination is His ability to work through mankind to accomplish His purpose. The host of unseen witnesses says, "You are going to do what? With them? No way". God says, "Way."

This man overslept, woke up with a headache, and missed his devotional time. He lost his temper this morning at his wife. He even said a bad word. He...is very fallible. How could God possibly use him? Because his God - our God - is an awesome God.

Throughout Scripture, God has continuously worked through humanity to establish His Kingdom, purpose, and will giving strength, guidance, and wisdom to those who respond to His call. Those who are willing to serve in his purpose to accomplish His will.

Therefore, I urge you, brothers and sisters, in view of God's mercy, to offer your bodies as a living sacrifice, holy and pleasing to God—this is your true and proper worship.(Romans 12:1 NIV)

They were not superhumans. They were normal people like you and me. Some were, in fact, pretty low on the totem pole in what we would regard as "spiritual". Read Judges.

Hands

Hands are amazing. There are so many things they can do. A hand can break a concrete block or paint a masterpiece. A hand can give a pat on the back or slap to the face. Give a high five, a V for Victory, or flip someone the bird. It can make a fist held up in defiance or reach down to lift someone.

Hands Evoke Emotion

Hands lifted in supplication. Hands lifted in praise. Hands lifted in futility.

You can say that our hands are an extension of our soul and thus by default an extension of our spirit as they express to the world our internal thoughts or expressions.

When I perform on stage I focus on what I do with my hands. The first time I watched myself perform on video it was embarrassing. I was used to holding a trombone or tambourine in my left hand. When singing lead, I would hold the mic in my right hand and not know what to do with my empty left hand. Talk about not letting your left hand know what your right hand is doing. My left hand had no idea what it was doing. It was just hanging limp. It looked weird. I began focusing on how I used my hands. I could hold the mic stand or put my hand at my side.

Later, when I taught drama with YWAM I would place a great amount of focus on awareness of our hands. Facial expressions are good but not very distinguishable from 30 or 40 feet away. The audience will follow your hands so it is important to not overuse them or they become visual noise. Use your hands wisely, "Grasshopper". Limit their use. They are a focal point.

"Uppy?"

I had recently gone through a divorce and due to certain circumstances, it was difficult to get time with Chon and Jamie, my two children from the marriage. One of my first mission trips was to an orphanage in Guatemala. Those kids won my heart. I had just been separated from my kids and now I got to work with these orphan kids. When I returned to the orphanage a year later, I brought specific gifts for each of those I had bonded with. None of those children were still there.

I asked where they were and was told they went back to their parents. "What? Back with their parents? I thought they were orphans." I was told, "Many of them are not orphans. The parents can't afford to take care of them so they drop the children off at an orphanage. We have them for a limited time. We know that when the children are old enough the parents will return to take them back and send them out to work. So we use that time to get the children as healthy as possible. We get them immunized. Teach them the Gospel. And, prepare them for life so that when they go back home, they're not floundering."

Something broke inside me. I suddenly didn't care. I was very disheartened not to see those kids, plus not seeing my kids.
I GOT AN ATTITUDE.

One Sunday I was asked to help chaperon the Children's Church bus as they were being driven to a different building for their Sunday School Service. I told them, "No, I don't want to do that. I don't want to have anything to do with kids." The response was " To be legal we need a certain amount of adults to be on the bus. Will you do it?" "Okay, I'll do it."

I am now seated on the bus thinking, "What am I doing with all these kids? What am I doing here?" Little Megan Lenz must have been four years old. She walked up to where I was sitting, raised her hands toward me, and said, "Uppy?"
Something changed in my heart. Something softened. The hardness left. I smiled, picked her up, and put her down on the seat next to me. I think I got a glimpse of the "Father Heart" of God. When we raise our hands to Him and say "Uppy?" "Will you lift me up?" "Will you hold me?"

Laying On of Hands
There is an aspect to our hands that reaches beyond the physical. A hug, a handshake, holding hands - there is some type of exchange or transfer. A connection that seems innate to hand contact.
Anointing for ministry.
Brothers and sisters, choose seven men from among you who are known to be full of the Spirit and wisdom. We will turn this responsibility over to them and will give our attention to prayer and the ministry of the word." They presented these men to the apostles,

who prayed and laid their hands on them. (Acts 6:6)

Healing power.

Is anyone among you sick? Let them call the elders of the church to pray over them and anoint them with oil in the name of the Lord. And the prayer offered in faith will make the sick person well; the Lord will raise them up. If they have sinned, they will be forgiven. Therefore confess your sins to each other and pray for each other so that you may be healed. The prayer of a righteous person is powerful and effective. (James 5:14-16)

[This verse doesn't specify laying on of hands; but, this is generally understood.]

And he laid his hands on her, and immediately she was made straight, and she glorified God. (Luke 13:13)

And God was doing extraordinary miracles by the hands of Paul, (Acts 19:11)

The gift of the Holy Spirit.

Then Peter and John placed their hands on them, and they received the Holy Spirit. (Acts 8:17)

For this reason I remind you to fan into flame the gift of God, which is in you through the laying on of my hands. (2 Timothy 1:6)

Our Hands Need to be Clean

Who may ascend the mountain of the LORD? Who may stand in his holy place? The one who has clean hands and a pure heart, (Psalm 24:3-4)

Draw near to God, and he will draw near to you. Cleanse your hands, you sinners, and purify your hearts, you double-minded. (James 4:8)

How Do We Get Clean Hands?

According to the Old Covenant, a physical ritual was done to accomplish this. The priests washed their hands before performing a sacrifice or entering the Tabernacle.

Aaron and his sons are to wash their hands and feet with water from it. Whenever they enter the tent of meeting, they shall wash with water so that they will not die. Also, when they approach the altar to minister by presenting a food offering to the LORD, they shall wash their hands and feet so that they will not die. This is to be a lasting ordinance for Aaron and his descendants for the generations to come."
(Exodus 30:19-21)

This was only temporary and needed to be done repeatedly. How do we get clean hands according to the new and better covenant? Our hands are already clean.

When Jesus washed the disciple's feet in John 13.
He came to Simon Peter, who said to him, "Lord, do you wash my feet?" Jesus answered him, "What I am doing you do not understand now, but afterward you will understand." Peter said to him, "You shall never wash my feet." Jesus answered him, "If I do not wash you, you have no share with me." Simon Peter said to him, "Lord, not my feet only but also my hands and my head!" Jesus said to him, "The one who has bathed does not need to wash, except for his feet, but is

completely clean. (John 13:6-10 ESV)

We have been declared clean. Hands, feet, our entire body - clean through faith and identification with the death and resurrection of Jesus Christ. As new creations, we are inherently qualified to be used as a point of Kingdom contact to the world.

"But, I don't feel clean."

My little children, these things write I unto you, that ye sin not. And if any man sin, we have an advocate with the Father, Jesus Christ the righteous: (1 John 2:1).

Slipped up a bit in your walk? Reach up your hands to the Lord and say, "Uppy".

If we confess our sins, he is faithful and just to forgive us our sins, and to cleanse us from all unrighteousness. (1 John 1:9 KJV)

Voila! - Clean Feet.

These are words to a drama we used to perform in the streets:

Hands, God gave us hands
Hands to create
Hands to love
Hands to give
Hands to protect.
But we have misused these hands:
Hands made to create now destroy
Hands made to love now hate
Hands made to give now take

Hands made to protect now attack.

Jesus came and held out his hands to a dying world.

But we took these hands and nailed them to a cross.

And said, "Stay there God!"

But he didn't!

Three days later he rose again.

And today he holds out his hands to you.

Will you listen to him or will you ignore him?

Will you accept him or will you reject him?

The answer is in your hands.

Feet

Our Spiritual Walk

Let's take a look at our spiritual walk.

The first mention of walking is in Genesis Chapter Three.

During the cool part of the day, the LORD God was walking in the garden. The man and the woman heard him, and they hid among the trees in the garden." (Genesis 3:8)

Unfortunately, at this point, Adam and Eve had already sinned. But, this does imply that the Lord was in the habit of walking with them in the garden.

Enoch walked faithfully with God; then he was no more, because God took him away. (Genesis 5:24)

Can two walk together, except they be agreed? (Amos 3:3)

There are paths or ways of behavior given by God that we are expected to follow. These are referenced as straight paths, paths of the righteous, level paths, and the "narrow path". We are called to walk in the light, walk in the spirit.

"Come, let us go up to the mountain of the LORD, to the temple of the God of Jacob. He will teach us his ways, so that we may walk in his paths." (Isaiah 2:3)

He restores my soul. He leads me in paths of righteousness for his name's sake. (Psalms 23:3)

We were buried therefore with him by baptism into death, in order that, just as Christ was raised from the dead by the glory of the Father, we too might walk in newness of life. (Romans 6:4)

...encouraging you, comforting you, and urging you to walk in a manner worthy of God, who calls you into His own kingdom and glory. (1 Thessalonians 2:12)

For we walk by faith, not by sight. (2 Corinthians 5:7 KJV)

So I say, walk by the Spirit, and you will not gratify the desires of the flesh. (Galatians 5:16)

These walks are internal and foundational to our mindset and patterns of behavior.

We can wander astray - run ahead - or fall behind. As we saw earlier, the Israelis were given a special guidance system in the wilderness. It manifested as a pillar of cloud by day and of fire by night. In this way, it was always visible. When it moved - they moved. Where it stayed -

they stayed. There was provision as long as they remained with the pillar.

Your word is a lamp for my feet, a light on my path. (Psalm 119:105)
Mark out a straight path for your feet; stay on the safe path. Don't get sidetracked; keep your feet from following evil. (Proverbs 4:26-27)
The LORD makes firm the steps of the one who delights in him; though he may stumble, he will not fall, for the LORD upholds him with his hand. (Psalms 37:23-24)

The generation that God brought out of Egypt rebelled against God and had to wander in the wilderness until the older generation had died - except Joshua and Caleb. During this time, God prepared the next generation for entry to the Promised Land by providing their needs - water, manna, quail, and guidance. All their needs were met for forty years. Their shoes and clothes didn't even wear out. He was guiding and training them from the start.

A "Seasonal Walk"

I have walked through many seasons with God. A few of them while "not holding His hand". But, He always held mine.

As we walk with God in our hearts and spirit we are also walking the earth. We "walk" at work. We "walk" at school. This is the physical part of our walk with God. As stated earlier, we carry the Kingdom of God within us everywhere we go.

A father told his son to get in the car. They were going on an adventure. They drove down to the beach and got into a sailboat. The father began their journey by teaching his son how to trim the sail, various types of knots, and more. Soon, the son was able to run the boat with only minimal supervision from the father. He said, "Well, I guess I am called to be a sailer." At this, the father pulled out a net and some fishing gear. He showed his son how to cast the net, properly bait a hook, and drop a lobster trap. "Oh, you taught me to sail so I could be a fisherman."

Back on land, the father set up a plow and prepared a field. They planted seeds, watered, weeded, and raised several different crops. "A farmer?" He followed his father to a nearby orchard - You can guess his next assumption. The journey continued through several other venues - sheepherder, miner, etc.

Together they climbed to a mountaintop where they could view all the areas they had visited. There was the sea, the fields, the flocks, and the orchards. The father said to his son, "Of all the places we have been and all you have learned which would you prefer?" The son thought hard. "I have become very adept at each of these and have enjoyed every moment. You taught me to fish. How to plant seeds. You showed me how to find wind for the sail. I could enjoy doing any one of these. But, the thing I enjoyed the most was time with you. That is what I want to do. I want to be with you. Where do we go next?"

Let's take a look at a few references to the importance of our feet. *Then he said, "Do not come near; take your sandals off your feet, for the place on which you are standing is holy ground." (Exodus 3:5)*

After the death of Moses the servant of the LORD, the LORD said to Joshua son of Nun, Moses' aide: "Moses my servant is dead. Now then, you and all these people, get ready to cross the Jordan River into the land I am about to give to them—to the Israelites. I will give you every place where you set your foot, as I promised Moses. (Joshua 1:1-3)

We saw earlier in "HANDS" that by living in the New and Better Covenant our feet are clean as our whole body has been washed in Jesus' blood. *(John 13:2-11)*

We can now boldly approach the Throne of Grace. *(Hebrews 4:16)*

Carry the Good News

As ambassadors of the Prince of Peace, we are to carry His peace wherever we go.

And your feet shod with the preparation of the gospel of peace; (Ephesians 6:15, KJV)

How lovely on the mountains are the feet of him who brings good news, who announces peace and brings good news of happiness, who announces salvation, and says to Zion, "Your God reigns!" (Isaiah 52:7)

Behold, on the mountains the feet of him who brings good news, who announces peace! (Nahum 1:15)

How will they preach unless they are sent? Just as it is written, "How beautiful are the feet of those who bring good news of good things!" (Romans 10:15)

Jesus sent out the twelve disciples, instructing them,

"...if the house is worthy, let your peace come upon it, but <u>if it is not worthy, let your peace return to you</u>. And if anyone will not receive you or listen to your words, <u>shake off the dust from your feet when you leave that house or town</u>. (Matthew 10:13-15 ESV)

After this, the Lord appointed seventy-two others and sent them two by two ahead of him to every town and place where he was about to go. He told them, Whenever you enter a town and they receive you, eat what is set before you. Heal the sick in it and say to them, 'The kingdom of God has come near to you.' But whenever you enter a town and they do not receive you, go into its streets and say, '<u>Even the dust of your town that clings to our feet we wipe off against you</u>. Nevertheless know this, that the kingdom of God has come near.' (Luke 10:8-11 ESV)

(note: some manuscripts say seventy disciples were sent out)

Jesus told them to shake the dust off their feet and the peace would not remain with them.

Our feet carry peace.

Rest In Peace *(Hebrews 4:10)*

If our feet carry peace and we are told to stand firm in the evil day then we are called to "stand in peace".

"Be anxious for nothing, but in everything by prayer and supplication, with thanksgiving, let your requests be made known to God; and the peace of God, which surpasses all understanding, will guard your

hearts and minds through Christ Jesus" (Philippians 6-7, NKJV).
"...Cast all your anxiety on him because he cares for you. Be alert and of sober mind. Your enemy the devil prowls around like a roaring lion looking for someone to devour. Resist him, <u>standing firm</u> in the faith," (1 Peter 5:7-9)

If you are in the faith you do not need to "prove it". If you feel you need to "prove" you are in the faith you are probably not in the faith. Remember the disciples' failed attempt to cast out the demon? It is not your job to psyche up a miracle. Or, know all the answers.

Never worry about anything. Instead, in every situation let your petitions be made known to God through prayers and requests, with thanksgiving. Then God's peace, which goes far beyond anything we can imagine, will guard your hearts and minds in union with the Messiah Jesus.

Finally, brothers, whatever is true, whatever is honorable, whatever is fair, whatever is pure, whatever is acceptable, whatever is commendable, if there is anything of excellence and if there is anything praiseworthy—keep thinking about these things. Likewise, keep practicing these things: what you have learned, received, heard, and seen in me. Then the God of peace will be with you.
(Philippians 4:6-9 ISV)

Are You In the Faith?
Examine yourselves to see whether you are in the faith; test yourselves. Do you not realize that Christ Jesus is in you—unless, of course, you fail the test? (2 Corinthians 13:5)

What is this test?
"they will pick up serpents, and if they drink any deadly poison, it will not hurt them;" (Mark 16:18)

Is this the test? Some denominations think so. They even handle snakes and drink poison to test their faith. They are only testing God's patience. When challenged by Satan *"If you are the Son of God"* Jesus replied, *"Thou shalt not tempt the Lord thy God". (Matthew 4:7-9)*

Mouth

The Scripture asks
"But how can they call on him to save them unless they believe in him? And how can they believe in him if they have never heard about him? And how can they hear about him unless someone tells them?" (Romans 10:14 NLT)

How is the Word of God going to manifest in the world unless we open our mouths and speak? How is the will of God going to be done on earth if not through us - His ambassadors? God promised to bless Abraham so he in turn could bless others. *(Genesis 12:2-3)* God has called us to feed the hungry and give food to the fatherless, the widow, and the foreigner. *(Isaiah 58:6 - Deuteronomy 10:18)*

This means more than just physical food. Scripture refers to the Word as bread, wine, water, meat, milk, and more. We have a Tree of Life growing in the gardens of our hearts producing abundant fruit for each season. This fruit is not for us to glut on. It is to be shared with the world. I want the will of God manifested in my life. I want the will of God to be accomplished in the world.

"Thy kingdom come, Thy will be done on earth as it is in heaven." (Matthew 6:10 KJV)

I will sing of the mercies of the LORD forever; With my mouth will I make known Your faithfulness to all generations. (Psalms 89:1 NKJV)

We have been talking about releasing the Kingdom of God within us into the world. Let's look at speaking the Kingdom into the world.

"So what shall I do? I will pray with my spirit, but I will also pray with my understanding; I will sing with my spirit, but I will also sing with my understanding." (1 Corinthians 14:15).

With My Understanding

We're taught so much to depend on our understanding that if we are not careful we will speculate in our minds the best approach to a circumstance. Then dictate that process to God. We will decide the best way for God to do something and then pray. Directing God on how best to handle it.

How are you allowing your voice to release the Kingdom of Heaven into the world around you? Are your words aligning with or blocking the work of the Holy Spirit?

"Let the words of my mouth, and the meditation of my heart, be acceptable in thy sight, O LORD, my strength, and my redeemer."
(Psalm 19:14)
" O generation of vipers, how can ye, being evil, speak good things? for out of the abundance of the heart the mouth speaketh. "
(Matthew 12:34)

Let's first define and lock in on our source.

Adversary vs. Advocate

We are caught up from our youth in the thought processes of the world system. An eye for an eye. A tooth for a tooth. You bad-mouthed me. Back at ya. I deserve better than this. *"Turn the other cheek"* You hurt me. I'll hurt you back. *"Love your enemy"*

There is a great disparity between the world system of thought and Kingdom thinking. When we allow our thoughts to align with the world system - an eye for an eye - we are standing on the side of the accuser. The Adversary - the Devil. If we choose to speak life in line with the Spirit of God we are standing alongside the Advocate - Jesus Christ. Your response will be rooted in agreement with one or the other. Life or death. Blessings or curses.

Bless them which persecute you: bless, and curse not.
(Romans 12:14 KJV)

Our body/flesh hears or sees a situation and transmits this information to our soul, Hap will respond directly to the situation from what he knows instinctively or look to our spirit for his response. Our spirit,

Shep planted in and in communion with the Holy Spirit through New Birth will respond in line with the Word while our flesh will respond in line with the world. Hap chooses the response. A renewed mind will agree with the spirit/Spirit and speak life.

Set a guard over my mouth, Lord; keep watch over the door of my lips. (Psalm 141:3-4)

We all stumble in many ways. Anyone who is never at fault in what they say is perfect, able to keep their whole body in check. (James 3:2)

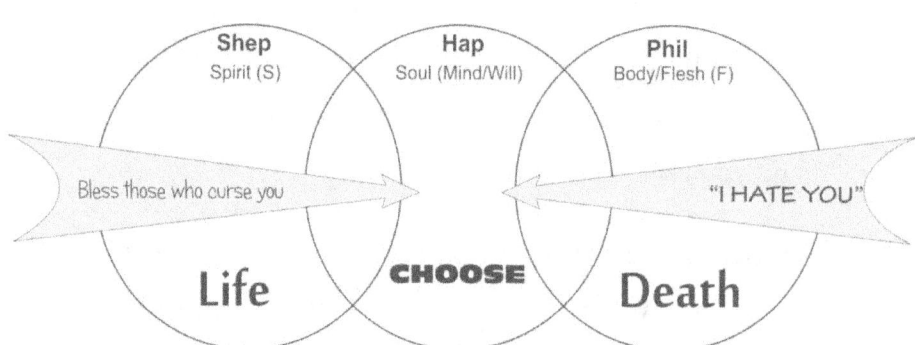

Let's look at a few circumstances where a guard placed over our mouth would be a great idea.

Personal Confrontation. This could be real or imagined.
I'm sure we have all been in situations where a discussion became heated to the point where we reacted to something the other person said and "it just came out of my mouth". Those words will never be able to be taken back. No matter how hard you try to rephrase it it has

been said. Did the conversation just happen to escalate to this point or was this argument predetermined by previous experience?

I don't know about you but I often find myself running conversations in my head triggered by memories of past conflicts or rough encounters with other people. Some are real and some are imagined. Let me explain. Let's say, I need to return something to a store. Something I purchased that broke. I bought it a while back and don't have the receipt. My brain starts looking for answers to the possibility that the cashier will not accept the return without the receipt. I tell them that it is defective and exclusive to their store. They respond. I respond. The argument in my mind escalates to the point where I am never going to shop there again.

I am still in the parking lot.

My Demons Know Your Demons

Whether the source is a demon whispering in your ear or just how the gears of our minds work; somehow these conversations seem to find and punch each other's buttons pushing the dialogue to a higher level of conflict. This is not the direction we want to go.

"A gentle answer turns away wrath, but a harsh word stirs up anger." (Proverbs 15:1)

Let me share a real story. First, a bit of background. I was involved in full-time missions with YWAM (Youth With A Mission) in Miami, Florida. One of my main supporters was ALF (Abundant Love Fellowship) in Cahokia, Illinois. This is the church that embraced me when I left the band. They ministered to me as I recovered from a divorce. Showed me that the Bible is more than Sunday School stories. More than memorization and rules. It is life. It is food. It is seeds planted in a garden. Christianity is not a religion. It is a relationship with the Creator God of the universe. Faith is not a psyche. It is trust in a relationship. The people of ALF became my family. I became involved with almost every aspect of that church. Worship team, Hospital Ministry, Children's Church, Editor of the Church Paper, Co-Youth Leader, Adult Sunday School Teacher, and eventually - Missionary. I cannot begin to share how important these people were to me and my spiritual development. Pastor Tim Ritzel is the first person I have ever called pastor. Yes, my father, Walden Owen was my pastor growing up. But, he was Dad.

Pastor Tim taught me how to put together a sermon using three to five points and be able to communicate that message in twelve to fifteen minutes. "If you can't teach it in that amount of time you don't know your subject well enough to teach it." The rest of the time - forty minutes or an hour - will allow you to go more in-depth, share a few stories, and strengthen your point. I can name many instances where this training was useful. I was asked to speak at a conference in Miami. We started with a big parade where I got to be one of the clowns. Upon arrival at the meeting place, I changed out of my costume and waited my turn to speak. Speaker after speaker droned on and on. We had been given thirty minutes each. The speakers were averaging forty minutes to an hour. By the time I was up the MC apologized and asked if I could keep it down to fifteen minutes. I told him I could do it in ten. My message went quickly and smoothly. It was well received by the crowd. The MC asked for my information and said he had several other events coming up and would I be available for them. He liked the message and my respect for the time allotment. This led to many opportunities in the Greater Miami area.

I share this because Pastor Ritzel and the ALFs were more than a family. They supported me. They laid hands on me on numerous occasions and sent me out into the world as an extension of them to share Christ with the world. With their support, I ministered in every country in Central America at least once, plus the Dominican Republic, Mexico, Canada, and India. I was always in their prayers and invited to their homes when I would return to Cahokia.

Okay. Here's the story.

I had an opportunity to come home to Illinois for a short visit. My monthly support check had not come in on the normal date. I waited several days and still no check. I had enough money to get home to Cahokia if I was careful with my finances. So I left. My mind was on hyper the entire drive. Why didn't the check come in? Should I have waited longer? Have they decided that they will no longer support me? I don't remember all the conversations that went through my mind during the drive. Let's just say I was hurt and confused. Had they dropped my support? In some of my "head conversations" I quit missions. I quit the church. Fortunately, by the time I arrived at the church, my spirit had won. I had peace. I had no answers. But, I had peace. God is my strength. He is my support. I set a guard over my mouth and walked into Pastor Tim's office.

Tim handed me an envelope. The first thought that came into my head was it was an explanation of why they were stopping my support. I opened the envelope. It was filled with cash. Much more than my monthly support check. Tim explained to me that they didn't want to take a chance on the check arriving after I had left town and me being in town without funds. So, they waited until I arrived. They had also prayed and the mission board had decided to raise my monthly support. Then he handed me some more cash and said, "This is from me. I want you to be able to enjoy your time at home."

Thank God the Spirit of God won the battle for my thought-life in this case.

Blessings or Curses
Jesus called the crowd to him and said, "Listen and understand. What goes into someone's mouth does not defile them, but what comes out of their mouth, that is what defiles them." (Matthew 15:11)
"With the tongue we praise our Lord and Father, and with it we curse human beings, who have been made in God's likeness. Out of the same mouth come praise and cursing. My brothers and sisters, this should not be. Can both fresh water and salt water flow from the same spring? My brothers and sisters, can a fig tree bear olives, or a

grapevine bear figs? Neither can a salt spring produce fresh water." (James 3:9-12)

There is an ongoing battle for our thought life and we need to determine which side we are going to follow. This is an area I deal with. I'll get into a confrontational situation and need to "bite my tongue" before I respond with a verbal attack. I am not always successful. Even when I successfully "guard my mouth" my thoughts sometimes get caught up in grumbling and murmuring against that person. Complaining to God about the treatment I just got. I am learning to do something that is consistently taught in YWAM - "Respond in the opposite spirit". Stop and speak blessing. Pray for peace and grace to that person. Turn the other cheek. Shalom. Right here we have the power to bless or to curse. Speak life or speak death into that situation.

The whole Israelite community set out from Elim and came to the Desert of Sin, which is between Elim and Sinai, on the fifteenth day of the second month after they had come out of Egypt. In the desert, the whole community grumbled against Moses and Aaron. The Israelites said to them, "If only we had died by the LORD's hand in Egypt! There we sat around pots of meat and ate all the food we wanted, but you have brought us out into this desert to starve this entire assembly to death." (Exodus 16:1-3)

The Israelites were saying to God, "You are not properly providing for us. You don't understand or care about our needs". "OUR WILL BE DONE"

But Paul tells us,
"Do everything without grumbling or arguing, so that you may become blameless and pure, 'children of God without fault in a warped and crooked generation.' Then you will shine among them like stars in the sky as you hold firmly to the word of life. And then I will be able to boast on the day of Christ that I did not run or labor in vain." (Philippians 2:14-16)

> The word in Hebrew for grumble is yalan. This means to worry, fret, complain. The word explains itself with its built-in commentary. It is spelled Yod, Lamed, and Nun. The Yod represents no foundation and irrational actions, the Lamed shows narrow thinking and self-importance, and the Nun shows a lack of faith.
> (SOURCE: https://www.chaimbentorah.com/2015/11/word-study-they-grumbled-%D7%99%D7%9C%D7%A0/)

It is quite a step to say "Thy will be done." with no contingencies. To trust in God's will. Any other position is a position of pride and would be based on the Tree of the Knowledge of Good and Evil rooted in the world system of thought. We decide what is good for us, and then dictate that to Him. Playing the role of God.
To dictate a better way of doing things, our way, to the planner and

creator of the universe, is the epitome of pride. *(Job Chapter 38)*
"Humble yourselves, therefore, under God's mighty hand, that he may lift you up in due time." (1 Peter 5:6)
"Humble yourselves before the Lord, and he will lift you up." (James 4:10)

I am not saying we can't come to God with our concerns, our fears, and circumstances we don't like. We are not to grumble or murmur. Rather, we are to petition. Jesus asked that the cup, if possible, would be taken from Him.
"nevertheless not my will, but thine, be done." (Luke 22:42 KJV)
Paul asked that the thorn in his flesh be removed.
"Three times I pleaded with the Lord about this, that it should leave me." (2 Corinthians 12:8)
God's grace was sufficient (2 Corinthians 12:9)

The Bible tells us, *"Do not be anxious about anything, but in every situation, by prayer and petition, with thanksgiving, present your requests to God"* (Philippians 4:6).

Just as the Israelites had to trust in the pillar of fire/cloud for guidance and provision we need to learn to trust in God's love, desire, and ability to provide. He is the lamp to our feet and the light to our path. Pointing us in the right direction and telling us when and where to place our next step.

With My Spirit

I spoke earlier about speaking in tongues. This is a prime example of how we can minister God's word into the world. The Spirit of God knows the will of God. Our spirit is rooted in the Holy Spirit. It would make sense that praying in tongues is allowing our spirit to speak the will of God directly from the Holy Spirit into the world.

In the past, thinking of being an interpreter for the Holy Spirit was to renew my mind to the word so that I can speak what the Spirit of God wants to teach. He speaks - I translate. This has served me well for many years. I am now looking at another level of interpreting. Directly speaking the words of the Teacher.

The Holy Spirit is not some power source to be tapped into to enhance our ministry or to further our agenda. He is an equal person to the Godhead. He has a will to be done on earth as it is in heaven. We say, Father, thy will be done. The Holy Spirit is in unity with the Father. He has been given to us as a comforter, as a teacher, to lead us into all truth. He has been given to us so *"I have much more to say to you, more than you can now bear. But when he, the Spirit of truth, comes, he will guide you into all the truth. He will not speak on his own; he will speak only what he hears, and he will tell you what is yet to come. He will glorify me because it is from me that he will receive what he will make known to you. All that belongs to the Father is mine. That is why I said the Spirit will receive from me what he will make known to you." (John 16:12-15)*

The Contemporary English Version says *"I have much more to say to you, but right now it would be more than you could understand."*

We have the Spirit of God within us. What better way for the Holy Spirit to communicate His will to the world than through our mouths?

Let's take another look at *Romans 8:26-28.*
Likewise the Spirit also helpeth our infirmities: for we know not what we should pray for as we ought: but the Spirit itself maketh intercession for us with groanings which cannot be uttered. And he that searcheth the hearts knoweth what is the mind of the Spirit, because he maketh intercession for the saints according to the will of God. And we know that all things work together for good to them that love God, to them who are the called according to his purpose. (KJV)

John tells us we can be confident that if we ask anything according to God's will He will hear us and will answer those petitions *(1 John 5:14-15)*. Back up to *Romans 8:28* and we see a promise that God is working out all things for the good in our lives. James tells us we need to ask; but, when we do ask we often miss the mark. *(James 4:2-3)* The catch here is we need to ask but we need to ask according to God's will. And, we need to believe He will answer.

As we saw earlier, the word translated infirmities is singular and not plural. We have one infirmity or weakness in this case. We don't know what to pray. Our finite, self-centered minds cannot come close to imagining what God's perfect will is. And, if we did have a glimpse of what He is preparing for us we might not want to ask. This is where

the Spirit of God comes alongside as a help-meet. He takes our groanings and speaks the perfect will of God. A better translation is *"And the Holy Spirit helps us in our weakness. For example, we don't know what God wants us to pray for. But the Holy Spirit prays for us with groanings that cannot be expressed in words. And the Father who knows all hearts knows what the Spirit is saying, for the Spirit pleads for us believers in harmony with God's own will."*
(Romans 8:26-27 NLT)

For he that speaketh in an unknown tongue speaketh not unto men, but unto God: for no man understandeth him; howbeit in the spirit he speaketh mysteries. (1 Corinthians 14:2 KJV)

For if I pray in an unknown tongue, my spirit prayeth, but my understanding is unfruitful. What is it then? I will pray with the spirit, and I will pray with the understanding also: I will sing with the spirit, and I will sing with the understanding also.
(1 Corinthians 14:14-15 KJV)

When we, in faith, allow the Spirit of God to give our spirit utterance we "hit the mark". In faith, we petition the perfect will of the Father and we have every confidence that He hears us, that He will answer, and that His will is going to be done.

Imagine you are in a war-torn country in a room surrounded by men with guns pointed at you. Your hands are tied behind your back. You don't know how you got there or why you are tied up. You cannot ask because they are speaking a different language and do not seem to understand yours. A phone rings and one of the men answers. There is a quick conversation and he hands to phone to you. The caller tells you he doesn't have time to explain. Just repeat his words to the gunmen and everything will be fine. He begins speaking in a language you have never heard. You begin parroting his words. You have no idea what you are saying. You might be confessing to a crime you have not committed. You decide to trust the caller and continue to speak. The men put their guns down and untie you.

This is similar to speaking in tongues. It is not a takeover of your mind or mouth. You have decided to trust the "caller" as He gives you utterance. Words of another language form in your mouth. It may sound like gibberish. It may sound familiar. Many human languages on this planet don't sound anything like English. Or, like any language at all to an English-speaking person. The Holy Spirit gives you *"utterance" (Acts 2:4)* and you speak trusting in that *"utterance"*. Trusting that the Spirit of God is not going to make a fool out of you. *(Luke 11:13)*

More Than All of You *(1 Corinthians 14:18)*

I just finished reading my journals from India where I saw the lame walk and blind eyes healed. Many miracles. Praying for the girl with the club feet I watched her toes straightening out. A very strong theme that is consistent throughout the journals is that I spent hours and hours every day praying in the spirit. I would pray what I knew in my mind. I would pray what I could think of. Then, I would pray in the spirit.

Something or someone would come to mind. A person's name might come to me. I would say whatever came to mind about that person. Then I would just pray in the spirit until I felt a release then move on. I also read the Word. I read lots and lots of scripture then continued to pray.

Look at Paul's ministry. He said,
I thank God that I pray in tongues more than all of you.
(1 Corinthians 14:18 NIV)
Forbid not to pray in tongues. (1 Corinthians 14:39 KJV)
What is it then? I will pray with the spirit, but I will pray also with the understanding; I will sing with the spirit, but I will sing also with the understanding. (1 Corinthians 14:15 Darby)
In *Jude 1:20* we see "...*building up yourselves on your most holy faith, praying in the Holy Ghost."(KJV)*

I believe that praying in the spirit not only builds our faith but is an opportunity for a very strong release of the will of the Holy Spirit using our tongue. Releasing the Kingdom of God from within us. In this case, you can be guaranteed that your prayers are effective and world-changing.
So shall My word be that goes forth from My mouth; It shall not return to Me void, But it shall accomplish what I please, And it shall prosper in the thing for which I sent it. (Isaiah 55:11 NKJV).

SPEAK A RIVER OF LIFE: 323

Prayer 323
    Micromanage 326
    Stem Cells 328
    You Promised 329
    Warfare 338
    India: 339
    Good Reports from Last Year's Crusade with Pastor Moses 340
    Regarding the Drought, I Mentioned in the Introduction 343

Speak a River of Life

Prayer

I recently saw an extremely vague post on Facebook requesting prayer. No specifics. Just "Please pray." How do you respond to that? I found myself wanting more information. I was tempted to message that person asking for more details. I grew up attending Baptist churches. The mid-week prayer meetings all had one thing in common. After a quick teaching, we would sit in a circle and share our prayer needs. Then, we would go back around the circle praying one after the other. Speaking out a list of those requests. Some expressed it better than others and some would add things like "The missionaries in Africa." But it seemed to me that we were just taking turns saying the same thing. I thought we could save time by having one person pray the list followed by the others stating "Amen". To make things worse, a few members of the prayer group would make an "unspoken" request. What do you do with that? "God, please do whatever for this person. And, for that person. Amen."

I have discovered a paradigm for those of us willing to pray but feeling a bit frustrated at the generality of the request.

For some people that prayer request may be either too personal to share publically. Or, to give a proper description or understanding of the request is just too involved. Like, "It started when I was three..." They might be so beaten down or discouraged that all they can do is

call for help. Maybe the issue is too embarrassing, "I have a problem with porn." Whatever the reason is they want and need prayer which is the whole reason we were there.
So, let's take it from there.

In cases like this, I look for the Spirit of God to know the specifics as I lift that person or situation to Him. Then, I pray for what comes to mind. I don't force details or teach or give counsel. I speak what comes to mind trusting the Holy Spirit to be the source.
Regardless - grace, peace, hope, supplication for the best outcome, and for God to be strong in their mind and heart are always good specifics we can add to prayer. Above all, we want God to be glorified.

We need to lift each other in prayer trusting that *"God's grace is sufficient for* (their) *today"*. Praying they will see God as their *"I AM"* confident that He is holding their hand as they walk together into the unknowns of tomorrow.

Pray for them to have a deeper understanding of Christ the *"Author and Finisher of our faith"* for God's mercy and grace to abound, and to be able to walk in peace with *"feet fitted with the readiness that comes from the Gospel of Peace" (NIV)*. I am not givinga checklist. I am not saying I pray every one of these every time for everyone. These are some things that come to mind. And, that is the solution. Ask the Holy Spirit to guide your thoughts. My pastor Tim Ritzel would sometimes ask which is the best spiritual gift. Is it healing? Is it wisdom? Is it prophecy? It is the gift that is needed at the time. I don't need you to prophecy if I am dying of a disease. I need the gift of healing. They need the words of the moment direct from the Holy Spirit's prompting. This should result in more effective prayer since so many of us tend to pray from our understanding more than from the Spirit. We are encouraged to *"by prayer and petition, with thanksgiving, present our requests to God." (Philippians 4:6)* But, we are also to pray *"Your will be done on earth as it is in heaven." (Matthew 6:10)*.

We are concerned that our prayers are sent out effectively. As a result, we potentially restrict our prayers by funneling them conditionally through our "own understanding".

But, the unimpeded power of the Spirit of God released in a prayer of faith will carry the grace, "God's enabling power" to meet the situation. When a person comes to mind, I tell myself "God knows their need" and focus on speaking peace, grace, and rest to that person. I pray that they hear His voice and will not follow the voice of a stranger. I pray that *"All things will work together for their good"* knowing that the Great "*I AM*" is walking with them through this life and is intimately involved in their every breath and every heartbeat confident that "*though he may stumble, he will not fall, for the Lord upholds him with his hand." (Psalm 37:24)*. Then, I pray that they will not let go of His hand. God cares and is aware of "every sparrow that falls". He knows the "number of hairs on our head" (for some of you we got a pretty good idea, too).

Micromanage

I have recently been looking at how prayer is used prayer in the Bible, specifically by the New Testament writers (e.g. Paul, Peter) to see how they prayed for those whose "life details" were not intimately known. So many times we tend to micromanage our prayers. We pray our idea of how God should answer rather than listening to what the Spirit of God would have us say. This ends up turning a spiritual practice into a mental process. The prayer now becomes a process of our intellect, moving into the realm of the soul. Limiting the prayer to our knowledge and imagination. God has intimate knowledge of this person's situation and a much greater imagination.

There is a beautiful little chorus we used to sing at Circle Church.
Silver and gold have I none.
But, such as I have give I thee.
In the Name of Jesus Christ
of Nazareth Rise up and walk.
He went walking and leaping and praising God.
walking and leaping and praising God.
In the Name of Jesus Christ
of Nazareth 'Rise up and walk'. *(Acts 3:6)*

Notice the words Peter spoke. "In the Name of Jesus Christ of Nazareth Rise up and walk." Peter didn't intellectualize the healing. It wasn't even spoken as a prayer. He just said, "Rise up and walk." Oh, yeah. Don't miss the part where he says, "In the name of Jesus Christ."

This is where the power is. It is in His name.

When Jesus raised the Jairus' daughter from the dead, He said *"Talitha cumi"* - *"Little girl, arise." (Mark 5:41)* He didn't say, "Okay. Let's get some brain activity going here. Heart. Start pumping. Soul, get back in the body...(etc.)" He took more of a stem cell approach.

Jesus spoke and the Holy Spirit released the power necessary for the result. She came back to life.

We pray - the Spirit flows - we see ministry results - we get excited - pray again - this time we try to psyche it - the Spirit of God flowing through humility is no longer the source.

We are pushing to "help" or "produce" through our spirit or soul. God cannot honor that.

Prayer, teaching, learning - *"all things pertaining to life and Godliness"* must be achieved and received in humility through God's grace and sourced in the Spirit of God.

Someone praying for healing to a knee injury, for example, might address in their prayer the cartilage, bone, and muscle tissue - neglecting the fact that nerve damage, blood vessels, and myriad more factors have not been covered.

Since the person praying decided to "be the boss" of the healing process, rather than trust the "Master Healer"; he has now put conditions and limitations on the prayer "according to his faith" and what seems best in his own mind.

At the same time, this person is introducing such factors as pride, spiritual independence, self-doubt "I hope I didn't miss anything", control "Who wears the crown, anyway?" and other unknown factors. All these limit the flow of the Spirit.

Better to take Christ's approach. Trust in the Spirit of the Original Designer and allow His power to work.

Stem Cells

A very basic look at stem cell therapy

Stem cells are "unimprinted" to any specific need. They are just "available" and able to adjust their coding to manufacture and reproduce pretty much any cell in the body. When the body sends out a call of "distress" for a certain cell type or organ to be restored, the stem cell adjusts to the necessary specifications for healing and restoration of that injury.

In a similar manner to stem cell therapy, whatever needs and actions are called for in the prayer circumstance, physical, emotional, or spiritual, the Spirit of God has the power and understanding available to produce the desired result. We need to trust in His knowledge and not "our understanding".

We can still be open to specifics brought about to be verbally expressed as the Spirit of God guides our thoughts. It is important to see these only as guides to help direct our request.

Many people use scripture almost as an incantation when they pray.

Buying a book of "promises" at the Bible Book Store and repeating those is not necessarily prayer. The power is not in the words. It is the "Word". *(John 1:1)*

"But when ye pray, use not vain repetitions, as the heathen do: for they think that they shall be heard for their much speaking." (Matthew 6:7 KJV)

The wise man built his house on the rock. Not on a bunch of little pieces of rock commonly known as sand.

You search the Scriptures because you think that in them you have eternal life; and it is they that bear witness about me, (John 5:39 ESV)

You Promised

I have been thinking about how our prayers can be given as a form of coercion. Like a spoiled child saying, "You promised."

There is no guarantee for the answer we seek except whether it is God's will or if it is best for us at this time for our growth or God's plan for us at the moment.

He won't let us get away with "I've been a good Christian so I deserve this." either.

Above all, He wants to protect us from spiritual pride. None of His workings are by our efforts *"lest any man should boast"*.

"But, I found a promise in the Bible."

Not every promise in the Bible is meant to be applied to your situation. Just because you decide to raise your son to not drink grape juice or cut his hair; does not mean he will have superhuman strength.

Some think the circumstance and/or result has already been established as God's will since creation, rendering prayer simply a moot act of obedience. "God already knows what is going to happen. He loves me so He has already made provision for me." If that is the case, why pray? "God has already determined if that person is going to be saved or not." Then, why share the Gospel?

Some think if they are spiritual enough, they can force it to happen. If not, "You lack faith. C'mon, psyche a little harder." ...They try to get more good deed weights placed on the prayer scale in an attempt to tip God in their favor. "If I pray hard enough. If I am good enough. If I can get more people on my prayer team. I need more prayer bucks." Don't get me wrong. Group prayer is effective.
For where two or three are gathered together in my name, there am I in the midst of them. (Matthew 18:20)
God is not impressed by how large your cheering section is. He responds to faith in the Name and the relationship we have with Him through Jesus Christ. And, the response is always conditional to His plan for our lives and according to His will.

How many times have you heard people quote *"I can do all things through Christ who strengthens me" (Philippians 4:13)*
All things? Let's look at the context.
Philippians Chapter 4 (NIV)
Verse 4: *Rejoice in the Lord always. I will say it again: Rejoice!*

Verses 6-7: ***Do not be anxious*** *about anything, but in every situation, by prayer and petition, with thanksgiving,* ***present your requests to God****. And the peace of God, which transcends all understanding,* ***will guard your hearts and your minds in Christ Jesus.***

Verses 8-9 *Finally, brothers and sisters, whatever is true, whatever is noble, whatever is right, whatever is pure, whatever is lovely, whatever is admirable—if anything is excellent or praiseworthy—* ***think about such things****. Whatever you have learned or received or heard from me, or seen in me—put it into practice. And* ***the God of peace will be with you****.*

Verse 12: ***I have learned the secret of being content in any and every situation,***

(Content. Why? Because, no matter the circumstance God is greater than that circumstance. And, He is willing and able to work all things for the good (*Romans 8:28*))

Verse 13: **I can do <u>all this</u>** (remain calm and content) **through him who gives me strength.**

I believe God responds to prayer according to the needs of our character development more than our temporal desires or needs of the moment.

He who began a good work in you will carry it on to completion (Philippians 1:6)

Consider prayer as conversation and problem-solving with a close friend. Knowing and sharing that friend's heart. At the same time, realize that your close friend is the All-Powerful Creator of all things with wisdom and insight beyond comprehension and trust in His final Word and decision as to the outcome.

Ask:

Ask, and it shall be given you; seek, and ye shall find; knock, and it shall be opened unto you: For every one that asketh receiveth; and he that seeketh findeth; and to him that knocketh it shall be opened. (Matthew 7:7-8)

Let us then approach God's throne of grace with confidence, so that we may receive mercy and find grace to help us in our time of need. (Hebrews 4:16)

Believe:

And without faith it is impossible to please God, because anyone who comes to him must believe that he exists and that he rewards those who earnestly seek him. (Hebrews 11:6)

This is based on the grace given by Christ's accomplishment - not ours. *"For I know the thoughts that I think toward you, says the Lord, thoughts of peace and not of evil, to give you a future and a hope. Then you will call upon Me and go and pray to Me, and I will listen to you." (Jeremiah 29:11)*

Trust:

And when you pray, do not keep on babbling like pagans, for they think they will be heard because of their many words. Do not be like them, for your Father knows what you need before you ask him. "This, then, is how you should pray:

"'Our Father in heaven, hallowed be your name, your kingdom come, your will be done, on earth as it is in heaven. (Matthew 6:7-10)
Trust that God's will is for your benefit.

"Trust in the Lord with all your heart, And lean not on your own understanding; In all your ways acknowledge Him, And He shall direct your paths." (Proverbs 3:5-6)

Expect His Best:

And we know that in all things God works for the good of those who love him, who have been called according to his purpose. (Romans 8:28)

The following is an excerpt from my friend Robert Zimmerman's book "Hope for the Hopeless: Finding Your Miracle in Plain Sight" which demonstrates a great point in petitioner prayer - "Don't pray for something you don't honestly believe will happen." You can't just psyche up a God-empowered answer to prayer. As the father of the demon-possessed boy in *Mark 9* responded to Jesus saying to him *"Everything is possible for one who believes." "I do believe; help me overcome my unbelief!" (verses 25-25).*

We need to pray from a point of belief. Not just hope. That point of belief can only come as a witness from the Holy Spirit in our hearts. *"Faith comes by hearing, and hearing by the word of God." (Romans 10:17)*

"Hope for the Hopeless: Finding Your Miracle in Plain Sight"
(Pages 3-6)

What I learned from the brutally honest assessment of my relationship with Jesus and the role of the Holy Spirit gave birth to a season of miracles I could never have experienced without the total stripping down of my perception of Christianity. Put simply. my death sentence obliterated religion in my life and replaced it with a relationship-a very one-way dependence.

I literally had nothing to offer Jesus. In fact, all that was left was need. There was no more. If you'll do this for me, Lord, I'll never (fill in the blank) again, or I promise to (fill in the blank) for You. Bargaining was absurd at that point. I laid in bed one night and admitted to Him that He was my only hope and my only help. I was back at square one, the utter helplessness I acknowledged the evening back in 1981 when I surrendered my life to Him. It was that raw, that naked.

Shortly after my conversion in 1981, a minister said something that stayed with me for this very moment. It incubated in me for decades, waiting in the deep recesses of my mind until circumstances came together, bringing it to life in my time of greatest need. As I started to wrestle with the prospect of fighting the cancer inside me, I returned to the discipline of falling asleep to sermons of ministers I knew, both historical and current, who had experienced the miraculous presence of God. I wanted to see what they had in common. And there it was, the same comment from a different minister. Paraphrased, the message was a simple one, yet life-changing: **"Don't pray for something you don't honestly believe will happen."** Let that sink in.

I have been around Christians since my rebirth that labor to make the faith message work for them by striving to confess things into being. I lived through the height of the so-called name-it, claim-it movement. Much of the movement has its roots in Kenneth Hagin's miraculous recovery from terminal illness by claiming Jesus' promise that anything asked in His name, believing, would be granted. Later in this book, I'll explain why this verse did manifest in his life the way in which Jesus said it would and why it hasn't in so many others' lives.

Be clear, I did not surrender to the idea of dying. Deep down I did not and do not believe that God intends for people to die from something for which He already paid the price. Even at the most basic level I knew that He died to bear the punishment for our sins and that by His wounds we were healed. The Psalmist said, "Bless the LORD, O my soul; And all that is within me, bless His holy name!

Bless the LORD, O my soul, And forget not all His benefits: Who forgives all your iniquities, Who heals all your diseases, Who redeems your life from destruction, Who crowns you with loving-kindness and tender mercies, Who satisfies your mouth with good things. So that your youth is renewed like the eagle's" (Psalm 103:1-5 NKJV). I had tumors, lots of tumors. Most of them were inside my body, but one was clearly visible on the left side of my neck and face. They were all the same flavor of cancer, so it stood to reason that whatever we saw the neck tumor doing, the others were probably also doing.

Before falling asleep one night, the seed that had been planted so long ago took root. If I wanted a miracle, it was up to me to commit to believing for it. I realized that I could not believe that I would wake up some morning and all my tumors would be gone. absolutely believed that happens for some people, but I could not convince myself that I was one of those people. <u>So lying there, I asked the Holy Spirit to show me what I could believe.</u> I really didn't have the answer to that question, but I figured He did. That very night, I dreamed about running the snowbanks at the elementary school I attended with my dog, Nikki. Every spring, I would take her to the school when the snowbanks were nice and tall. 9:24 We would run up and down them and across the tops until we both wore out. We did this in the spring because Wisconsin winters were just too cold. Every year, the snowbanks got smaller and smaller with each day's warming sun until all we had left was a parking lot full of water. By then, it was warm enough to play basketball outdoors, so Nikki and my time together was through or at least different.

I awoke the next morning with full recall of the dream, which is rare for me. I know I dream, but I almost never remember them. I told my wife that the Lord had shown me that my tumors were going to melt like the snow in spring. I shared my expectation with the oncologist at Ochsner that was overseeing my treatment the next time I saw him.

Within three weeks we all noticed that my head/neck tumor was getting smaller and looking less violent. He was thrilled. Before two months had lapsed, the tumor was almost completely gone. He decided it was time for a scan to see if the inside tumors were doing the same. They were. I went from dozens of tumors in my chest cavity, on my heart, lungs, and spine to a very few, and they were decreasing in size as well. Within another couple of months, there were almost no detectable tumors left inside or out.

He had his entire staff in the room when he showed me the results of my last scan so they could celebrate with us and

I could thank them personally for all their work and compassion throughout the process. He called it a miracle and made it very clear he never uses that term. He had no better explanation. The same was true for my surgeon and my radiologist. By consensus of medical professionals who do not use the term miracle, I was a walking miracle. That experience blew the doors off of a season of miracles for me and a newfound understanding of how my relationship with the Holy Spirit could look. Without the need, there were no miracles in my life. But the need was not enough. I also had to believe the things for which I prayed and not doubt.

I have learned so many powerful lessons when it comes to experientially knowing the love and miraculous power of the Lord Jesus. This is just one of the life-changing truths of the Scripture hidden in plain sight.

Robert Zimmerman - "Hope for the Hopeless"
(You can find this book at Amazon.com, Barnes & Noble, and more) I highly recommend reading his book...

Warfare

Prayer is warfare against the pride of life. Jesus said, "When you pray..." "When you fast..." and "When you give..."

All that is in the world - Lust of the eyes (give vs. greed). Lust of the flesh (Fasting - give up physical food for spiritual nourishment). Pride of Life (who wears the crown in your life? Prayer is placing yourself in the position of seeking what is right in God's mind vs. "What is right in your mind.")

It is not the vehemency with which you pray. It is not the faith behind your prayer that releases power. It is the Who that you are placing your faith in and your relationship with that person. The person of Jesus Christ. Prayer does not need to be complicated. It is not a ritual. It is not a psyche. It is a statement of faith. A statement of trust.

India:

One night, after teaching, a couple brought their daughter to me for prayer. She had club feet. Her toes were pulled down so tight that her feet looked like fists. As I began to pray her toes slowly started to move into a normal position. My interpreter got excited and grabbed her head. He started speaking quickly and loudly while shaking her head around. Her toes immediately snapped back down. I put my hand on him and told him to stop. I began praying again. Slowly, calmly. Her toes began to move. To stretch out. Her feet were beginning to look normal. My interpreter did it again. He grabbed her head and started shaking it while praying very loudly and fast. The toes went back into fists.

I calmly asked the parents to stay with their daughter while I went out of the room with my interpreter. I said, "Let me take a few moments and pray for you." I placed my hands on his head and began praying, nice and easy. Then, I suddenly raised my voice and began to violently shake his head around. I increased the volume of my voice and the shaking. Then I stopped. He was visually shaken. I asked how he felt. He was not happy. I said, "How do you think this little girl felt when you just did that to her? Can you expect her to be open to receiving anything from someone treating her like that? This is a little girl. A little girl asking for help. Asking for healing. And you are terrifying her. Her feet were healing. You saw it. You grabbed her and freaked her out. Twice."

If you are dealing from a point of authority you don't need to shout and get all worked up. You only need to speak. Power is inherent with authority. Jesus said to lay hands on the sick and they shall recover." *(Mark 16:18)*

Jesus is the Word. He is the power. He has given us the authority to stand in His place as His representative. If God is going to do a work, He will do it. No amount of physical or emotional exertion is going to add anything to God's workings. All we are is a point of contact for the Spirit of God.

'Not by might nor by power, but by my Spirit.' (Zechariah 4:6)
I went back into the room and prayed some more. The toes didn't move this time. I laid my hands on the parents, prayed, and told them to continue trusting God. They had seen the beginnings of her healing. I told them not to give up faith. They saw how I had prayed. Continue praying for her healing.

Good Reports from Last Year's Crusade with Pastor Moses
Monday, September 7, 1987 - 2nd India Journal:

Pastor Moses came to visit and gave me an update on the crusade I had done on my previous visit to India in 1986. This is the same crusade where I had so much trouble with the interpreter arguing with me. "Oh, no. You cannot say that. They will not understand." I told him this is my crusade and please just trust that I know what I am doing. He ended up ignoring me and preaching his sermon while pretending that he was interpreting mine. I finally told him to sit down and asked Pastor Moses (my sponsor for the crusade) to interpret for me. Each night as I was headed to the platform to speak I would be called over to pray for an elderly lady. She would be sitting on a pad. I was told that she was crippled and wanted me to pray for her. I would lay hands and pray. She would say something. I would ask what she said. The answer each night was, "She said she feels stronger."

This is his update on that woman.
"That woman had been lame in both legs for many years. She heard two women talking about a man from abroad who was manifesting the powers of God and praying for the sick. (Me)
She thought, "Why don't I go and get healed?"
She came every night of the crusade and when I prayed for her she would feel stronger.

After I left she continued to get stronger and eventually became completely healed. She is now a member of his church.

Pastor Moses tells me she is uneducated and knew nothing of the Bible but began sharing the testimony of her healing with others and praying for them.

She began casting out demons and people were being healed.

She would say, "The blood of Jesus heals you." Pastor Moses told me, "She is just a simple woman. She only knows how to believe."

Another entry from the same day: (India 1987)

Yesterday the power went off and it stormed all night. The air was so humid and it was so hot I couldn't sleep and spent most of the night fanning myself and praying in the spirit. I was very tired and almost fell asleep in church. The teaching went well and that afternoon I received my first testimony of the day.

A lady had been having pain in her right arm for several years and got healed during the teaching. We visited several homes that afternoon to pray for people and a woman walked for the first time in years. A man was healed of a stroke (paralysis of one side of his body).

Another man who had been bedridden for more than five years received the strength to get up and walk around. That night, as I was preaching on healing, a woman was walking by on her way to the Doctor. Her son had been running a fever and she had given up trying to take care of him herself. As she was passing she heard me saying that those who believe will lay hands on the sick in Jesus' name and they will recover. She thought, "Why not?" She placed her hands on her son, prayed in Jesus' name, and the fever left.

Oh, yes. Regarding the drought from the year before. Pastore Moses had a great report on that.
First, a bit of catch-up.

Regarding the Drought, I Mentioned in the Introduction

It was finally time for the crusade to start. As I prepared to enter the platform I was advised that the area was in the middle of a drought and the locals were concerned they would lose their crops. They asked me to pray for the drought to break. Nothing like a bit of added pressure. A pressure that I had to immediately turn over to God. I had no power over the weather and even less power over God. But, I could ask.

I began the service by mentioning the prayer request. I told the crowd that I have no special power; but, I do have a wonderful friendship with the One who does. The God who created the earth and all that is in it loves and cares for all people. *"He causes his sun to rise on the evil and the good, and sends rain on the righteous and the unrighteous." (Matthew 5:45)*

According to God's written word, the Bible, we can only become righteous through faith in Jesus Christ, and the provision He made for us by His death on the cross and His resurrection. "I want all of you to join with me - Muslim, Hindu, Christian - all of you, in asking God to send rain. To break this drought and save your crops. Father, we stand before you Muslim, Hindu, Christian - righteous and unrighteous - and ask in the name of Jesus that you break this drought and, by the power of your Spirit save the crops."

The next evening, about an hour before the crusade, there had been a gentle rain of about 30 minutes. I was hoping for more than that; but, it was something. The next night and the next was a bit more and a bit longer. I left never seeing the rain I had hoped for.

I asked Pastor Moses about that when he came to visit. He said the rains continued to increase for several more days and, then it poured. The crops were saved. He said the gentle rains were needed to soften the ground and prepare it for the rain. If there had been a downpour (that I had been hoping for) the seeds would have been washed away and the topsoil eroded. God knows better than me.

I mentioned earlier how Jesus spoke for healing. When he raised the girl from the dead, He said "Talitha cumi" - "Little girl, arise."

One more example from scripture of a simple and yet powerful prayer. *As Peter traveled about the country, he went to visit the Lord's people who lived in Lydda. There he found a man named Aeneas, who was paralyzed and had been bedridden for eight years. "Aeneas," Peter said to him, "**Jesus Christ heals you**. Get up and roll up your mat." Immediately Aeneas got up. All those who lived in Lydda and Sharon saw him and turned to the Lord.* (Acts 9:32-35)

Hope is the handle by which we lift a situation or circumstance.

Trust is the compass that directs us toward the answer.

Faith is the application of that situation to the answer source.

Where is your "Trust Compass" directing your hope? Money? Drugs? Your Job? The Lottery? "Universal Positive Vibrations?"
Or, the Creator of the Universe through the path provided by Jesus Christ.
Jesus Christ is the True North.
The *"author and finisher of our faith".* (Hebrews 12:2)

Bless the LORD, O my soul: and all that is within me, bless his holy name.

Bless the LORD, O my soul, and forget not all his benefits:

Who forgiveth all thine iniquities; who healeth all thy diseases;

Who redeemeth thy life from destruction; who crowneth thee with lovingkindness and tender mercies; Who satisfieth thy mouth with good things; so that thy youth is renewed like the eagle's.

(Psalm 103:1-5)

MIRACLES: HOME & FIELD: 349

- The "Non-Obvious" Per Bristow 350
- In The Faith 351
- Miracles at Home 353
- I Need A Job TX 9-473-139 (02-27-2025) 354
- A Recovering Heathen 360
- A Different Chon 362
- TONGUES - MAURY, EL SALVADOR 363
  - I Will Sing With My Spirit 367
  - Stop Petting Your Peeves 370
- ACTS TWO EXPERIENCE 370
  - Maury 370
  - El Salvador 376
  - The Baptism of the Holy Spirit 378
- ANGEL UNAWARES? 379

Miracles: Home & Field

If any of you lacks wisdom, you should ask God, who gives generously to all without finding fault, and it will be given to you. But when you ask, you must believe and not doubt, because the one who doubts is like a wave of the sea, blown and tossed by the wind. That person should not expect to receive anything from the Lord. Such a person is double-minded and unstable in all they do. (James 1:5-8)

A friend recently asked, " You have seen many miracles. You have laid hands on the sick and seen them recover. Why can't you heal yourself?" My "unspoken" answer was, "Why don't you ask Elisha when you get to heaven? He had twice the anointing of Elijah but died of sickness. He had so much of the Spirit of God in him after he died a dead man's body touched his bones years later the man came back to life."

Now Elisha had been suffering from the illness from which he died. (2 Kings 13:14)

Now Moabite raiders used to enter the country every spring. [21] Once while some Israelites were burying a man, suddenly they saw a band of raiders; so they threw the man's body into Elisha's tomb. When the body touched Elisha's bones, the man came to life and stood up on his feet. (2 Kings 13:20-21)

I was nice and kept my mouth shut. But, this left me wondering the same thing. What was different? What was I doing then that I was not doing at other times?

If you're thinking that was the Old Covenant. Now, we have a better covenant allowing us to come boldly before the throne with our petitions. That is true. But, we need to remember that God is more interested in our total well-being. He meets our needs, not our wants. When Jesus healed the paralytic in *Luke 5:17-39* He first met the man's deeper needs. *"Friend, your sins are forgiven."*

We boldly make our requests trusting that God will respond in the best timing and way according to his knowledge, will, and plan.

Everyone didn't get healed in the N.T. either.

Paul did many miracles and was commissioned personally by Jesus. But, under his care, Epaphroditus got sick and almost died. *(Ephesians 2:25-27)* Also, read *1 Timothy 5:23* and *2 Timothy 3:19-21*.

The "Non-Obvious" Per Bristow

Why is it that you can go out on the golf range or go bowling and get a tremendous score only to completely fail on your next endeavor? As a singer, I would sing on karaoke night and totally "nail" the song. Next week, same song, same venue - I would not come close to "owning" that song. A few years ago I purchased a singing course by a fellow by the name of Per Bristow (https://www.perbristow.com/sing-with-freedom/). [I highly recommend this series]

Per Bristow has a way of pointing out the "non-obvious". I say non because once he points it out, it makes so much sense that it is totally obvious in retrospect. As I said, I would have good song nights or songs that worked well; but on other nights, I would miss the mark.

It is like perfectly hitting the golf ball on the driving range; then slicing and hooking the rest of the bucket. What did I do right? What am I doing wrong? We burden ourselves with so many do's and don'ts, tweaks, and hacks it can be bewildering. Per Bristow focuses not on avoiding what you are doing incorrectly. Rather, he shows you how to focus on removing all those little "helps" that hurt you in the long run. To allow your vocal cords to function as they were designed to function. And to sing and enjoy singing.

As "Per" his instruction (pun intended), I began following his breathing techniques and per his advice began trusting my voice. I had been listening too hard to my voice and was constantly overcorrecting my tone, pitch, etc. I was burdening myself with distractions rather than relaxing and trusting my vocal cords. There is much more to his training videos. But, this is where I want to focus for now.

I have not lost my voice or had problems since Lesson One of the "Singing with Freedom" series and have consistently increased my range by over half an octave.

In The Faith

I cannot emphasize enough how our peace and focus have got to be sourced in Jesus' work on the cross. Trusting in His work is all that is needed. Our "works" cannot accomplish anything. Yes, "works" are necessary. But, should be an outward manifestation of our faith. *(James 2:17-20)*

The same approach can be taken in our daily walk. Remove our focus from "religious" distractions and place it on those things that matter. *(Luke 10:42)*

We need to get down to the basics. Find those few principles that encompass all the others. Jesus narrowed the Law to the first two commandments stating that all else hinges on these.

I can grab a tree by gathering the branches in my arms. I grab one branch, then another, then another. The first branch slips out as I reach for a fourth. Or, I can seize the trunk and have the entire tree in my grasp. The "Rock". The "Root" of our salvation is this.

For I determined not to know any thing among you, save Jesus Christ, and him crucified. (1 Corinthians 2:2 KJV)

Jesus spoke of the wise man who built his house upon the rock. *"Therefore everyone who hears these words of mine and puts them into practice is like a wise man who built his house on the rock. The rain came down, the streams rose, and the winds blew and beat against that house; yet it did not fall, because it had its foundation on the rock. But everyone who hears these words of mine and does not put them into practice is like a foolish man who built his house on sand. The rain came down, the streams rose, and the winds blew and beat against that house, and it fell with a great crash."* *(Matthew 7:24-27)*

As Christians, we tend to piece our foundation together from things we learned in Sunday School, favorite verses, experiences, a book we just read, or last week's sermon - our latest epiphany. These are all good.

But, they are bits of the "Rock." Sand. When the storm comes we try to hold these together but unless we see these teachings as facets of Jesus "The Rock" - unless we are holding on to Him in the storm our foundation may wash away.

Jesus said, *"You study the Scriptures diligently because you think that in them you have eternal life. These are the very Scriptures that testify about me," (John 5:39-40)*

The burden Jesus gives us is light. It is not a life of following rules. It is following the One who rules.

Miracles at Home

I would like to share a few things that happened back when I was seeing miracles occur, not just in India and other countries; but in the United States. First, allow me to say that I was in an environment that was very conducive to the expectation of answered prayer. I was attending a non-denominational, spirit-filled church, Abundant Love Fellowship (ALF) in Cahokia, Illinois. There was a very strong emphasis on faith; but also, an emphasis on balancing that faith with love *(1 Corinthians 13:2)*. The Bible was presented as more than a bunch of stories and things to do. The Bible was full of seeds to plant in my heart, and water to nourish my soul. Milk, honey, wine, and bread to feed my spirit. I couldn't seem to get enough of God. In addition to my daily reading through the Bible, I was reading Proverbs and Psalms each month. Proverbs - one chapter a day (31 chapters) and Psalms - Five chapters a day. I would finish each book on the last day of the month. Prayer was introduced to me as a first resort rather than "Well, nothing left to do but pray."

I Need A Job

Something that has become a mainstay for me is seeing God as my source of *"all things pertaining to life and godliness" (2 Peter 1:3 NKJV)*. That means He is my source of employment and He determines where I am to get my paycheck.

Right after I left the band, Millennium, and stopped playing music for my full-time employment in 1984 (nine years full-time) I was concerned about finding regular work.

Even before I left the band people would come up to me in the clubs and ask what was different. "I hear you got religion." "No, I got 'relationship'. With Jesus." We would have Bible studies between sets at the clubs.

Although these Bible studies were great I began to feel that it was time to leave the band and move more strongly toward ministry. A good friend, David Vaughn was very inspirational in me developing a heart for missions. He had written a booklet called "The Fast of Isaiah 58".

"Is not this the kind of fasting I have chosen: to loose the chains of injustice and untie the cords of the yoke, to set the oppressed free and break every yoke?

Is it not to share your food with the hungry and to provide the poor wanderer with shelter when you see the naked, to clothe them, and not to turn away from your own flesh and blood?

Then your light will break forth like the dawn, and your healing will quickly appear; then your righteousness will go before you, and the glory of the LORD will be your rear guard.
Then you will call, and the LORD will answer; you will cry for help, and he will say: Here am I. (Isaiah 58: 6-9)

Dave invited me to accompany him on a mission trip to Guatemala.

I had given my notice to the band and was helping them work on a replacement. All the while visiting the local employment office daily, seeking work. I kept seeing openings for tuck-pointers. I had no idea what that was and no one I spoke with knew, either. The closest answer I got was, "I think it has something to do with bricks."

My notice to the band was almost up and I was getting frantic. One day my prayer time was a bit more intense. I knelt and prayed for several hours that day. At one point, I felt a release. I decided to go to the swimming pool. I had reached the realization stated above. I was going to consider God as my source of employment. I even told someone that if God wanted, He could have someone I don't even know call over the phone and offer me a job. I felt at peace.

The next evening, I was at a prayer session at Randy and Laurie Cutrell's house. I hadn't even brought up my need for a job. During a lull, the phone rang. The caller was looking for a laborer for one week, mixing mortar for a tuck-pointer. I was leaving the next week for my first mission trip. Guatemala. This was perfect.

I took the job and worked the week. The owner liked my work so well that he asked me to come work for him full-time when I got back.

My one-week check was way more than it should have been and was signed by Beverly Owen. That is my mother's name. The owner's wife who signed the paycheck was Beverly Owen. The company was Owen Tuck-Pointing and Chimney Company. The owner, Tom Owen had told his wife to make the check out for $600.00 because he wanted to help with the mission. Talk about God confirming His provision.

I worked there from 1984 to 87. Every job since then has had obvious orchestration by God.

Owen Tuckpointing and Chimney did more than brickwork and repair. We also installed fireplace inserts and stainless steel and aluminum round pipes. They had a series of various size patterns hanging on the wall to make elbows, tees, etc. Tom or Kenny would tell me to go make a five-inch round T or an elbow for today's job. They had many patterns hanging on the wall. One pattern might say "cut on outside of line" while another said, "cut on inside of line".

They had purchased various items and cut them apart to make these patterns. It was very frustrating. I would sometimes need to make two or three pieces to get one that worked. I went to the local library and borrowed a book on triangulation. I bought some flexible poster board, made a large compass, and taught myself triangulation Eventually I had a decent pattern for a five-inch tee. I used my paper pattern to make a five-inch tee from some scrap metal during a lunch break and showed it to the owner, Tom. He said, "You stay here today. You are now the sheet metal man."

Nice. It was winter and I didn't have to go out anymore in the snow and the cold. I began making new patterns to replace those on the wall. I also began doing custom work for specific installations.

I took three months off to work with Jack Harris Ministries in India. I wasn't sure what I would be doing; but, my pastor Tim Ritzel felt it would be a good thing and that I would not only be a benefit to them but would benefit greatly from the experience. They were doing healing crusades in the evenings while training local pastors and doing children's ministry during the day. One of their teachers had to leave and I was asked to teach about baptism. I guess it was well received because they asked me to stay on as one of the teachers. I was offered an opportunity to go up into the mountains and lead a crusade with one of the Indian pastors from the class, Pastor Moses. This is where I had my experience with the interpreter and determined to be an interpreter for the Great Teacher. That sure did take a lot of pressure off of me. I didn't have to do anything except be sensitive to the Spirit of God. Listen to my heart. I would pray and trust God to fulfill the need. No amount of psyche on my part could produce anything. I was just the point of contact for God's work. I saw many prayers answered. Miraculous healings. Blind eyes healed. The bedridden walking.

More and more, I am thinking that this should be our expectation. Look at the lives of the apostles. They started as disciples. Then, Jesus sent them out as apostles. An apostle is defined as one who is sent on a mission. Jesus said, *"Go into all the world and preach the gospel"* (Mark 16:15) *" Heal the sick, raise the dead, cleanse those who have leprosy, drive out demons." (Matthew 10:8)* As disciples of Christ, seeking to go out into the world to minister the Gospel, to carry the Kingdom within us, and to preach that Kingdom we need to see ourselves as apostles. Going out with authority. To do miracles. To manifest the Kingdom of God into the world.

Back home in Cahokia, Illinois; I had no reason not to expect a continuation of the same. After all, even before my time in India, I had seen many answers to prayer at my home church in Southwest Michigan - Coloma Circle Church. We were meeting at Cribb School on M-140 in Watervliet during that time.

Upon my return from India, I resumed my position as the sheet metal man at Owen Tuck-pointing and Chimney.
One day, I got a call to drive out to a job site. Our team was having difficulties installing a fireplace insert. They were not allowed to remove the mantle nor were they able to reach up into the chimney far enough to put the various pieces together. They needed a single piece that could slide up and attach to the pipe coming down from the roof and then attach to the fireplace insert at the bottom. Tom, the owner,

sent me to the location to take measurements for that piece. As I was taking measurements and making notes the customer asked if I thought I would be able to make the piece. I told him I was praying and assured him that God would give me the right design. He looked a bit dubious.

I returned to the shop and began working on the piece. There were several places where I just looked at the template and drew lines where I thought they should be because I didn't know how to connect some of the measurements. I called Kenny and told him I had the template finished and was starting the actual build. He asked me to add an extra inch to the length just to be safe. They could always cut it shorter if need be. I added the inch. They picked the piece up and returned a few hours later. It fit like a glove. Oh, yes. Kenny told me they had to cut an inch off.

I share this not because I am a great innovator. I share this because this is how we should function as having been created in the image of the creator. I was functioning as one in my trinity. The way God designed and intended for us to function. I was in the Word and *"praying without ceasing."* A great part of that prayer was in tongues " *But ye, beloved, building up yourselves on your most holy faith, praying in the Holy Ghost," (Jude 1:20)*

I was very much in touch with my spirit and with the Holy Spirit *"But the Helper, the Holy Spirit, whom the Father will send in my name, he will teach you all things..." (John 14:26)*

I was asking and trusting for an answer.

"Ask, and it will be given to you; seek, and you will find; knock, and it will be opened to you. For everyone who asks receives, and the one who seeks finds, and to the one who knocks it will be opened." (Matthew 7:7-8)

If any of you lacks wisdom, you should ask God, who gives generously to all without finding fault, and it will be given to you. (James 1:5)

A Recovering Heathen

Tom, the owner, Kenny the manager, and I were pretty outgoing in our conversations and much of the talk around the shop was about prayer, healing, and other spiritual things. One of the workers, Sean, was very attentive to these conversations.

One day Sean hit his hand with the pointy end of a brick hammer. He came up to me and asked if I would pray for his hand when I got home. It had been hurting all day. I asked if I could pray for him right now. He asked, "Can you do that? I thought you had to do things like that during prayer time." I said, "It hurts now. Let's pray now". I put my hand on his thumb and began to pray. He jerked his hand back exclaiming, "Praise the Lord. It's healed. The pain just went away." He began listening even more attentively to our discussions.

Sometime later, Sean asked after work if I would pray for his car to start so he could drive home. It had been acting up on him.

This is where things become simple and complicated. As I stated earlier, I believe I was unconsciously functioning as one in my trinity. As a situation came up I would look back into my spirit for a proper response and would pray accordingly. If my spirit witnessed a yes, I would follow up. Sometimes, it would be a no. I never tried to psyche anything. Whether in India praying for a man to receive his sight or praying that a car would start in St. Louise, Missouri; if anything was going to happen it would be God's work and God's grace. I could do nothing to make it happen except to ask, trust God, and allow the Kingdom to enter that circumstance.

I went out and laid hands on his car and it started up. A few days later his car wouldn't start again. Again I prayed. After several episodes of this, I told him you need to get your car fixed. A while after that, Sean came up to me and said some girls down the block were having trouble starting their car. Would I go pray for them? It was dark and I wanted to get home. I walked over to the car. The hood was up. They were cranking the engine. I said "Start" and blew on the engine. It started right up.

One evening, Sean and I were working on a hanging scaffold about five stories up tuck-pointing a building (repairing the mortar between the bricks). I am left-handed so I was working on the left side of the scaffold and trying to reach the last bit of repair. It was getting dark and there was just a bit more to do to finish the job. I was hanging outside the scaffold trying to reach the last bit. Sean would put mortar on my joiner and hand it to me so I could strike the mortar between the joints of the brick. There wasn't enough time left before dark to break down and reset the scaffold. If we couldn't finish tonight we would have to come back in the morning to finish a few square feet of work.

Sean said, "Why don't you just ask your God to move the scaffold over?" I thought, "Why not?" I prayed out loud asking God to move the scaffold so we could finish the job. There was no wind that night. The scaffold moved about three feet to the left placing the last section directly in front of me. I struck the mortar in, brushed it off, and the scaffold went back into place.

Sean began to listen more attentively to our conversations joining in at one point with a comment of "us Christians". Kenny asked, "Did you receive Christ?" to which Sean replied, "Let's just say I'm a recovering heathen."

A Different Chon

My son, Chon, had become accustomed to seeing answers to prayer. As situations would come up I would just say, "Let's pray about it." Things were happening and many prayers were being answered. One day Chon called and said, "Dad, can you come over and pick up my friend with his bike? It's raining. He has to be home by a certain time and he can't ride home in the rain. He can't leave his bike here overnight, either. Can you come over and get his bike and take it to his house?" I wasn't in a position to drive over as it was about 40 minutes one way.

A solution came to me. I checked my heart and felt a confirmation this would be okay. So I told Chon, "Tell you what. I'm going to pray for it to stop raining long enough for your friend to ride his bike home. He can ride home and not have to ride in the rain. Okay?" He said, "Okay". I started praying. Chon interrupted, "Dad, the rain just stopped." I said, "Good, tell your friend to leave now. I don't know how long it's going to stop, but I prayed it would stop long enough for him to ride his bike home. Don't dawdle. Tell him to leave now." A while later, Chon called back and said, "Dad, my friend just called and said he got home, got his bike in the garage, and it started raining again."

A week or so later, Chon called and said, "Dad, I want to go outside and play. Will you, pray for it to stop raining?" I looked at my heart and didn't get a witness. I said, "No Chon. I don't think that's the right reason for praying for something like that. Figure out something to do inside." I didn't pray for the rain to stop because my heart didn't bear witness.

Tongues - Maury, El Salvador

Regarding 1 Corinthians Chapter 14 speaking in tongues:
Paul states in verse 2 *"For anyone who speaks in a tongue does not speak to people but to God. Indeed, no one understands them; they utter mysteries by the Spirit."*
"Anyone who speaks in a tongue edifies themselves,"(verse 4)
For if I pray in a tongue, my spirit prays, but my mind is unfruitful. So what shall I do? I will pray with my spirit, but I will also pray with my understanding; I will sing with my spirit, but I will also sing with my understanding." (verses 14-15)
[Jude v. 20 "But you, dear friends, by building yourselves up in your most holy faith and praying in the Holy Spirit, "]

"I thank God that I speak in tongues more than all of you." (verse 18)
I would like every one of you to speak in tongues, but I would rather have you prophesy. The one who prophesies is greater than the one who speaks in tongues, unless someone interprets, so that the church may be edified."(14:5)
Yes, to prophesy in a group setting is much more edifying than to speak in tongues. But, this is in a congregational setting.
Let's look at verse 39 *"Therefore, my brothers and sisters, be eager to prophesy, and do not forbid speaking in tongues."*

For those who say that the gifts mentioned here (including tongues and prophecy) are not for today 1 Corinthians is the only epistle that explicitly targets more than a single group or person. Titus is addressed to Titus. 1 and 2 Timothy are addressed to Timothy. Romans to the Church at Rome. Philippians to the congregation at Philippi etc. We apply the entire New Testament as relevant to Christians today. But, for some reason, many say that the charismatic gifts of the Holy Spirit are no longer relevant or manifested "in this age".
1 Corinthians Chapter One Verse 2 *"To the church of God in Corinth, to those sanctified in Christ Jesus and called to be his holy people, together with all those everywhere who call on the name of our Lord Jesus Christ—their Lord and ours:"*
ALL THOSE EVERYWHERE WHO CALL ON THE NAME OF

OUR LORD JESUS CHRIST. Paul has specifically called out this epistle as timeless.

Regarding spiritual gifts given by the Holy Spirit:
All these are the work of one and the same Spirit, and he distributes them to each one, just as he determines. (1 Cor. 12:11)
There is a difference between a gift from the Holy Spirit e.g. faith, miracles, healing as a ministry, the working of the Holy Spirit in a corporate situation, or through an individual for a particular circumstance.
Example: *"People brought the sick into the streets and laid them on beds and mats so that at least Peter's shadow might fall on some of them as he passed by. Crowds gathered also from the towns around Jerusalem, bringing their sick and those tormented by evil spirits, and all of them were healed." (Acts 5:15-16)*
This was a ministry or "gift of healing" working in Peter via the Holy Spirit.
At the same time James 5:14-15 states *"Is anyone among you sick? Let them call the elders of the church to pray over them and anoint them with oil in the name of the Lord. And the prayer offered in faith will make the sick person well; the Lord will raise them up. If they have sinned, they will be forgiven."* This would be a corporate situation where the Spirit of God works in the body; but, not necessarily as a "Gift of the Spirit".

At a third level, the individual seeking personal healing for themselves or a dear one can ask for and receive healing.

"who himself bore our sins in his own body on the tree, that we, having died to sins, might live for righteousness — by whose stripes you were healed." (1 Peter 2:24)

The Gift of Tongues can be used to bypass a language barrier as in Acts Chapter 2. It can be used in a corporate situation to edify the body along with interpretation. Or, on a personal level for edification, *"building yourselves up in your most holy faith". (Jude 1:20)*
However, as it is written: "What no eye has seen, what no ear has heard, and what no human mind has conceived" the things God has prepared for those who love him, these are the things God has revealed to us by his Spirit.
The Spirit searches all things, even the deep things of God. For who knows a person's thoughts except their own spirit within them? In the same way no one knows the thoughts of God except the Spirit of God. (1 Corinthians 2:9-11)

We cannot comprehend the details of God's plan for us. But, the Spirit knows.

For the word of God is alive and active. Sharper than any double-edged sword, it penetrates even to dividing soul and spirit, joints and marrow; it judges the thoughts and attitudes of the heart. (Hebrews 4:12)

Our body/flesh hears or sees a situation and transmits it to the soul which either reacts directly or passes the information to our spirit for a response. The God-planted human spirit in communication with the Holy Spirit responds in alignment with the Word of God. The soul then determines to follow the spirit's counsel (Tree of Life - Fruit of the Spirit) or react to the Wisdom of the World (Tree of the Knowledge of Good and Evil - What seems right).

As Jesus "God in the flesh" spoke and did the "will of the Father" so our flesh speaks and does the "will of our soul". Producing either life or death depending on which fruit our soul partakes.

With the tongue we praise our Lord and Father, and with it we curse human beings, who have been made in God's likeness.
Out of the same mouth come praise and cursing. My brothers and sisters, this should not be.
Can both fresh water and salt water flow from the same spring?
My brothers and sisters, can a fig tree bear olives, or a grapevine bear figs? Neither can a salt spring produce fresh water. (James 3:9-12)

I Will Sing With My Spirit

Believe it or not, for years I had difficulty singing in the spirit. I know that sounds crazy. I have been playing music since third grade. I have been playing and leading worship for most of my adult life. I have been a professional touring musician, in both the secular and Christian genres since the early 70's. Why should this be difficult for me? Exactly. I was so used to performing and improvising that I was concerned that I might be manipulating the melody. I didn't want to interfere with the flow of the Spirit.

I was thinking about how we used to improvise Psalms 150 back at Cribb School with the Coloma Circle Church worship team. Which was the root of the Testimony Band. We didn't sing the words. Mary Sliter would read them.

I will give a general scenario. It varied from time to time. But, would go something like this.

Praise ye the Lord. Praise God in his sanctuary: praise him in the firmament of his power.
Art Attila begins improvising on the bass guitar.
Praise him for his mighty acts: praise him according to his excellent greatness.
Dale Owen comes in on keyboards.
Praise him with the sound of the trumpet: praise him with the psaltery and harp.
I would jump in with my trombone. Ray Massey begins riffing on his guitar.
Praise him with the timbrel and dance: praise him with stringed instruments and organs.
Judy "Miller" Toth, Debbie Sink, Sherrie "North" Messenger, and Debbie "McNabb" Tarantino (Circle of Joy) would begin singing.
Praise him upon the loud cymbals: praise him upon the high sounding cymbals.
Ed Skjordal jumps in on drums. He would already be playing softly;

but, would kick everything up a few notches.

Let every thing that hath breath praise the Lord. Praise ye the Lord.
We are in full-tilt jamming and worship.

The sequence might change. Different or more musicians might be involved. But, it was the same scripture. The same God. The same Spirit. I decided to try singing a chapter from the Book of Psalms. I sang it slowly. I sang it again fast. Two different styles. Two different melodies. Same Scripture. Wow!

What is it then? I will pray with the spirit, and I will pray with the understanding also: I will sing with the spirit, and I will sing with the understanding also. (1 Corinthians 14:15 KJV)
That was with the understanding. We knew the words. What about singing with the spirit? I began to sing while entrusting the Holy Spirit to provide the words. But, in an unknown tongue. A melody came with it. Was the score of the melody written by the Holy Spirit? Did I "create" the melody inspired by the Holy Spirit and using the musical talent God gave me? Does it matter?

Just sing. Sing freely. Enjoy. Worship. Above all - don't overthink. (That last part is for me.)

I share this because if it was an issue for me. It might also be an issue for someone reading this book.

Stop Petting Your Peeves

This is a major point in spiritual warfare brought down to its simplest form.

The car in front of you is stopped at a red light in the left turn lane. His left turn signal is on. The light turns green. One - Two - Three - Four - Five...seconds.

Where do your thoughts go? What comes out of your mouth?

You have two trees growing in the garden of your heart. The Tree of Life and the Tree of the Knowledge of Good and Evil. Which tree are you going to eat from?

A man's belly shall be filled with the fruit of his mouth; With the increase of his lips shall he be satisfied. **Death and life are in the power of the tongue; And they that love it shall eat the fruit thereof.** *(Proverbs 18:20-21)*

I just about have this "pet" euthanized.

Acts Two Experience

I have experienced manifestations of Acts Chapter Two on two occasions.

Maury

The first experience occurred around 1971 or 72. The Jesus People movement was starting to hit big in our area. Circle Church would sponsor the JPUSA (Jesus People USA) when they toured our area of Southwest Michigan. They had a music group that toured with them

called the Resurrection Band. Now, known as the REZ Band.
At that time, it was a three-piece group and tended toward folk and light rock. The band consisted of a conga player, bass guitar, and guitar. The Resurrection Band would play at our "Circle Church" rallies and stay in our homes. Around that time, two girls and two guys from Europe were hitchhiking through the USA. I don't remember the guy's names because they were there for only a few days. But, the two girls were named Elyon and Mauricette (Maury). Elyon was from Switzerland and spoke French and English. Maury, from France, spoke several languages but not English.

Elyon had, earlier accepted Christ and received the Baptism of the Holy Spirit with the gift of tongues. During the prayer part of a church service, Elyon stood up and spoke in tongues.

Maury became very angry with Elyon and asked her later, "Why didn't you tell me you speak that African dialect?" Elyon responded that she had no idea what she had said. She just stood up in faith believing she was supposed to speak and she spoke.

Maury had been touring the world writing a book on the occult. She would go into a trance while sitting at her typewriter and type what she had experienced during the day and whatever else came to mind. She had spent quite a bit of time in Africa, studying tribalism, and had learned enough of this particular African dialect to communicate. When Elyon stood up and spoke in tongues, God was telling Maury, "Maury put away childish things. Put away this book and follow Me." I am not sure of the exact words: but, this was the gist of the message.

Elyon left soon after to finish her tour of the United States and return to Switzerland. But, Maury stayed. I don't remember if she was staying at our house at that time. She accepted Christ and received the Baptism of the Holy Spirit and soon after began manifesting demons The entire church became involved in prayer leading up to a 24-hour prayer meeting.

I came over late that evening to pray. We had hired a French interpreter because Mauri didn't speak English. He got weirded out by the manifestations and left.

So here we were, sitting around, praying, praying, praying for this girl who is majorly manifesting demons. We had no idea what to do being very new to this whole thing.

As I was praying a thought entered my mind. I had recently received the gift of tongues. My father, a graduate of Wheaton College and Moody Bible Institute, had been raised that speaking in tongues was not for today. Acts Chapter Two was a one-time happening. At seminary, he was taught to skip certain passages as not pertinent for today. He had recently become interested in an organization called Full Gospel Businessmen and began attending meetings. Curious, I attended one of the meetings with him. The "FULL GOSPEL" was presented including the Baptism of the Holy Spirit along with the gift of tongues.

After reading and rereading these "new" Scriptures that had suddenly popped into the Bible, I went out to the barn that same night and prayed to receive. A warmth and glow filled my being like I had never imagined and I was convinced that a change had occurred in me. I asked for the prayer language adding, "If this is right and really from You: please let it sound like a real language and not some 'Yadda Yadda Yadda' stuff." As I began speaking in faith trusting that, although my mind did not comprehend, my spirit was somehow communicating to the physical world in a prayer sourced by the Spirit of God and understood by God. I thought, "How convenient. I can pray perfect prayer without my mind interfering."

The words coming out of my mouth sounded a lot like French to me.

Flash forward to the prayer meeting with Maury. Everyone was getting tired. It was very late and we were getting nowhere. I thought, "Hey, my prayer language sounds like French. I think I'll go up and speak to her in French".

I walked up to her and began speaking. It was kind of a bold move, I guess. And I felt a bit foolish. A "Who do you think you are?" type of thought. But, why not trust God? So I started speaking in tongues. Maury got excited, grabbed a pen and paper began writing notes. After about forty minutes I felt like there was nothing more to say and sat down. So**meone else** got up and spoke for about 15 or 20 minutes in tongues. Maury continued taking notes. After he stopped I went back over for about another 15 minutes. I was very tired. I had to be at work early the next day. So I left.

I was later informed that God had been giving Maury scriptures through these speaking sessions. The language being spoken was, indeed, French. God had been giving direct scripture and describing incidences in her life where He wanted to heal and guide her. He would say, "Remember when this happened? Remember when that happened? I want you to read this scripture. I want you to do this. I want you to pray this".

Mauri had received deliverance through speaking in tongues. This was not just a fly-by-night experience. Mauri continued to grow in her walk with Christ. She became very involved in missions. I heard she later became involved with Youth With A Mission (YWAM).

I had an opportunity to meet Mauri years later when she came to our house to visit. She had learned to speak English. I decided to try to speak French to her in tongues again. I just started speaking in tongues.

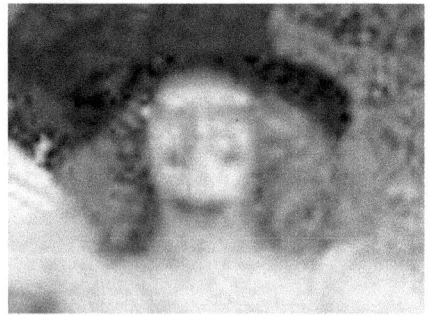

Mauri used to call me Poilu (hairy in French). She probably called me this because my hair was very long (to my lower back when wet - shaggy and curly to my shoulders when dry and I had a mustache and beard that I would sometimes braid). She said, "Oh, Poilu. Your French is so terrible. It used to be so perfect. Such perfect French. But now it's so terrible." Throw that in the mix.

I posted this story on Facebook mentioning that I am including it in my book in the section on speaking by the power of the Holy Spirit. Several friends responded saying they were there that night and remembered.

A long-time friend, Michelle Brodock sent the following to me about a similar experience she had with Maury around the same time as my "bad French" episode.

> I was new to speaking in tongues in the mid- to late seventies so I often didn't know when I had a word or prophesy. I would simply feel unction by the Holy Spirit to sing in my prayer language and usually an interpretation or an understanding would come through someone else moments later. One Sunday evening at Twelve Corners Church, where Circle Church was meeting, I felt the urging to sing in my prayer language, and the French woman, Maury understood the words. Maury said that it was in Italian (it may have been French) as I recall and it was a word to her from the Holy Spirit. My friend Sara Carlson says that the word was asking Maury why she was playing games with Him. Maury never told me what was said, but it was a personal message to her as she told us.

So that's one story.

El Salvador

My next story occurred in El Salvador. I was working with Para Vida Ministries. Desplazados (displaced families) had taken over a sugar mill and the government wanted to use it. These families were living in the mixing tanks, under desks, and any place where they could find a bit of privacy. No running water or electricity. The government granted a section of land next to it for development into houses, a medical center, and two wells. I helped dig one of those wells. It is a very strange feeling being lowered by rope into a hole that is approximately four feet wide and you are about 15-20 feet down. I would dig some earth and dump it into a bucket which was attached to a rope and pulled up by hand.

One day we took some time off to visit the town square and buy souvenirs. It was a large area about the size of a football field in the middle of town and surrounded by shops and houses. It was literally, a town square. We were each paired with a person who spoke Spanish. As we were walking around, I felt an urge to go to the center of the town square. I turned to my interpreter friend and told him where I was headed. He was busy and said he would follow me as soon as he was free. I walked to the middle of the town square thinking, "Okay, why am I here?"

A lady walked up to me and started speaking in Spanish. I looked around for my interpreter. I wasn't sure what to do. I didn't know any Spanish. I knew how to ask about the location of the bathroom, and say "Hello, how are you?" "What is your name?" Not conversation level. At McDonald's, I would still say "hamburgerasa" instead of "hamburguesa" with the H silent when ordering a hamburger.

I decided to make a bold move and began speaking in tongues. The lady got excited and started nodding her head repeatedly. She smiled, said something, and hurried away. Right about that time, my interpreter showed up. I asked him, "Did you hear what I said?" He said, "No, I just got here." I asked, "Did you hear what she said?" He said, "Yes, I heard what she said. She said, 'Thank you. That's what I needed to hear'".

I mentioned earlier how I asked God that my prayer language would sound like a real language.

I don't believe a "prayer tongue needs to be a known or currently spoken language. Before Babel, there was only one language. God created new languages for and from each family group. The Hebrew tongue came through Eber or Heber descended from great, great grandfather Shem from whom we get the term Semite.
(Shem - Arphaxad - Shelah - Eber/Heber).

A prayer language could be unique to that person's spirit as they are a "new creation". After all, we are speaking mysteries sourced by the Holy Spirit's searching of our hearts, "*dividing asunder of soul and spirit." (Hebrews 4:2)* What better way to pray than in a way that only God and our spirit understand; giving no advantage to the enemy or inhibition to our mind?

Just because it may sound meaningless to us or even non-linguistic to the ear; does not mean it has no message. "Ayúdame. Ayúdame. Ayúdame. Ayúdame" would not make much sense to someone who didn't know Spanish. (Ayúdame means "Help me")

How about Bāng wǒ (Chinese) or meree madad karo (Hindi) repeated over and over? These all say "Help me".

By the way. Shunda or Shanda is Yiddish for embarrassment, shame, or disgrace. It comes from the German Schaden to damage.

"Let me not be put to shame, LORD, for I have cried out to you; but let the wicked be put to shame and be silent in the realm of the dead." (Psalm 31:17)

"Lord, you are righteous, but this day we are covered with shame— the people of Judah and the inhabitants of Jerusalem and all Israel, both near and far, in all the countries where you have scattered us because of our unfaithfulness to you. (Daniel 9:7)

Who are we to judge someone else's prayer?

"I thank God that I speak in tongues more than all of you." (1 Corinthians 14:18)

"...and do not forbid speaking in tongues." (1 Corinthians 14:39)

The Baptism of the Holy Spirit

I have heard so many people tout a prayer language and the baptism of the Holy Spirit as something given to a certain few upon them reaching a higher level of holiness or sanctification. It is not some type of step up on the ladder of spiritual hierarchy or sanctification. Rather, it is a step of faith. An unmerited gift.

The "seed" of our dormant spirit was planted in the Holy Spirit during the process of New Birth activating our Tree of Life which, if nurtured, will produce the fruits of joy, peace, patience, etc.

Just as in water baptism our flesh was immersed in water, in the Baptism of the Holy Spirit our spirit is immersed in the Holy Spirit. *"If ye then, being evil, know how to give good gifts unto your Children: how much more shall your heavenly Father give the Holy Spirit to them that ask Him." (Luke 11:13)*
"I am the vine; you are the branches. If you remain in me and I in you, you will bear much fruit; apart from me you can do nothing." (John 15:5)

Speak from your spirit and the Spirit.

Angel Unawares?

One Last Story.
It was my second mission trip to Guatemala. I had learned that my parents were in Antigua. They had recently joined Youth With A Mission and were in Guatemala to learn Spanish. The procedure is to live with a family that doesn't speak English for several months. You have to learn Spanish to survive. We had a day or two off coming up, and I mentioned this to a fellow mission worker. He told me he had been wanting to go see Antigua, so why don't we go? We were working in Guatemala City (Guate) so the distance didn't seem too great. We got permission to go. Did I mention the fact that neither of

us spoke Spanish? No problem. My friend told me he had a Spanish phrasebook. "We should be fine." We got on the bus to Antigua and, after several hours arrived at an enormous bus terminal where we were to change buses to continue the trip.

There were at least 100 buses at this location. As we looked around trying to determine which bus was next on our route to Antigua I said, "Why don't you pull out your phrase book and we'll ask someone?" He pulled out this little book that was about two inches by one inch and maybe 12 pages. Like something you might get out of a Cracker Jacks box. It had phrases like "Where is the bathroom?" and, "How much does this cost?" But there was nothing near how to ask directions to Antigua. Now, I am in a real dilemma. I'm praying. I'm asking, "Lord, what do we do?" Then, I heard this voice and turned to see a Guatemalan lady standing to my left. She looked maybe in her twenties. I don't know. She was dressed in the typical colorful garb of someone from up in the Guatemalan mountains. In perfect English, she pointed to the right and said, "Get on the bus number 100. Take it to Antigua. When you get to Antigua, don't get off at the first stop. Wait until you pass - [she described a certain store.] After you have passed that store you will come to this particular street. Get off there. Go down one block. Turn left. [I don't remember the exact directions, but they were very explicit. A much better description than the ones I am giving.] When you arrive at the house knock on the door. Your mother and father are there."

I turned to my friend and said, "Hey, this lady over here..." When I turned back toward her she was gone.

We got on bus 100 and followed her directions. My buddy exited at the town square. Now, I was alone. Of course, I was never alone. I reached the house, knocked on the door, and asked, "Are Walden and Beverly Owen here?" Moments later, my mother and father came to the door, looked out, and said, "Jon, what are you doing here?"

All the years since I have wondered if that was an angel. Perfect American English. She knew what I needed to know. Gave perfect directions. Then, was gone. I have decided to share the story in this section because whatever it was, it was a work of God.

I see three things in scripture that might line up with this story. It may have been an angel that God sent to guide us. Another one, which is a little bit farfetched is the story of Balaam and his donkey. God gave the donkey the ability to speak. Not to relegate her to a donkey, but it could have been a person who just turned and spoke. Except, Balaam's donkey spoke what was on his mind. God enabled him to say, "Hey, buddy, I was trying to protect you." Concept number three just struck me yesterday which is why I'm putting it in this section. Maybe, just like me speaking French to Maury. Or, speaking Spanish in El Salvador. Like Michelle Brodock speaking Italian to Maury. It is possible that this lady just spoke in tongues and I was on the receiving end this time. It was perfect American English. All I know is what I have shared. Possibly, just like with me, God told her to go over to me and speak in tongues. Then she left.

THOUGHT LIFE - OR DEATH? 385

- *SINtrusion - A Bee in Your Bonnet* 385
- LEAVEN/YEAST 386
  - *Beware of the Leaven* 386
  - *A Two-Way Street* 389
- HEART GARDEN 390
  - *Triggers* 390
  - *Break the Connection* 392
- IDENTIFY AND ISOLATE 392
  - *Wiggle Your Ears* 392
  - *AA Motto - One Day at a Time* 393
  - *A Stone of Remembrance - Ebenezer* 396
- BREAKING THE CONNECTION 399
  - *Stop Smoking* 399
  - *Pick Your Habit* 400
- NEW HABITS 401
  - *Smile* 401

Thought Life - or Death?

SINtrusion - A Bee in Your Bonnet

Paul gives a great description of our spiritual armor in Ephesians Chapter 6. Those reading his letter were very familiar with the Roman army and their armor. Rome had conquered most of the known world and its soldiers were everywhere. When we think "Helmet of Salvation" an image comes up of a solid metal object devised to protect the head from the blow of a sword or battle ax. For the sake of our next discussion, I would like to replace that helmet with a beekeeper's

bonnet. As the beekeeper works with the hive the bees swarm his head and body. They are unable to sting the beekeeper because the bonnet has a netting surrounding it. If the beekeeper removes the bonnet or if there is a breach in the netting the bees would be able to enter and sting the beekeeper. Like swarming bees, we have thoughts and voices continually hovering around our minds seeking access. Screaming fear and hopelessness. Whispering seduction. Demanding entry into our thought process. Telling us that God's grace is not sufficient. Or, we are not good enough to deserve it. Telling us what Jesus accomplished on the cross is not complete and we must complete it with "works". I want to look at a few types of what I term SINtrusion or, how that thought got into my head. Worse yet, how did it get into my heart?

Leaven/Yeast

Beware of the Leaven

Without going into some long scientific explanation of how yeast works; let's just say you put some in the mixture and it spreads. As long as the environment is conducive the yeast will feed and spread. According to Dictionary.com, there are around 600 known species of yeast. All yeast is not the same.

> Yeasts are single-celled fungus that metabolize sugar for energy and create carbon dioxide and alcohol. (BakerBettie.com)

Jesus' influence was growing. His teachings were spreading like yeast in bread dough. It was getting to the point where even some of the religious leaders were secretly beginning to follow Him.

Yet at the same time many even among the leaders believed in him. But because of the Pharisees they would not openly acknowledge their faith for fear they would be put out of the synagogue (John 12:42) The chief priests and the teachers of the law heard this and began looking for a way to kill him, for they feared him, because the whole crowd was amazed at his teaching. (Mark 11:18)

The King James Version uses the word leaven whereas other versions translate the word as yeast. Jesus warned about the leaven of the Pharisees.

Then Jesus said unto them, Take heed and beware of the leaven of the Pharisees and of the Sadducees. (Matthew 16:6 KJV)

Be careful," Jesus said to them. "Be on your guard against the yeast of the Pharisees and Sadducees." (Matthew 16:6 NIV)

Woe to you, teachers of the law and Pharisees, you hypocrites! You travel over land and sea to win a single convert, and when you have succeeded, you make them twice as much a child of hell as you are. (Matthew 23:15)

In the above-mentioned type of reference, we can conflate yeast to a mental, spiritual, or emotional state. Let's define a few more types.

When Abel gave a "better sacrifice" in Genesis Chapter Four his brother Cain was angry. God approached Cain and warned him to beware of the "leaven" of anger.

Then the Lord said to Cain, "Why are you angry? Why is your face downcast? If you do what is right, will you not be accepted? But if you do not do what is right, sin is crouching at your door; it desires to have you, but you must rule over it." (Genesis 4:6-7)

James warns us about this type of leaven.

But each person is tempted when he is lured and enticed by his own desire. Then desire when it has conceived gives birth to sin, and sin when it is fully grown brings forth death.(James 1:14-15 ESV)

As depicted in the graphic above, these thoughts are continually "buzzing" around us. In the songs we listen to. On the radio or TV. They might come at us from a passing aroma. A word spoken. Whatever the source, we are continually bombarded with thoughts demanding a response. Hoping to get in. Hoping to find a place to land. To take root in our hearts.

Above all else, guard your heart, for everything you do flows from it. (Proverbs 4:23)

and do not give the devil a foothold. (Ephesians 4:27)

For the sake of simplicity, I am going to refer to these thoughts as "yeasts". The "helmet" depicted in the graphic has a screen or filter. What is our first line of defense against the yeasts?

Finally, brothers and sisters, whatever is true, whatever is noble, whatever is right, whatever is pure, whatever is lovely, whatever is admirable—if anything is excellent or praiseworthy—think about such things. (Philippians 4:8)

Ask yourself, "Does this thought agree with the Spirit of God?" How we respond with our mouths is important. Remember, James' admonishment to speak blessings and not curses.

Out of the same mouth proceedeth blessing and cursing. My brethren, these things ought not so to be. (James 3:10 KJV)

The word curse here is not to be confused with a cuss word. It is a response aligned with the accuser, not the advocate. The spirit of the world, not the Spirit of God. The Holy Spirit will always initiate blessing.

Your speech must always be with grace, as though seasoned with salt, so that you will know how you should respond to each person.(Colossians 4:6 NASB)

As we saw in "**Three Points of Kingdom Contact - MOUTH**" there is a strong connection between your mouth and your heart.

For it is with your heart that you believe and are justified, and it is with your mouth that you profess your faith and are saved. (Romans 10:10)

A Two-Way Street

A yeast may enter our awareness via our ears, our sight (a tee shirt with a repugnant phrase), a whiff of perfume, or just a vagrant thought. The source is not important. How we respond is. I am not trying to give a literal explanation of this process. But, I want to give a word picture that helps me with my responses.

When your mouth responds with a curse you are opening a pathway allowing that yeast access to your heart and mind. It feeds on the fruit of the Tree of the Knowledge of Good and Evil like a fruit fly and spreads its message as yeast does.

If, however, you speak in line with the Spirit of God, words sourced from the Tree of Life, then the Sword of the Spirit is released to destroy that thought. Words of love, joy, peace, forbearance, kindness, goodness, faithfulness, gentleness and self-control.

We are destroying sophisticated arguments and every exalted and proud thing that sets itself up against the [true] knowledge of God, and we are taking every thought and purpose captive to the obedience of Christ, (2 Corinthians 10:5 AMP)

Heart Garden

Unfortunately, some of these "yeasts" have already gotten in and are embedded in our thought lives. Thorny vines and weeds in our "heart garden".

The yeasts outside have a connection with their inside counterpart which can be great or small depending on how long or widely it has been allowed to dwell in our thought life and how rooted it has become. We may have even come to accept it as inevitable or comforting, almost like it is our true self.

Triggers

I will refer to the connection between the yeast outside and its garden counterpart as a trigger and response.

In "**Miracles at Home and in the Field**" I touched a bit on Pet Peeves. I would like to expand on that a bit. We looked at how these "peeves" trigger negative thoughts and responses. We are so familiar with many of these situations and responses that we accept them as a status quo. Recently, my brother Dale posted a poem on Facebook. I don't remember the whole poem, but it began "I named my pet peeve Steve". The key word here is "trigger'. I don't mean Roy Rogers' pet horse Trigger. Seeing these peeves as triggers we can lump them in with other "triggers" we covered earlier in "**Voices**". In terms of spiritual warfare, we could also term these as booby traps. James talks about sin entering by way of our thought life as we "play around" with worldly self-centered thoughts. Even something as tame as comparing our lives to someone else. Wishing we had what they have.

But each one is tempted when by his own evil desires he is lured away and enticed. Then after desire has conceived, it gives birth to sin; and sin, when it is full-grown, gives birth to death. (James 1:14 BSB)

As we saw in the BakerBettie.com definition, there are different types of yeast. They work similarly but produce different results. A different byproduct. The byproducts of the yeasts we are referencing are behaviors. They may be a reaction like anger, or resentment. Or, they might stir up an attitude such as pride or envy. This type of thinking can develop trigger points.

When we allow a trigger to hit its trigger point it is like an earthquake resulting from two land masses pushing against each other for many years finally reaching the point of disruption.

You may not think you're doing any damage when you respond to a peeve. You're just venting at that driver who cut you off on the road. Or, venting at the fact that you are the only one who replaces the toilet paper. "What is wrong with those people?" What you're doing is allowing yourself to speak curses. You are not venting. You are speaking curses. Just as we are learning to recognize and filter out ungodly voices and their demands we need to identify these triggers and break them.

Break the Connection

The longer we allow these to interact in our thought processes and emotions the more entrenched they become and the more damage they incur affecting our behavior and responses. Some expose themselves as flare-ups with physical reactions ranging from the before-mentioned curses or worse yet physical violence against someone else or yourself. This behavior develops into a habit, or, depending on the root message and how we deal with it an addiction.

An addiction or habit can have multiple triggers acting upon the same behavioral pattern. To break the habits or addictions we need to identify the triggers and break the links to the habit.

I want to share with you a few techniques I have learned over the years that enable me to identify, break, and combat these "yeast beasts" that ravage the gardens of our hearts.

Identify and Isolate

Wiggle Your Ears

When I was a kid, I knew a guy who could wiggle his ears. I was impressed. I asked, "How do you do that?" He said, "Just wiggle your brain." When I got home I went into the bathroom, looked in the mirror, and asked myself, "How do I wiggle my brain?"

I began moving everything on my face and head. Scrunch nose. Squint eyes. Make every possible motion with my mouth. I moved everything I could as hard as I could until I saw my ears move. Just a little. Then more. And more...I began isolating the things I could move. Stop flaring my nose. Stop moving my lips. Stop gritting my teeth. My eyes. Until only my ears were moving.

Then I knew which muscles moved my ears. I got good at it. One day a kid asked me, "How do you wiggle your ears?" Rather than, say, wiggle your brain I described the process I just shared and told him to practice in front of a mirror. He left and came back 10 or 15 minutes later, wiggling his ears. When you remove the distractions you will be able to focus on the important things.

If you find yourself dealing repeatedly with the same thoughts, the same issues, and the same sins, you may want to take a look at what you are exposing yourself to. Possibly that 60s or 70s music channel has songs that are stirring memories. Some bad. Some good. Is it wrong to listen to these music stations? Maybe. Maybe not. *All things are lawful for me, but all things are not expedient: all things are lawful for me, but all things edify not. (1 Corinthians 10:23 KJV)* Put your antennae up and see if some of the songs are triggering unpleasant or pleasant memories that might be leading your thoughts in a direction they shouldn't go. Like discovering a sniper's cover, this may help you locate the target so you can better deal with it. Identifying the external triggers and their internal counterparts can be a great start in the battle for your thought life.

AA Motto - One Day at a Time

The first time I broke a bone was at a wrestling match in high school. I got thrown down on the floor landing with the back of my left hand toward the mat. The bone in the middle of my left hand split in half. I thought it was never going to heal. It took a while; but, it did heal. The next time I broke a bone, I knew it would heal because the first one had. Every time I have broken a bone since - my nose several times, a rib, I subflexed my Achilles tendon, crushed both my heels - each time it was easier to be patient and wait for that healing process to complete.

I say this because one of the first issues we have when we're trying to break a habit or get away from an appetite is that thought, that voice that says, you're going to fight this the rest of your life. I would crave a cigarette and fear that a year from now I would still be battling the same craving. Five years from now. Ten years from now. The idea of battling this for the "rest of my life" was self-defeating. But you can disregard that voice by looking at the other side of the effort.

Let us hold fast the confession of our hope without wavering, for he who promised is faithful. (Hebrews 10:23 ESV)

And he said unto me, My grace is sufficient for thee: for my strength is made perfect in weakness. Most gladly therefore will I rather glory in my infirmities, that the power of Christ may rest upon me. (2 Corinthians 12:9-10 KJV)

Here is a clip from another book I am working on "A Journey of Worship: Point A to Z - Alpha to Omega". (still working on the title) In 1987, I had the privilege of helping lead a worship tour with a YWAM group called "Alegria" out of Cambridge, Ontario. This was a month-long tour through Honduras led by David Hinds. Some members of the group asked if I would mind leading a few worship sessions. They wanted to see how I led worship. One of the songs I used was "Horse and Rider".

> I will sing unto the LORD, for he has triumphed gloriously,
> the horse and rider thrown into the sea.
> I will sing unto the LORD, for he has triumphed gloriously,
> the horse and rider thrown into the sea.
> The LORD, my God, my strength and song, has now become my victory.
> The LORD, my God, my strength and song, has now become my victory.
> The LORD is God, and I will praise him, our covenant God, and I will exalt him.
> The LORD is God, and I will praise him, our covenant God, and I will exalt him.

Sing the song and imagine you are standing before the Red Sea along with the Israelites. Pharoah's army is behind you. You are standing in faith. You have no idea how but you trust that God has a plan and can get you through this. Amazingly, the water parts and you along with the entire nation of Israel walk between the waters to the other side on dry land.

You look back and see the water crash over the Egyptian army. Repeat the song. This time it is not the Red Sea standing between you and freedom. Your habit or addiction is pursuing you and the barrier is your struggle. Not a lifetime of struggle. Just this this struggle. Right now, the focus is to make it through this time. To cross the "Red Sea" of the moment.

Therefore do not be anxious about tomorrow, for tomorrow will be anxious for itself. Sufficient for the day is its own trouble. (Matthew 6:34 ESV)

A Stone of Remembrance - Ebenezer

We have several references in the Old Testament to the term "Ebenezer". It is a point of remembrance of God's work in our life.
Afterward, Samuel took a stone and set it upright between Mizpah and Shen. He named it Ebenezer, explaining 'The Lord has helped us to this point. (1 Samuel 7:12)
In some hymnals, you will find a song entitled "Come, Thou Fount of Every Blessing" by Robert Robinson. Verse Two states:
Here I raise my Ebenezer; hither by thy help I'm come;
and I hope, by thy good pleasure, safely to arrive at home.
Jesus sought me when a stranger, wandering from the fold of God;
he, to rescue me from danger, interposed his precious blood.

Robert came from a troubled home and had been hanging out with a bad crowd. He received Christ at a George Whitfield evangelistic meeting and wrote this song to commemorate the turning point his life had made. God had met him, changed him, and turned him to a course of life where before he had been in a life of sin.

Remembering my survival of the first broken bone helped me exist through the next. As we continue to grow in Christ, it is important to set up and remember personal "Ebenezers". Times when God met us in a crisis and brought us across the Red Sea leaving the enemy behind and defeated. By God's grace, you made it through this test. Set up an "Ebenezer" for this particular habit.

Each time you pass through this particular "Red Sea" you strengthen your Ebenezer. Your testimony of God's victorious grace working in your life.

Sing the song again knowing that where God came through for you before He is able and will do it again. God cares about you more than you can imagine.

I have loved you, my people, with an everlasting love. With unfailing love I have drawn you to myself. (Jeremiah 31:3 NLT)
He wants you to be free.

"And it shall come to pass in that day, that his burden shall be taken away from off thy shoulder, and his yoke from off thy neck, and the yoke shall be destroyed because of the anointing." (Isaiah 10:27)
The word anointing here means grossness or fatness. The life in a planted seed once activated develops and grows. But, it is contained in a shell. It grows to the point where the shell can no longer contain it. The grossness - the fatness - the anointing bursts through the shell and

the life is released. Now, the plant can grow.

In this case, the seed is our hope and the shell is the shackle that is binding us to this habit. Imagine God has broken the shell. Life is flowing. A spring of living water is flowing from your spirit. This is not a psyche thing. Not a "name it - claim it". You are trusting Scripture.

"Anyone who believes in me may come and drink! For the Scriptures declare, 'Rivers of living water will flow from his heart.'" (John 7:38)

This is not hype. Just a release of faith. It has nothing to do with how Christlike you are doing. Whether you lost your temper this morning. Your faith is based on Jesus and His faithfulness. Not on yours. His success - not your failures. But take caution here. This is not an excuse to sin.

What shall we say, then? Shall we go on sinning so that grace may increase? By no means! We are those who have died to sin; how can we live in it any longer? (Romans 6:1-2)

We should always be pushing forward.

For this very reason, make every effort to supplement your faith with virtue, and virtue with knowledge, and knowledge with self-control, and self-control with steadfastness, and steadfastness with godliness, and godliness with brotherly affection, and brotherly affection with love. For if these qualities are yours and are increasing, they keep you from being ineffective or unfruitful in the knowledge of our Lord Jesus Christ. (2 Peter 1:5-8 ESV)

You need to feed from your Tree of Life. The fruits of hope, patience, faith, and perseverance will sustain you. Substitute the habit with a different behavior and that voice will become quieter and quieter. Until it finally is just a muted voice on the other side of a closed door.

Breaking the Connection

Stop Smoking

These "yeasts" buzzing around your helmet instigate and activate more than peeves. They activate habits and awaken thought patterns that are not aligned with the Spirit of God. One habit can have many triggers. This is why many are so difficult to break. We talked earlier about trying to grasp a tree by its branches. You can only grab so many branches before they start slipping out of your grasp. You need to take hold of the trunk or the root.

I'll never forget my first fight. We had just moved to the house on Winchester Road in Ft. Wayne, Indiana. So, I must have been about six or seven. I heard yelling and crying coming from the backyard and ran around the house to check it out. Three neighborhood boys were beating up my younger brothers - Bruce and Dale. I jumped in to help. I ended up taking on all three of them as Bruce and Dale sat down over to the side and watched. I decided to focus on the biggest one. Great idea! Not! While I was working on this one the other two were "impeding" my progress. One had sat down on my feet wrapping his legs around mine and kept grabbing my arms while the other kept hitting me with a brick. They weren't the real danger: but, were distracting enough that I was getting pummeled. I grabbed the brick from the youngest one and hit him with it. Then, I hit the other one. They ran off crying and the big one gave up. Then I beat up my brothers for not helping. Just kidding. I did yell at them. My brothers and I were discussing this years later. I asked why they didn't help. The answer? "You were doing such a good job." The other brother? "Yeah. We were so impressed we just watched and learned."

We ended up being best friends with the neighbors. One of them and their sister are friends with me on Facebook.

Why is this story relevant? We often fail because we're attacking the habit. We are fighting the addiction while their triggers attack us seemingly from nowhere. Just as you think you have this thing licked a trigger sneaks in from behind and smacks you with a "yeast-brick". You turn and are tripped by a "yeast-vine". We need to discern our triggers and break the connection between them and our habits. Then, we will be ready to dismantle the big boy.

Pick Your Habit

Let's begin by choosing a habit and locating its triggers. Since all of these work in the same way, rather than attempt to distinguish between peeves, habits, and addictions I will categorize them under the term habit.

This is how I stopped smoking. I carried a small notebook with me and every time I wanted a cigarette I wrote it down. Back when you could smoke in restaurants, waiting for the waitress to bring the food was a trigger. During a break playing music. As I walked off the stage I'd light a cigarette. Trigger. Bored. Trigger. I had thirteen triggers activating the craving for a cigarette. Many triggers - one habit. I started the process of nullifying these triggers one at a time by replacing them with something else. I was told, "If you quit smoking, you'll start eating and get fat." I said, "No, I'll pick out something else besides food. If I want a cigarette - I'll drink a glass of water." I drank a lot of water.

I began breaking these triggers one at a time. It took me a year. I reached the point where I would wait the whole day and only smoke a cigarette after the first set of music. We would normally play five sets a night six nights a week. When I wanted a cigarette, I'd say, "You can have one later, but not now." I kept pushing the "later" until I was only smoking on Friday and Saturday nights. And, no smoking after leaving the club.Then, every other weekend. When I lit up my first cigarette after two weeks of abstaining it was disgusting. That was my last one. I turned 71 this year. My last cigarette was on my 27th birthday.

New Habits

Smile

When Atlantic City Steel Pier first began touring and later with Circus Maxx, we would hire professional groomers to work with us on stage presence, musical arrangements, choreography, and microphone technique. We paid a set fee and provided a motel room. A few notable groomers we worked with were Johnny Rico from The Characters while we were living in Las Vegas and Tiny Barge (Tiny

Barge and the Big Chill). The first few nights they videotaped and took notes during our performance. Then, we started doing sessions during the day where we would watch the videos while they pointed out the good and the bad, advised, and trained.

The groomers all had one thing in common. One thing they stressed above everything else. "SMILE. And make it look natural." "How do I smile and make it natural? It feels weird." They would say, "Look in the mirror and practice smiling until it becomes natural. Work on it until it becomes a habit. Until it becomes natural."

I believe the concepts discussed in this book are crucial to a successful spiritual walk. Removing or disciplining our "high places" is a high priority. These activities waste our time, distract, and glut our souls. *(Mark 4:19)* Building a spiritual appetite is another big priority. *"No one after drinking the old wine immediately desires the new" (Luke 5:39)*

We just looked at how triggers and pet peeves consciously or unconsciously invade our thought process demanding curses instead of blessings in our speech. Voices prophesy despair and futility. Hopelessness. The *"roaring lion seeking whom he may devour"* *(1 Peter 5:8)* We must war against these voices. These impulses. *"take no thought for tomorrow" (Matthew 6:34)* *"Trust in God with all your heart and He will direct your path." (Proverbs 3:5-6)*

Trusting in God's acceptance of us based on the work Jesus did on the cross *"it is finished"*. His works and His alone. Nothing we do can add to that work *(Ephesians 2:9)*. A successful spiritual life must be premised on His success - not ours because we will always fail. God loves us and is constantly working in our lives.

And we know that for those who love God all things work together for good, for those who are called according to his purpose.
(Romans 8:28)

We have no idea the extent and complexity of His workings on our behalf but need to trust Him to the point of praying *"Thy will be done on earth as it is in heaven" (Matthew 6:10)* And, when we do not know how to pray, Jesus has given us a help-meet to pray on our behalf. The Holy Spirit of God.

If you decided walking or running for ten minutes or an hour a day was beneficial you would make it a priority. Rain or cold would not stop you. You might join a gym or walk around a mall with friends. You would find a way not to be deterred.

It's the same when you are working on new habits. It's time to retrain the brain.

NEW HABITS: 405

Habit One: Practicing God's Presence 405
    Footprints and Fingerprints 406
    Roadtrip 408
    "Worth-ship" 408
    Worship: Ground Zero 410
    Pizza 413
For Such a Time as This 413
    The Nudge 415
    More Habits to Learn 417
    Parable of the Seed (Matthew Chapter 13) 417
    Develop an Appetite for God 420
    God is Your "I AM" 421
    Build New Triggers 422

New Habits

Habit One: Practicing God's Presence

Though all of the haze of my busy days I'm finding your love again
Like a child that was lost in a big city park and then finding a long-lost friend.
Days have been long with no hope in sight.
Time dragging on. Oh, where was the light?
I hear your voice whispering softly to me And I'm feeling your arms hold me tight.
And I realize Lord that you always were there in spite of the darkness of night.

And oh, how lovely to be here Letting your love draw me near
By mercy and by grace I now stand in this place.
And worship you God face to face

Time wore on faith I thought it was gone I see now as I look in your eyes
Yes, the hope is still there, and you always have cared.
It was I who had turned to the side.
There may be times when my heart just can't go.
But when I rely, then your power will flow

And oh, how lovely to be here Letting your love draw me near
By mercy and by grace I now stand in this place.
And worship you God face to face.
To see you face to face. I will stand by mercy and grace.
By mercy and by grace I will stand in this place.
I worship You, God, I worship You, God, I worship You, God.
I worship you Holy Lord Face to Face.
Face to Face - Mary Johnson

Footprints and Fingerprints

According to Gail Giorgio's 1995 biography Mary Stevenson wrote the poem "Footprints in the Sand" which was later the theme for a song sung by Edgel Groves.

> One night I dreamed I was walking along the beach with the Lord. Scenes from my life flashed across the sky. In each, I noticed footprints in the sand. Sometimes there were two sets of footprints; other times there was only one. During the low periods of my life I could see only one set of footprints, so I said, "You promised me, Lord, that you would walk with me always. Why, when I have needed you most, have you not been there for me?"
> The Lord replied, "The times when you have seen only one set of footprints, my child, is when I carried you."
> Lyrics: https://www.geneseo.edu/~heap/footprints.html

Following is an excerpt from a review of the book "Fingerprints of God: His Hand in History and in Human Hearts" by Franklin S. Nauman.

> Evidence for the presence of God can be found in history, human experience, and in Holy Scripture. Fingerprints of God relates contemporary situations to biblical precedents and personalities from Genesis to Revelation in search of Truth. The author follows the footsteps of others who found the fingerprints of God's hand in their lives. With

illustrations from literature, biography, and his own personal experience, he shares insights of pastors and teachers who guided his own faith journey. The reader follows the foibles and faith of Old Testament characters leading to the person and work of Jesus Christ, the finger of God among us (Luke 11:20).

https://uic.redshelf.com/app/ecom/book/1050569/fingerprints-of-god-his-hand-in-history-and-in-human-hearts-1050569-9781467094368-franklin-s-nauman

These two concepts have impacted my thinking so profoundly that I have lived most of my adult life with an awareness of God intimately working in my life. Picking me up and carrying me. Nudging me in one manner or another. Always, drawing me with His love.

Yes, I have loved you with an everlasting love; therefore with loving-kindness have I drawn you. (Jeremiah 31:3)

But, at times allowing me to reap the consequences of my wandering ways.

Do not be deceived: God cannot be mocked. A man reaps what he sows. (Galatians 6:7)

He has always been there when I called out. He has never left me or forsaken me.

Another major impact was a sermon by my pastor, Tim Ritzel titled "God: Inside Minded and Outside Minded". Teaching us to be aware of God in our thought life and equally aware of His interactions with our external circumstances. And to approach our behavior accordingly.

Roadtrip

As I look back I see so many places where God has touched my life when I was seeking him and when I was not. If I was a glass of water I don't think you could see me for His fingerprints.

I referred earlier to these interactions as Ebenezers. If we were to map out our Ebenezers we would see a trail filled with twists and turns where our way was sometimes purposedly blocked and diverted, possibly avoiding a pit, held back - waiting for resources or the cavalry? We might see a trail scattered with avoided precipices, detours, and pitfalls not unlike the forty-year wandering of Israel in the wilderness.

Over the years I have come to think of my life as a road trip with God as my partner. A "Road trip into Eternity".

"Worth-ship"

I like to think of worship as "worth-ship". How do you show someone how much they are worth to you? By spending as much time with them as you can and avoiding anything that might interfere with that time. You choose how you spend your time. I talked about my daughter, Jamie wanting to be with me even though it was going to be a boring day at the car repair.

Remember the boy who spent time with his father? They went sailing, and fishing, they planted crops, and much more. What was the important part of their time together? It was being together. Time with his father.

God walked with Adam in the Garden of Eden *(Genesis 3:8)*. Jesus walked with His disciples *(Luke 24:13-35)*. When God had His talk with Job He made a few interesting points.
"Have you journeyed to the springs of the sea or walked in the recesses of the deep? (Job 30:16 NIV)
"Do you know when the mountain goats give birth? Do you observe the calving of the does? Can you number the months that they fulfill, and do you know the time when they give birth, when they crouch, bring forth their offspring, and are delivered of their young? Their young ones become strong; they grow up in the open; they go out and do not return to them. (Job 39:1-4 NIV)
God is intimately involved in His creation and wants to be intimately involved with us. Every aspect of our lives is important to Him.
What is the price of two sparrows—one copper coin? But not a single sparrow can fall to the ground without your Father knowing it. And the very hairs on your head are all numbered. So don't be afraid; you are more valuable to God than a whole flock of sparrows.
(Matthew 10:29-31 NLT)
How much does He love us?
O Jerusalem, Jerusalem, the city that kills the prophets and stones those who are sent to it! How often would I have gathered your

children together as a hen gathers her brood under her wings, and you were not willing! (Luke 13:34 ESV)
But God demonstrates his own love for us in this: While we were still sinners, Christ died for us. (Romans 5:8)

When Saul/Paul had his encounter with Jesus on the way to Damascus Jesus didn't ask why he was persecuting His followers. He said *"Saul, Saul, why do you persecute me?" (Acts 9:4)*
That is how closely Jesus relates to each of us.

Worship: Ground Zero

Many of us have relegated worship to gathering with a group of people once or twice a week and singing, "God, you are worthy. God, you are worthy." What do we do with the rest of our week? Are we 24/7 aware of God? Putting His interest first? Are we thinking of how to please Him? How not to displease Him or displease the Holy Spirit? Are we having the mind of Christ to do the will of the Father? Or are we doing our own will? Doing what looks best in our mind and then asking God to bless it? I would say this is the root of worship.
"Worthship".Thanking Him daily for everything. Petitions granted. Fingerprints.

There are many references to our relationship with Christ as bride and groom. Can you imagine a relationship where the man ignores his wife all week long? Then, once a week he brings her flowers and spends an hour telling her "You're beautiful. You're wonderful. I love you so much. You're amazing. You're fantastic." After which he hurries out of the house to eat lunch with his buddies.

But during the week he expects her to be there for him. He's not serving her. He's not keeping her in mind. He's not, wooing her. Seeking out her presence. Setting aside time for her. That's not much of a relationship.

Yet we come in once a week. Do our praise and worship thing for God. Listen to a sermon. Hope the sermon doesn't go too long. Gotta zip on out to Bonanza or McDonald's. Gotta hurry and get there before the other church congregations fill up the tables.

We go about our business until Sunday night, Wednesday, or Thursday night. Maybe a special meeting. We get our God-time in. Are we giving God worth? Are we living a lifestyle that says You are worthy of my time? You are worth seeking out. There is nothing wrong with scheduling time to gather with other people in a congregational setting to worship God.

For where two or three are gathered together in My name, I am there in the midst of them. (Matthew 18:19-20 NKJ)

Worship is not a ritual. It's a lifestyle. It is sharing the most intimate moments of our day with our most awesome God and Creator, the most awesome intellect in the universe, who, despite the vast difference between us and Him, wants to spend time with us.

Worship is personal. It's intimate. It's time with your Father. Time with your Creator. Time with your Savior. Time with your Lord. Time with your friend. Time that should top all other demands. Yes, we have to live our lives. We have to work our job. But we still have our thought life. And that's where we have been going in this book. We're taking a look at our thought life. What and how we process in our mind, how we react to things, how we use words, where we go, and what we do with our hands. Because that's the root of spiritual warfare. Who is Lord? What is our relationship with the Lord?

Another point I would like to relegate to the category of worship is trust. Jesus told us not to worry about tomorrow.

Therefore take no thought, saying, What shall we eat? or, What shall we drink? or, Wherewithal shall we be clothed? (For after all these things do the Gentiles seek:) for your heavenly Father knoweth that ye have need of all these things. But seek ye first the kingdom of God, and his righteousness; and all these things shall be added unto you. Take therefore no thought for the morrow: for the morrow shall take thought for the things of itself. Sufficient unto the day is the evil thereof. (Matthew 6:31-34 KJV)

God is intimately interested in our well-being and is constantly working on our behalf.

And we know that to them that love God all things work together for good, [even] to them that are called according to [his] purpose. (Romans 8:28 ASV)

People ask me all the time, "How's it going?" I tell them, "Better than I know." Because I know that God cares about my well-being more than I can ever imagine. Keep in mind, that God is interested in our "needs." Not necessarily our "wants". Israel wanted a human king. They needed God as their king. He is with us. And, we are with Him.

Pizza

If your father invites you to go with him for pizza, do you spend your time wondering how you're going to pay? No. It was his idea, His plan. He will take care of it.

When I was going to India for the first time people kept asking me, "Do you have the money for your plane ticket?" I said, "No". "But, what if the money's not there in time to purchase your ticket?" I answered, "I'll stay here and eat at McDonald's. I'll swim in the pool, hang out with my friends, and go to my church. But if God is sending me to India, He'll provide."

A week before I was to leave someone I had never met wrote me a check for $1,000 which was what I needed. If God is leading He will provide. He is our Jehova Jirah *(Genesis 22:14)*

Trusting that God will provide is another form of worship. When you pray or sing, "You are worthy." Know that He is worthy of everything, including our trust. Trust for today's needs and your needs for tomorrow. *"Thy will be done."*

For Such a Time as This

As we witnessed in the story about the Koschai people (**Chapter 12 - A Mind for Battle**), God had given a plan to two young men to translate a portion of the Gospel of John into the Koshkai language.

Things didn't seem to be going well for them until a Muslim man showed up in his pajamas at 3:00 AM at the bridge where their car had broken down and said, "I came to get the information about Jesus." The tapestry of God's workings is so remarkable we can only stand in awe of His plan.

The Book of Esther is a perfect example of His workings. The best works of fiction can barely compare with the level of intrigue and drama covered in this book. This wasn't a whodunnit engineered in the mind of some author. God orchestrated this in real time using admittedly fallible mankind.

King Xerxes gave a lavish 180-day banquet for all his military leaders, nobles, and officials to show off the wealth of his kingdom. Then, he gave an additional seven-day banquet for all the rest of his subjects who resided in Susa. This was the same Xerxes from the movie 300. *Xerxes who ruled over 127 provinces stretching from India to Cush (the upper Nile region) (Esther 1:1)*

He wanted to show off his queen and called for Queen Vashti to attend. She refused him. He deposed her.

Esther's Uncle Mordecai a prominent figure in the Jewish community had adopted the orphaned Esther and raised her to honor God.

From his entire empire, Xerxes chose Esther to replace Vashti as queen.

Mordecai overheard a plot to kill Xerxes and reported it saving the King's life.

Xerxes decided to promote Haman above all his other nobles.

Standing up for his principles, Mordecai refused to bow down before Haman who upon learning he was a Jew went to the King and got a law passed for all Jews to be killed.

One night, the King couldn't sleep so he ordered the record of his reign to be read to him. They just happened to read the part where Mordecai saved his life so the King decided to honor him. [FAST FORWARD] Mordecai told Esther to talk to the King. Here she hits a "not my will but your will" dilemma.

Then she instructed him to say to Mordecai, "All the king's officials and the people of the royal provinces know that for any man or woman who approaches the king in the inner court without being summoned the king has but one law: that they be put to death unless the king extends the gold scepter to them and spares their lives. But thirty days have passed since I was called to go to the king." (Esther 4:10-11)

Mordecai responded.

"Do not think that because you are in the king's house you alone of all the Jews will escape. For if you remain silent at this time, relief and deliverance for the Jews will arise from another place, but you and your father's family will perish. And who knows but that you have come to your royal position <u>for such a time as this</u>?" (Esther 4:13-14)

Coincidence? Or, orchestrated by God in real-time with fallible humans?

The Nudge

If you are a member of the Body of Christ God has a plan for you. Your life is being woven into the fabric of His work. You may be called to save a nation like Esther was. You might be called to nurture a nation's savior like Esther's Uncle Mordecai who trained her up in the way she should go. *(Proverbs 22:6)*.

The Lord told Phillip to go down from Jerusalem to Gaza. A desert area. He may have wondered why. But, went anyway. When Phillip arrived he saw a eunuch from Ethiopia riding on his chariot reading from the Book of Isaiah. Phillip shared Jesus with him and the eunuch accepted Christ. *(Acts 8:26-40)* Ethiopia is the second-oldest Christian country in the world. Guess who introduced it to the Christian faith? The same eunuch from Acts Chapter eight. You might say he was the first Christian missionary to Ethiopia.

I doubt if Mordecai, Esther, Phillip, or the Ethiopian Eunuch had any idea of the impact they would have on the world. That is for God to know. Our part is to be ready to respond to the leading, the "nudge" of the Holy Spirit. Go here. Stop there. Speak a word of encouragement to this elderly couple at McDonald's. Share your lunch with that hungry person at the park. Stop and pray for someone whose name comes to your mind. You may be instrumental in the start of a world change. Or, you might be helping one person take the next step toward an eternity with Christ.

Like Esther, this moment may have been orchestrated for "such a time as this". Be attentive. Be ready. Be one of the wise virgins. *(Matthew 5:1-4)*

More Habits to Learn

Faith cometh by hearing and hearing by the Word of God (Romans 10:17 KJV)

If you know it is the Spirit of God speaking and it lines up with the Word of God you should feel comfortable praying it. But, unless you read it in the Scripture for yourself and allow it to become life in you it will always dwell in the realm of hearsay. I can't say how many times I have heard people attribute things to Jesus that are not scriptural. It causes me to wonder if they have read the Bible or at least any of the Gospels.

You need to read the Scripture. Get into the habit of daily Scripture reading. Don't make it difficult. A Bible study is great but every reading doesn't need to be a Bible study just like every meal doesn't need to be a three-course meal. You grab a sandwich or a salad at work during a break. You eat a bowl of cereal in the morning with your coffee. How about replacing that bowl of cereal with a chapter from the Bible? Or, eat that bowl of cereal with your coffee and read that chapter instead of reading the cereal box for the fifteenth time? Commit to a minimum of one chapter each day. You are nourishing your soul. Feeding your spirit. This is eternal food. The Word is bread, milk, wine, honey, and water.

Parable of the Seed (Matthew Chapter 13)

We normally attribute this parable to individuals. Some are ignorant, some hardhearted, some are caught up in seeking riches or pleasure, and some have good soil and receive the Scripture gladly. I propose that all four of these instances can be found in each of our hearts. We all have areas in our lives that for some reason we will not or cannot release.

Jesus explained to the disciples that the seeds that are sown represent the word of God.

Understanding

In verse nineteen the seeds were snatched up because the person didn't understand. How do we get "understanding"? Ask. Seek.

yes, if you call out for insight and raise your voice for understanding, if you seek it like silver and search for it as for hidden treasures, then you will understand the fear of the Lord and find the knowledge of God. (Proverbs 2:3-5 ESV)

I recommend reading the entire Bible from Genesis to Revelation. When I started Greenwich Ministries in 1989 as a part of YWAM Miami I knew that graphics and music would be a major part of the ministry and was looking for a better way to do graphics. Windows WYSIWYG (What You See Is What You Get) had just come out. It was a graphic overlay for the computer's disk operating system. Even with the graphic overlay I still needed to learn the disk operating system. I decided to go with Microsoft and bought a book on MS-DOS (Microsoft Disk Operating System), borrowed a computer from my close friend Barret Hart, and began reading. It was very difficult. I would be on page 20 reading about a program that would refer to another program on page 80, which led to page 45. It was confusing, to say the least. After quite a bit of jumping around in the book, I decided to read the book cover to cover. "Don't try to figure out all the details. Just read the book." After a few read-throughs, the book began making sense. I would read something and think, "Oh, I saw that on page 45." This was very similar to how I would study Scripture. I wrote various topics of interest in the back of my Bible and would add scripture references and notes to these. When I finished reading that Bible I would photocopy the pages and start with a new Bible. A different version - Amplified, NIV, KJV, ESV, etc. To this day, I continue to get more and more "understanding" in my daily reading. I have been doing all my reading online for the past several years. When something jumps out at me I copy and email it to myself. Then I place that into a subfolder. This is a long way to say read your Bible. All of it. Don't just word study or search out certain topics. Yes, do that. Get all of the Word in you. Cover to cover. Like in baptism, you want every part of you to be filled and immersed. Like an open cup placed under water.

All Scripture *is breathed out by God and profitable for teaching, for reproof, for correction, and for training in righteousness,*
(2 Timothy 3:16 ESV)

Stony Heart - *(verses 20-21)*
You may have stony areas in your heart garden. Areas where your heart is hardened possibly by hurts, unforgiveness, or just being stiffnecked. You have given certain parts of your life to God but you are holding onto these areas. Reading Scripture will take care of that.
Is not my word like fire, declares the Lord, and like a hammer that

breaks the rock in pieces?(Jeremiah 23:29 ESV)

Allow the Word to break those stony areas down into dust. Ask the Spirit of God to breathe life into those areas of your heart. To make them good soil.

then the Lord God formed the man of dust from the ground and breathed into his nostrils the breath of life, and the man became a living creature. (Genesis 2:7)

Cares of the World - *(verse 22)*

Anxieties and cares of this life - bills, relationships, chasing the American Dream - can choke out your growth. They can hold you back from the fullness of God's plan and workings in your life.

Don't worry and say, 'What will we eat?' or 'What will we drink?' or 'What will we wear?' All the people who don't know God keep trying to get these things. And your Father in heaven knows that you need them. The thing you should want most is God's kingdom and doing what God wants. Then all these other things you need will be given to you. So don't worry about tomorrow. Each day has enough trouble of its own. Tomorrow will have its own worries.(Matthew 6:31-34 ICB)

Develop an Appetite for God

Work to develop an appetite for spiritual things. Turn off the radio. Speak to God while you are driving. If there are others in the car you may want to talk quietly in your head.

God is Your "I AM"

And Moses said unto God, Behold, when I come unto the children of Israel, and shall say unto them, The God of your fathers hath sent me unto you; and they shall say to me, What is his name? what shall I say unto them? And God said unto Moses, I Am That I Am: and he said, Thus shalt thou say unto the children of Israel, I Am hath sent me unto you. And God said moreover unto Moses, Thus shalt thou say unto the children of Israel, the Lord God of your fathers, the God of Abraham, the God of Isaac, and the God of Jacob, hath sent me unto you: this is my name for ever, and this is my memorial unto all generations. (Exodus 3:13-15 KJV)

Line up Your Ebenezers.

The God of your Ebenezers was there in your moment of need. He was and is your "I Am" at every moment of your life.

Petition God with your concerns.

Feed Your Mind

If you YouTube, subscribe to channels like "The Bible Project", "Answers in Genesis", "Expedition Bible", "CSLewis Doodle", "Evidence 4 Faith", "Genesis Apologetics", "Patterns of Evidence", and more. These videos will get you thinking and feed your mind with scientific and archeological evidence of Scripture.

Pray Without Ceasing.

If you can sit down and pray for one hour each day, that is wonderful. I have never been able to do that. I guess if that was my full-time job it might be easier. Even when I was a licensed minister working full-time in missions and while on the mission field, there were so many demands my prayer time was limited. I have had times when I prayed for hours at a time. But, I am speaking of continuous prayer.

Build New Triggers

Behold, I will send for many fishers, saith the Lord, and they shall fish them; and after will I send for many hunters, and they shall hunt them from every mountain, and from every hill, and out of the holes of the rocks. (Jeremiah 16:16 KJV)

Think of prayer as hunting. You place yourself in the appropriate location and wait for the animal to pass by. In this case, the appropriate location is a mindset of listening. Being attentive to the Spirit. If someone's name comes to mind pray for them. Pray what comes to mind. If you are not sure what to pray, pray in the Spirit. Allow the Spirit of God to *"make intercession for us" (Romans 8:26)* When that song gets stuck in your head pray for the band members or people who may be listening to that song right now. Use that song as a trigger to pray.

God is our refuge and strength, a very <u>present</u> help in trouble. (Psalm 46:1 KJV)

A hunter doesn't fire thirty rounds into the air with the hope that they hit ducks on the way down. You shoot the target as it passes by.

Be *"instant in season and out of season." (2 Timothy 4:2 KJV)*

You may be joining God in an "I Am" moment building an Ebenezer for someone else in this moment of prayer.

Or, replace that song with a song of praise or worship. Allow that song to trigger you to turn your thoughts toward God.

Finally, keep in mind that you are three personalities living as a trinity. Each of you has a function in who you are in Christ.

Hap/Soul is the decision maker. He is the arbiter between Shep/Spirit and Phil/Flesh. He determines the direction of the flow. From the spirit or the world. Always place your spirit as your top priority. You cannot depend on Phil for anything eternal.

Phil will let you know when it is time to eat, blink your eyes for you when the dust blows, and duck that swinging tree branch. But the flow needs to come from your spirit rooted in the Holy Spirit. He has the final say.

Finally, brethren, whatsoever things are true, whatsoever things are honest, whatsoever things are just, whatsoever things are pure, whatsoever things are lovely, whatsoever things are of good report; if there be any virtue, and if there be any praise, think on these things. (Philippians 4:8 KJV)

Give others the benefit of the doubt and respond in love.

Charity suffereth long, and is kind; charity envieth not; charity vaunteth not itself, is not puffed up, Doth not behave itself unseemly, seeketh not her own, is not easily provoked, thinketh no evil; Rejoiceth not in iniquity, but rejoiceth in the truth; Beareth all things, believeth all things, hopeth all things, endureth all things.
(1 Corinthians 13:4-7 KJV)

Keep your thoughts toward eternity. Eternity for you. Eternity for others.

The world and its desires pass away, but whoever does the will of God lives forever. (1 John 2:17)

Choose Life

BEYOND THE GATE: 427

Freedom *427*

Jonbo *427*

Find Your Jungle *429*

Rambo *432*

The "What-if Giant" *434*

Beyond the Gate

Freedom

How beautiful upon the mountains are the feet of him that bringeth good tidings (Isaiah 52:7 KJV)

In 1974, Hiroo Onoda, a Japanese army intelligence officer, caused a sensation when he was persuaded to come out of hiding by a former comrade on the Philippine island of Lubang.

Mr Onoda, now 83, wept uncontrollably as he agreed to lay down his rifle, unaware that Japanese forces had surrendered 29 years earlier. He returned to Japan the same year, but unable to adapt to life in his home country, emigrated to Brazil in 1975.

https://www.theguardian.com/world/2005/may/28/secondworldwar.japan?CMP=share_btn_url

Hiroo didn't know the war was over. Someone needed to tell him.

Jonbo

I got my nickname, Jonbo around 1985. I had posed with some Guatemalan soldiers while in the Ischil Triangle building homes for widows and presenting the gospel with a team led by my friend and mentor David Vaughn.

When I got back home, I had the photo blown up to a poster and put it in the youth room. That was the same year Rambo: First Blood Part Two came out.

Someone said, "Like Rambo."

The same day I saw a postcard with Ronald Reagan's face over a bare-chested soldier labeled Ronbo. I pasted my face over his and put a "J" over the "R".

JONBO. The name stuck.

Even though it began almost as a joke as I thought about it my life began to focus on Isaiah Chapter 42.

God promised a servant, a chosen one who will "*be a light to guide the nations. Open the eyes of the blind. Free the captives from prison, releasing those who sit in dark dungeons*". (*v.6-7 NLT*)

Describing His people as "*robbed and plundered, enslaved, imprisoned, and trapped. They are fair game for anyone and have no one to protect them, no one to take them back home.*"

(v.22 NLT) That servant is Jesus Christ.

There are many today who have never heard this message. Or, have heard a partial message of Christ as Savior but not as Lord. A message that "saves them from hell" while they continue to live life their way. As followers of Jesus, we are to continue in His footsteps. To open the eyes of the blind both physically and spiritually by bringing them the whole Gospel. The Good News of Salvation through His life, death on the cross, and resurrection. Bringing them into the Kingdom of Light with Jesus as their Lord. Encouraging all to walk in His light. I took this as my mission.

Find Your Jungle

Thou preparest a table before me in the presence of mine enemies:(Psalm 23:5 KJV)

This may be for life. It may be for a season. But, God will give you the appetite for your calling.

> Disciple:
> Definition - Merriam-Webster: "a pupil or follower of any teacher or school."
> [i] A true disciple is not just a student or a learner, but a follower: one who applies what he has learned.

Jesus commissioned His disciples to
"*Go into the world. Go everywhere and announce the Message of*

God's good news to one and all." (Mark 16:15 MSG)
Disciples? I guess that includes us.

As I have stated earlier in the book; I don't believe we are all called to go into the jungles of Africa or the Amazon. We are all called to go into the jungle of the world system in an attitude of responsiveness to the leading of the Holy Spirit and be *"prepared to preach the word; be instant in season, out of season; reprove, rebuke, exhort with all longsuffering and doctrine. (2 Timothy 4:2 KJV)*
And these signs shall follow them that believe; In my name shall they cast out devils; they shall speak with new tongues; They shall take up serpents; and if they drink any deadly thing, it shall not hurt them; they shall lay hands on the sick, and they shall recover.
(Mark 16:17-18 KJV)
"But, I'm not a preacher. I haven't attended seminary. I'm not eloquent. I wouldn't know what to say." Let's deal with that.
"When they drag you into their meeting places, or into police courts and before judges, don't worry about defending yourselves - what you'll say or how you'll say it. The right words will be there. The Holy Spirit will give you the right words when the time comes."
(Luke 12:11-12 MSG)
In this case, Jesus was referring to you being dragged into court possibly on trial for your life. If the Holy Spirit can give you the words to say when your life depends on it you can trust Him to give you the words when someone else's life, eternal life, depends on it. Remember, The Spirit of God is the one speaking. You are merely His interpreter.

We often tend to think of a "preacher" as someone who stands on a soapbox or corner and yells at people. Or, the pastor of a church who preaches on Sunday. Just be ready to share the Word as the Spirit leads.

For I say, through the grace that was given me, to every man that is among you, not to think of himself more highly than he ought to think; but to think as to think soberly, according as <u>God hath dealt to each man a measure of faith</u>. (Romans 12:3 ASV)
What is your measure of faith? Maybe we can conflate this to the appetite God has given you to seize hold of His grace, His power to enter your "jungle" undismayed by the perceived "giants".

The other day I mentioned to God that I needed more grace to handle a few things that are going on in my life. He asked me how much water could I drink from a spring. "Can you drink the spring dry? If you drink until you are satisfied do you think you have come near depleting the water supply? My grace is infinite."
My grace is sufficient for you, for my power is made perfect in weakness. (2 Corinthians 12:9)
What weakness is that? Any weakness whether it be lack of knowledge or lack of faith.
"Lord, I believe; help thou mine unbelief." (Mark 9:24 KJV)
How much power do we have to heal or speak a word of knowledge? For that matter, how much power do we have to live a victorious life? Little to none in every case. In Exodus Chapter Three *Moses said unto*

God, Who am I, that I should go unto Pharaoh, and that I should bring forth the children of Israel out of Egypt? (v. 11 KJV)

God assured Moses *I will be with thee (v. 12 KJV)*. In Chapter Four *the Lord said unto him, What is that in thine hand? And he said, A rod. And he said, Cast it on the ground. And he cast it on the ground, and it became a serpent; and Moses fled from before it. (v.2-3 KJV)*
That is all you need. God being with you and empowering what you already have. Who you are.

The Holy Spirit is with you and in you. This is why Jesus told the disciples to wait for the Spirit.
But you will receive power when the Holy Spirit comes upon you. And you will be my witnesses, telling people about me everywhere (Acts 1:8 NLT)

Rambo

In Rambo First Blood Part 2 John Rambo was sent into the jungles of Vietnam to find and free American prisoners of war. The war was over. The prisoners were technically free. But, they didn't know. Hiro Onada had never been told of the war's end. He didn't learn about this until a former comrade told him. From the same above article: In 1972, Shoichi Yokoi was found on the island of Guam and returned to Japan, where he died in 1997. Like Mr Onoda, he had no idea that the war had ended. From World War Two and the Vietnamese War, we move to a different type of war.
A "World War" that has been going on since the Garden of Eden. A

spiritual war. A war for the souls of men. A war for their eternity. A war waged against the god of this world and his tactics.

For God did not send his Son into the world to condemn the world, but that the world might be saved through him. (John 3:17)

The battle has been won. Jesus has conquered death and sin through His shed blood and death on the cross, and His resurrection from the dead. The war is over but there are still countless millions who have not heard that "Good News".

Isaiah 42 says that we are anointed (as co-laborers with Jesus) to free the captives.

Isaiah described these captives as people held in chains and prisons. As Jonbo it has been my mission to go into the jungles (spiritual or physical) as a soldier of Christ to bring this message of freedom. Freedom from the imprisoning power of the enemy. This is the mission we all have been given. The ministry of reconciliation.

In the movie. these prisoners were being held illegally. The war was over and they were supposed to have been freed. The Bible says this war is over and Satan has been declared as defeated and yet he still holds power over many people.

God has reconciled the world to himself *(1 Corinthians 5:19)*.

It is our job to go out and enforce that action as ambassadors for Jesus. We must declare the good news to those who are ...*plundered and despoiled; all of them are trapped in caves or are hidden away in prisons; they have become a prey with none to deliver them, and a spoil, with none to say, "Give them back!" (Isaiah 42:22)*

We all need to add the letter "B" from "Be" and the letter "O" from "Obedient" and become a spiritual Jonbo, Bonbo, Jimbo, Whoever-BO and Be Obedient to His call.

As Isaiah said in chapter six verse eight, *"Here I am. Send me".*

The "What-if Giant"

But, what about we who have heard and accepted the message? Are we free?

The purpose of this book is to present a more intimate perspective on this spiritual battle we were born into. The battle of choices we engage in every moment of every day. How we respond in word and thought. There are millions of Christians in the world who have received Christ as Lord and Savior. Many are living their lives in line with the teachings of the Gospel. Yet, their spirits are withering inside. Their spirits are imprisoned and relegated to a small voice, their conscience in the background. Silenced by the many voices and reasonings coming from the world system of thought initiated and cultivated by Satan, the god of this world.

Jesus has called us all to be free. Free to walk in the light. To walk in the Spirit. To walk while it is yet day. We have crossed the Jordan River. We are in the the Promised Land. Where do we go from here? What is our next step to be? Go to church? Be good? Don't smoke, drink cuss, or chew...? There is a "Land of Milk and Honey" ready to be explored. Nations to conquer. Giants to drive out of the land of our lives and the lives of others. Ten of the twelve leaders sent to spy out the land of Canaan feared the giants. They were afraid to enter the Promised Land because of this fear. *(Numbers 13)* Joshua and Caleb on the other hand were unfazed and exhorted Israel to enter and conquer by God's favor. *(Numbers 14:6-9)*

Let's be like them.

Have I not commanded you? Be strong and courageous. Do not be frightened, and do not be dismayed, for the Lord your God is with you wherever you go." (Joshua 1:9 ESV)

God is able to make all grace abound to you, so that having all sufficiency in all things at all times, you may abound in every good work. (2 Corinthians 9:8 ESV)

we know that for those who love God all things work together for good, for those who are called according to his purpose. (Romans 8:28 ESV)

You are called.

His divine power has granted to us all things that pertain to life and godliness, through the knowledge of him who called us to his own glory and excellence, (2 Peter 1:3 ESV)

I pray that out of his glorious riches he may strengthen you with power through his Spirit in your inner being, so that Christ may dwell in your hearts through faith. And I pray that you, being rooted and established in love, may have power, together with all the Lord's holy people, to grasp how wide and long and high and deep is the love of Christ, and

to know this love that surpasses knowledge—that you may be filled to the measure of all the fullness of God. (Ephesians 3:16-19)
Now to him who is able to do far more abundantly than all that we ask or think, according to the power at work within us, to him be glory in the church and in Christ Jesus throughout all generations, forever and ever. Amen. (Ephesians 3:20-21 ESV)

I pray that this book provides a process to help set us on a path of unity within ourselves and unity with the Father, the Son, and the Holy Spirit as we walk this earth carrying and sharing the Kingdom of God everywhere we go.

As we become more and more free to be who we were created to be and to walk as God intended let's see how many others we can bring along with us.

We all have a long way to go. But, through Christ, we can walk victoriously bringing others along the way on our road trip to eternity.

Not that I have already obtained all this, or have already arrived at my goal, but I press on to take hold of that for which Christ Jesus took hold of me. Brothers and sisters, I do not consider myself yet to have taken hold of it. But one thing I do: Forgetting what is behind and straining toward what is ahead, I press on toward the goal to win the prize for which God has called me heavenward in Christ Jesus. (Philippians 3:12-14)

A Spiritual Legacy

"Peep Eye" Gramma was always fun and interesting. She brightened up the world for those around her. Keeping us enraptured between laughter and suspense as she quoted the poetry of James Whitcome Riley. The children she speaks of and those who came after were similarly wonderful and fun as aunts and uncles. Well, almost all. One of them, the youngest, was not an aunt or an uncle. She was Mom. Here is the story. It is entitled:

"Journeys of Faith"
by Ida Keith as told by Jean Reder.

Shots. Gunshots in the middle of the night, followed by the pounding on the door, then epithets, and the sound of scurrying feet. Terrified, I gathered my small brood around me and prayed. My husband was at work on the railroad and I was alone in Calumet City, Illinois, a wide-open town on the outskirts of Chicago. Bootlegging was in full swing, and Al Capone's thugs were doing business as usual.

We were totally alone, my three girls and I - a hundred miles away from family and friends. It was 1927 and my husband had brought us here because of his work.

Fear was the dominating force in my life. When I was five years old, my mother died of measles, Left with six children to raise and on the verge of losing his farm, my father committed suicide by slashing his throat. We were separated, some of us, never to see each other again for thirty years.

A well-to-do aunt and uncle who were childless took my sister and me to raise, and even though we faithfully attended church every Sunday, there was a darker side. Aunt Edna was a big woman with a violent temper who flew into rages and threw things, leaving Mattie and me cringing in fear.

Upon graduation from high school, my sister and I went to work in the office of the ice cream factory our uncle owned. Looking back, I see this as one of God's wonderful provisions for my life later on. We were both exceptional typists and enjoyed working for our Uncle Scott. He trained us well in office procedures.

Mattie married and so did I. However, something happened that changed our destinies forever. Mattie and her husband accepted the Lord Jesus as their personal Savior and gave themselves wholeheartedly to Him. It wasn't long before 1, too, came to a living faith.

The Fort Wayne Bible College was holding evangelistic meetings, and we went night after night, absorbing the teaching, learning the hymns, and witnessing the power of God when prayers for healing were offered.

I now knew the Bible was true. I had such a hunger to know it, to read it, to study it. Little by little, I began to change. Although fear was still a constant companion, I began to trust - to have hope.

After graduating from chiropractic college, my husband set up his practice in Hammond, Indiana, a bustling railroad town where he got a job as a switchman on the railroad. It was a slow process getting himself established as a chiropractor, and he had to keep food on the table.

That's how it happened that during this time of isolation from everything I held near and dear this time of terror in a city of violence and lawlessness - that I had a nervous breakdown.

My health had always been poor and my eyesight was so bad that I had to wear very thick glasses. Homes were heated with coal in those days, and during the winter were usually drafty and cold. So when the children got sick, I didn't know what to do. Then I, too, got very sick with tuberculosis. There was no money to go to the doctor and no one to turn to. I cried for days. My husband didn't know what to do. He thought I was going to die and so did I.

Then one night something happened - something strange and wonderful. Neal had gone to work, but I was afraid to go to bed because when I fell asleep, I stopped breathing. I knelt beside the bed and prayed all night long.

"What will become of my babies?" I asked God. "If I die, who will take care of them?" I had overheard my husband tell someone that "if she dies, I'll have to put the kids in an orphanage."

"Jeannie, you and Nita and Lorraine come pray with me and keep me awake," I told my daughters, ages 4,3 and 2. "Don't let me go to sleep. If I do, wake me up."

They did pray, but they were just little girls and couldn't stay awake. Suddenly, sometime during the night, a light appeared up near the ceiling in the corner of the bedroom. It grew brighter and brighter, and then a voice spoke to me. "you will get well, but it will come slowly." And then it faded away.

There was a message of hope. A promise I could trust. I would get well. My God knew all about me and He was here with me in my difficulties. I went to sleep and woke up the next morning feeling rested and strengthened.

The following year, we had another baby girl. We moved back across the street to Hammond, and shortly afterward, our only son was born. The year after that, we had another little girl-six children in eight years! And the Great Depression was just beginning.

Work on the railroad was sporadic. My husband was on the extra board and sometimes worked only three or four days a month. People didn't have much money to spend on chiropractic treatments and we were barely getting by. We planted a garden and canned the vegetables. Friends gave us hand-me-down clothes. Somehow, God always provided.

And so we survived - and thrived. The children were healthy and bright. My husband's practice became successful. One by one the children graduated from high school, but another crisis loomed on the horizon. My marriage had been in difficulty for a long time, and now after 25 years, Neal and I separated. I was shattered.

Having done nothing but keep house and raise children all this time, I was totally unprepared to take care of myself. But God was there all the time, helping me, showing me the way. I went to live with a married daughter who sent me back to business college to brush up on my skills. My training at the ice cream factory now stood me in good stead.

At 53, I was hired by a Christian businessman as a dictaphone operator. I worked there for 25 years. During all that time, I never missed a day's work except for one day following a fall. God's promise to me had come true.

My children, too, have a living faith. They have become Sunday School teachers, missionaries, and steadfast Christians. My son and his wife served the Lord in the heart of the Amazon for thirty years. My youngest daughter and her husband have trained young people in short-term mission work, sending teams to Costa Rica, Panama, Guatemala, and Mexico. Two of my grandsons are pastors and several others are missionaries.

God is faithful. He will do what He says He will do. And I can do what He says I can do.

"I sought the Lord and He heard me, and delivered me from all my fears." Psalm 34:4

Note: Jean Reder

In 1979 Ida Keith went to be with the Lord Jesus at the age of 80 surrounded by her children and grandchildren. She was in her right mind, articulate, and still had her wonderful sense of humor. We all held hands in a circle around her bed and offered prayers of praise and thanksgiving for her exceptional life.

EXTRAS: 445

Never let it be said that a life serving God is boring: 445

Jesus Film - "Daya Sagar" 448

Word Bird 451

Toymaker and Son 455

Panama, Central America 457

Dominican Republic - February 1986 459

McAllen, Texas 464

Tribal People - India 465

Coffeehouse Ministry 468

Goa, India 470

More Fellow Workers - India 473

Churchmouse Twins 475

More Pics & Brochures 479

EXTRAS

Never let it be said that a life serving God is boring:

I have showered under a waterfall in the jungles of India with wild monkeys running around. I spent a day at the southern tip of India and watched the sunrise on the Indian Ocean and set in the Arabian Sea. I swam with dolphins on a tiny fishing boat in the Bay of Bengal, rode horseback in Belize, toured with music groups across Honduras, Canada, and the United States was on national television in the Dominican Republic as a clown, snorkeled in the Caribbean, walked through coffee plantations in Panama, Central America, spelunked in Missouri, North Carolina, and Kentucky.

I have picked olivine crystals from the lava rock at the summit of Hawaii's Kilauea volcano where my cousin Dick taught me to surf, bathed in Lake Atitlan, Guatemala, watched Niagara Falls from the Canadian side, baptized new converts in the Arabian Sea, and more. All of this while working on missions.

Between 1981 and 1983 70 to 90% of the villages in the Ixil region were razed by the Guatemalan military. Thousands of men, women, and children, an estimated 5.5% of the Maya Ixil population were killed. (GHRC-USA.org) This was genocide at its worst. My friend David Vaughn began taking teams down to Guatemala to help restore these people and share the Gospel of Jesus Christ.

My First Mission Trip was in 1985 with one of those teams. We worked in two villages - Chajul and San Juan Cotzal sharing the Gospel and built several homes for the widows and orphans of many who were killed. After that, I was hooked. Since then, I have worked on missions in every country in Central America at least once. I have also worked in Mexico, Canada, Dominican Republic and toured the US presenting the Gospel of Christ. I have lived in India and Canada studying and performing in missions.

In 1989 I attended a Discipleship Training Course (DTS) in Miami, Florida followed by an Arts in Ministry (AIM) in Cambridge, Ontario, Canada where I majored in Theater, Dance, Mime, Clowns, and Analogue Sound Recording. After this, I returned to Miami where I joined the staff as the Arts Coordinator and founder of Greenwich Ministries, eventually helping to start the YWAM base in Orlando, Florida. During that time I commuted between Orlando and Miami for about a year; eventually settling in Orlando.

I have used various venues such as Preaching, Worship Ministry, and Children's Ministry. I trained Mission and Church Youth groups in Clown, Drama, Mime, Dance, Puppets, Sound Reinforcement, and Computer Graphics, and organized and led various teams and tours throughout North America.

I have worked in soup kitchens in the US and Canada. On various trips, I worked with teams to build Medical Centers in El Salvador, Guatemala, Panama, and Costa Rica, and a feeding center in Brownsville, TX. I helped dig two wells by hand in Colima, El

Salvador, and build cement block houses for 60 families (Desplazados) who had lost their homes due to guerrilla fighting.

I built homes for widows in San Juan Cotsal and Atitlan, Guatemala. I did various work at orphanages in Guatemala, Costa Rica, India, and Nicaragua.

I set up three film teams - edited the films, organized tours, designed billboards, and trained the teams to present the first Jesus film performed by Indian actors and in the national language, Hindi.

Here are a few stories and pictures from those travels.

Jesus Film - "Daya Sagar"

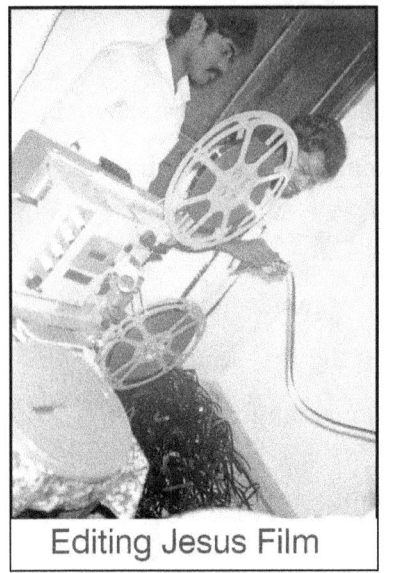

Editing Jesus Film

I set up three teams to show the film. It was the rainy season. By the time we reached reel four, the rain would start and everyone would scatter. I edited the film from five reels to three. Problem solved. Of course, in the process of "problem-solving," I had to purchase a kit and learn how to edit 16 MM film. No YouTube in those days. I purchased two more kits so each team could do repairs as needed. I designed posters and flyers and set up itineraries using contacts from the year before.

I went out with the first team for about a week training them on setup and film repair, making sure things were going smoothly, and

Editing 16MM Film

helping with any issues that came up. Then I returned to Madras (now Chennai) for local ministry and to start a new team. I repeated the process with the second team and then the third.

During one of these breaks, I flew to Goa on the West Coast to help Shelly O'Sullivan and Pastor Kotbagi counsel a group of new Christians who

Watching Jesus Film

were being pulled into a cult (**see Goa - India**). While working with one of the teams in Tamil Nadu I was near Kanyakumari - the southernmost tip of India so I took a day off to watch the sunrise over the Indian Ocean and set on the Arabian Sea.

I went out with each of the film teams several more times to be sure things were going well and to show my support.

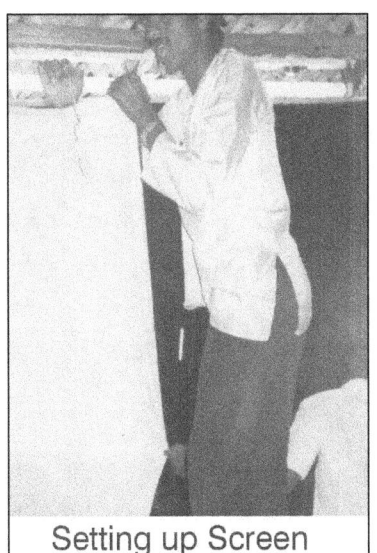

Setting up Screen

Wherever I went to minister I always promoted the local pastors and churches. I didn't want this to be about a man from America. I wanted it to be about men of God who were Indian Nationals and were there for life. Special thanks to Jack and Sherrie Harris (Global Messenger Service) for setting up and funding this venture. Also, for entrusting me with this responsibility. The last I heard about the film several million people had watched it with many making life-changing decisions to follow Christ.

Word Bird

Riding on the van to draw a crowd

On my first India trip in 1986, I had the opportunity to work with Ron Zupcic (Ron Zupcic Ministries) doing child evangelism. I don't know if you ever heard of Willie George from Tulsa, Oklahoma. He put together a terrific curriculum for Children's Ministry - "Faith Roots." Ron was permitted to translate that curriculum into Tamil as part of his ministry in India.

Another part of Ron's Children's Ministry was "Word Bird". Kind of like the San Diego Chicken. (see photos). I had the opportunity to perform as "Word Bird".

Ron would tell a story and I would act out what he had just said during the interpretation. Our Indian friend, Charles Chandran, was our interpreter.

We had very good ministry results with lots of children making

I act out the story as the interpretater speaks

commitments to Christ. I would like to share one story in particular. This story is not about the children. It is a lesson I learned while wearing that costume.

Sometimes I would climb up on a van, stand, and wave at the kids while they were running behind the van following us to the meeting place. Upon arrival at our destination, I would climb down off the truck or van and we would do our show. One day they asked me if I would stand on the parked van and wave people in to build a larger crowd. It was very hot in that costume; but, I told them that I would be fine.

As I stood on top of the van with the heat building up in the costume. I said, "God, it's so hot up here. I don't know if I can handle this." I felt like Jesus said, "I wasn't very comfortable on the cross either." I said, "You're right. I'm sorry. I won't complain again." Just as I said that, a cool breeze somehow found its way into the costume cooling me off.

The red box is where I would change into Word Bird

After that, it wasn't too bad.

Changing into the costume was always a challenge. Depending

on where we were, I would sometimes change at someone's house. Sometimes they would set up a large box with PVC pipe and cloth next to the ministry area.

When it was time for the performance, Ron would tell the kids Word Bird was very shy and they needed to call for him to come out. He would get them cheering and calling for Word Bird.

"Hey, Word Bird, come out.."

I would come running out acting shy. The kids would cheer and the stories would begin.

When Ron returned to the United States he turned everything over to Charles Chandran including the Word Bird costume. Charles was now the storyteller and interpreter. I would act out during the interpretation like before.

Ron Zupcic - the Story Teller

I spent some time with Charles on my return the following year and he shared a great story with me.

Charles was doing Word Bird ministry in an area called Orissa. It is so remote that it's not unusual for a tiger to walk down through the middle of the village. When they got to the part where the children called for Word Bird to come out and this giant bird ran out of a house the entire village ran away. They were freaked out. They had no idea what it was. The performer finally had to take off the head and convince everyone that it was a person in a costume. They thought some giant bird had invaded their territory. Of course, Charles was laughing as he told me the story.

Toymaker and Son

While studying theater and dance at the Academy of Performing Arts in Cambridge, Ontario I became acquainted with the director, Colin Harbinson. He had written a musical called "Toymaker and Son" which was being performed around the world by various YWAM teams. It is an allegory of creation, the fall, and the restoration of mankind back to God through the death and resurrection of Jesus Christ. Humanity is depicted as loving toys built by the toymaker and his son. Their apprentice is jealous and leads some of the toys into rebellion. Toymaker was later redone as Toymaker's Dream. You can find it on the Internet.

YWAM Miami did two tours of Toymaker. I was in both. In the first tour, I played a pirate. I played two roles in the second tour - a pirate and a cruel teddy bear. I had to run off stage and do a quick makeup change for that.

Because a majority of the performers had been on the previous tour and I had studied drama and dance at the Academy of Performing Arts Colin entrusted me with training and grooming the second tour. I was told this is the first time they let someone do this who had not been specifically trained and vetted to do this.

The tours ranged from Miami, Florida to St, Louis, MO. to Southwest Michigan, and back by way of Tennessee.

Still the Pirate

Panama, Central America

Mixing Cement

We built a medical center in Bejuco, Panama, Central America. We were there at the time of Noriega's false coupe. It was so hot I sweat so hard that I didn't have to urinate for three days. I just drank a lot of water and perspired everything out. We cut out the footers for the building with machetes because the roots are so bad.

We mixed the cement directly on the ground. Wheelbarrows of gravel with sand dumped on top. Mix with hoes. Add cement and mix well. Dig a hollow in the top and pour water. Mix

Laying the Foundation

furiously and don't let the water wash over the side and erode the cement away. This is how the cement work was done on all the projects I was involved with - orphanages, medical centers, feeding centers. In McAllen, TX I mixed my mortar in a wheelbarrow. What a luxury.

A new way to blow up a baloon

Break Time

We still found time for clown ministry.

Dominican Republic - February 1986

My first mission trip with a YWAM group was to the Dominican Republic. I always loved clowning around. For the first time in my life, I got to do it dressed as a clown. I chose a big rubber nose, huge shoes, and a Bozo-type outfit. Bad choice. Very hot. I had to put a cotton ball in the prosthetic nose because my sweat would build up and fill the tip of the nose while I was

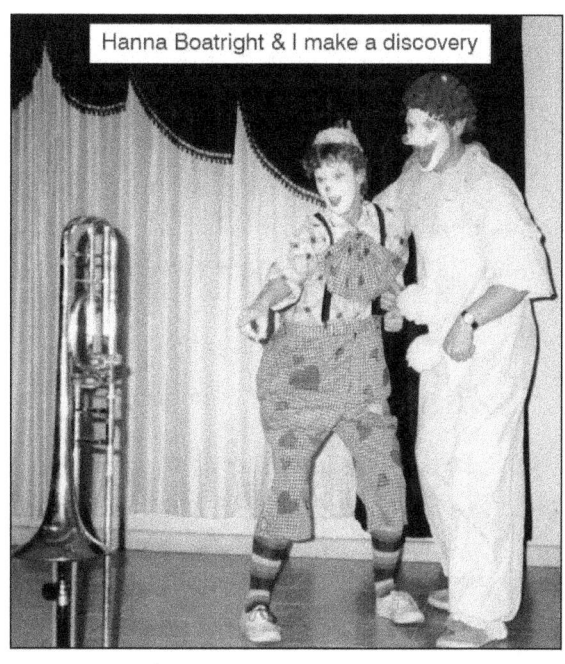

Hanna Boatright & I make a discovery

performing. Then, if I raise my head the liquid would run down my face and my make-up would run. I drastically changed my clown style after that mission.

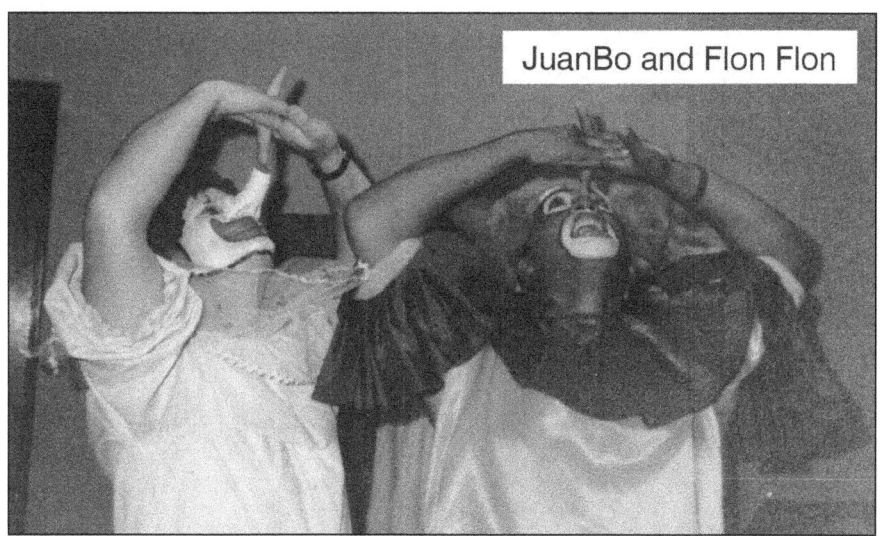

JuanBo and Flon Flon

Once while playing with a group of kids one of them reached up and grabbed my nose pulling it off. I didn't want to break character so I put one hand over my face, grabbed the nose out of his hand with the other, and pretended to pray. Then, I stuck the nose back on my face. He looked like he was going to faint. That was almost 40 years ago. He is probably in his 50's. I wonder if he tells the story to his grandchildren. "The time I pulled the nose off a clown's face." Good thing he didn't pull my finger.

Here is a short clip from my Journal from the Dominican.

> 02/09/86
>
> Friday was a wild evening.
>
> We were to start at 7:00 pm but suddenly the power went out.
>
> In the "ensuing confusion," a man jumped up on stage from the crowd and took control of the children like a pro. He just "happened" to be in the crowd. He just "happened" to be the number one clown and kiddy show host in the country, on the number one station and number one children's show in the Dominican Republic. I was dressed like a clown and went out and entertained with him alone then brought out my brother, Dale. Dale is terrifically talented. Dale and I did go into some impromptu routines we had just "happened" to think up in the past few days, playing around. About the time we ran out of ideas, the power came back on. We were able to go through our prepared group performance; but had made a new friend.

This man, Radamez, had become involved. His interest was peaked. He enjoyed the evening before so much we were invited to his T.V. station to film a show with Him. My brother Dale, Hannah Boatright, and I performed as clowns while my cousin Terry Keith translated.

Flon Flon & his sidekick Tolon

This show will be televised nationally next Sat. (the 14th) and viewed by virtually every child in the Dominican Republic (D.R.) and many of their parents. We did a skit on love from Jesus as being a light "Liviana" burden compared to unforgiveness, hatred, envy, etc. which is "pesado" heavy. We did some clown skits that were just plain fun and at the end, He asked if we wanted to say something. I said yes (Terry translated) "I look happy because I'm a clown. It is not the makeup I wear on the outside that makes me happy. Inside I am also very happy because Jesus is in my heart. If you let Jesus in your heart you can have this same happiness."

God can do anything. He got us on national television, just like that. For His purpose and glory. They have asked u to return next week with the entire team to perform.

An improve ending in "How Great Thou Art"

That following Saturday, Flon Flon (his clown name) was presented with an award for number one clown in the country. That was two days before my 33rd birthday. What a birthday.

> Another quick clip from my journal. Something I just remembered. A little over a year ago, Tuesday, February 4th; I was praying and had a vision (in my heart) of myself in whiteface performing mime and playing my trombone with hundreds of little Latin children following me like I was the pied piper. It was so unusual, that I wrote it in the back of my Bible. That is exactly what I've been doing, in

fact, today possibly (easy estimate) 2,000,000 people saw me perform as a clown and on my trombone on national television and heard me share about Christ. Next week we won't even be here but they are speaking of possible future "reruns".

My brother Dale & Me on set

McAllen, Texas

After returning from the Dominican Republic I got on my Kawasaki 150 and rode to McAllen, Texas to help work at a feeding center. I hopped on my motorcycle and hit the road.

I laid a lot of bricks and led worship locally. We took a trip to Reynosa, Mexico, down just a little bit across the border from McAllen for more worship, clowns, and general children's ministry.

Laying Brick

Tribal People - India

Cooling off on our way to minister to the tribal people

After a long train ride followed by a long ride in a van, we parked along the side of the mountain for a long walk to reach a small tribal village that a church in that area had been working with.

On the way, we passed a waterfall. It

Wild Monkeys

was a very hot day so we stripped down to our skivvies and took a nice long shower under the waterfall.

There were wild monkeys with tails climbing in the trees and running around us.

When we got to the village, there was no one there. The group I was with apologized for taking up my time and decided to go back. I asked them to wait while I set up my trombone and started playing.

I started playing and they came dancing from the woods

People began coming out of the surrounding jungle, dancing and smiling. We had a decent crowd after a while.

The people I was with had brought food, bread, and various amenities with them as gifts. They were speaking to the people and the people were shaking their heads. And I asked, what was going on? They were trying to convince the people in the village to let them take the children back with them to become educated.

I said, "You don't like it when Americans try to make you American Christians. They don't want their children to become City Indian Christians. They want to keep their children. You are doing to these tribal people exactly what you resent foreign missionaries doing to you. Why don't you let them just be who they are? Leave them alone and let God take care of them.

So I preached out of Romans Chapter One.

For what can be known about God is plain to them, because God has shown it to them. For his invisible attributes, namely, his eternal power and divine nature, have been clearly perceived, ever since the creation of the world, in the things that have been made.
(Romans 1:19 ESV)

I told them they could have a relationship with the God who created the heavens and the earth through the work that Jesus Christ had done on the cross. God knows everything about everything because He created everything. By the power of the Holy Spirit that would be birthed within them, they could have access to God's knowledge and wisdom. He could guide them where to fish, where to hunt, how to take care of things, and how to behave and live properly.

His divine power has granted to us all things that pertain to life and godliness, through the knowledge of him who called us to his own glory and excellence. (2 Peter 1:3 ESV)

The entire village accepted Christ.

Coffeehouse Ministry

I have been playing trombone since sixth grade. I broke my hand during a wrestling match in high school and was moved temporarily to sousaphone. I picked up the trumpet and French horn while working on my music degree at Lake Michigan College.

I thought at the time you needed a guitar for worship music. You can't just walk into a coffee house and start playing the trombone. Well, you can. And you will get a lot of attention. I bought a guitar and started playing.

Coffee House

Later on, I proved the trombone thing wrong. I have since sat in with many a worship team. I brought my trombone with me everywhere I went. I would bring it to conferences I was attending. I would ask the worship team if I could sit in with them while they practiced and they would usually ask me to perform with them on stage.

I would play and sing a couple of songs that I wrote then play trombone with the worship team. The team was: Art Attila on bass guitar, my brother, Dale Owen - on keyboards and lead vocals, and Ed Skjordal on drums. They went by the name "Testimony Band". Judy

Miller-Toth and Sherrie Norris-Messenger filled out the rest of the team. They were later joined by Debbie Sink and Debbie McNabb-Tarantino to form "Circle of Joy". You can hear their harmonies on my YouTube channel by searching (theJonboix the Seed).

I was playing in a band called Nevada at the time. When Nevada broke up Andy Kendall - trumpet and I joined the Testimony Band along with Jim Sink on guitar to form the Atlantic City Pier Band (ACSP). Our first official Circle Church - Cribb School Ministry road trip was to Zinnia, Ohio. We called ourselves the "God Squad".

Our 1st Cribb School Trip

Goa, India

In 1986 I teamed up with Shelley O'Sullivan. Shelley led worship and played guitar. I played my trusty trombone and sang.

I got a call from her the following year. She was working in Hubli, Goa (on the West side of India) with Pastor Kotbagi. Goa used to be a Portuguese colony so it is mostly Catholic. A group of Catholics had started a Bible study and were trying to live by what the Bible said and not necessarily what they had been taught to believe.

Leading Worship with Shelly O'Sullivan

Unfortunately, a group of people, similar in effect to the Judaizers were trying to bring these new seekers under the law. Telling them now that they were Christians they weren't supposed to marry or eat certain foods, and many other strange rules. The new group of believers was becoming confused and struggling.

They were being rebaptized as adults. They were searching scripture for the right path to follow. They wanted to be good Christians but were being pulled out of grace and under the law. A law that wasn't even close to Biblical.

Shelley asked if I could come up and help counsel and help her lead worship. So I got on a plane and flew to Goa. 7:00 AM on the dot there would be a knock at the door of my motel room. I would open my door to a waiting group of people. The counseling would run as late as 2:00 AM.

Samuel Kotbagi was very much led by the Spirit. The people there called him Father because of their Catholic upbringing. I remember

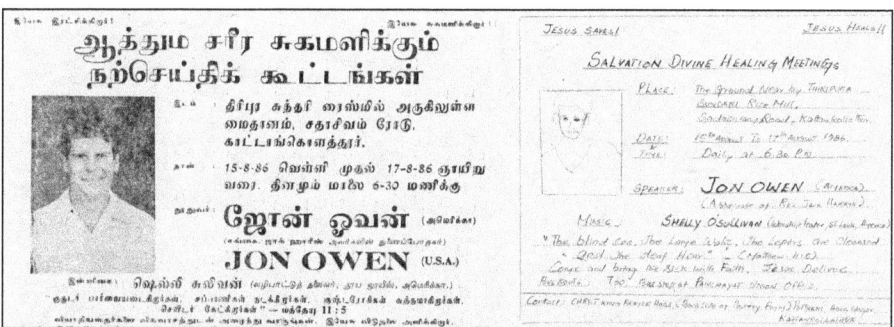

one time, a lady came in and asked him to pray for her for healing. He shared Christ with her and offered to pray but she had to remove the idol from her house.

She said, " I have accepted Jesus and I got rid of all my idols. He said, "No, you still have an idol in your house." When she argued that she didn't have any idols he asked, "Have I ever been to your house?" She said, "No, you have not been to my house."

Pastor Kotbagi then proceeded to describe her house. It went something like this.

"Okay. You walk in the front door and go down the hall. Then you turn left and go to the second room then turn right. There is a cabinet there. Inside that cabinet, you have an idol." "That is not an idol. That is blessed holy water from the cathedral." "You're using that as an idol. There is no power in that holy water. The only power is in the name of Jesus Christ and His work on the Cross. If you want to be fully healed, you have to get rid of that."

He would continually do things like that. Dave Vaughn used to get words like that too.

More Fellow Workers - India

Jill and Charlie LeBlanc (charlieandjill.com) came over and worked with us doing worship ministry. They do excellent ministry and are still going strong.

Jill and Charlie LeBlanc

Jack and Sherrie Harris (globalmessenger.org/) are the people I worked with both times in India. From the headhunters in Borneo to the tattooed bikers on the streets of Sturgis they are still going strong in ministry. Sharing the Gospel worldwide.

Jack Harris & Interpreter

I had a lot of fun with their three girls and Roger Marlin's two children during times off. (We made whiskers with my shaving cream)

Churchmouse Twins

My friend Dave Vaughan, was a recording producer, promoter, and former executive at MCA Records, Sound Impressions, and Paramount Records. Promoting quite a few well-known artists during the sixties and seventies. He left the business after miraculously receiving Christ. But, not before he had shared the Gospel with many of the top music artists of the time.

When I first met Dave he had recently written a booklet "The Isaiah 58 Fast"

Is not this the fast that I have chosen? to loose the bands of wickedness, to undo the heavy burdens, and to let the oppressed go free, and that ye break every yoke? Is it not to deal thy bread to the hungry, and that thou bring the poor that are cast out to thy house? (verses 6-7 KJV)

Dave was leading a discipleship class with a focus on Missions. You can say that this is where I got my passion for missions. God had called him back into the music industry where he used his knowledge and talents to set up independent labels for and promote various Christian artists such as David and the Giants and Phil Driscoll. Dave was one of the first promoters to receive a Dove Award.

On one of my many visits to the Greater Nashville area, Dave showed me a cassette tape and coloring book in his office that he was producing - Sparkle and Jay Jay: the Churchmouse Twins. I got permission to put together a tour based on those materials. I had some costumes made, built a sound system, and off we went.

The first tour was mostly in the Greater Miami area with John and Kami Fournier performing. I had new costumes made by a lady who built costumes for Disney and Universal Studios for the second tour. This tour ran from April 9 through June 4 and traveled from Orlando, Florida to Ontario, Canada, and back.

These pictures are from the second tour with Laura Perlini as Sparkle and me as Jay Jay.

Both tours went well with many children touched and confessing Christ. The costumes are still being used by the YWAM Knoxville Base. Rob and Chris Ellis, from

my Pursuit Band, are the directors and founders of that base. Rob - Keyboards and Lead Vocals

Chris - Bass Guitar.

This is enough for now. I have many more stories to share including our YWAM touring band "Pursuit". I plan to talk more about that in my next book "A Journey of Worship: Point A to Z - to Alpha and Omega".

Meanwhile, you can listen to a few songs from the album by searching YouTube - theJonboix Pursuit Band.

Song titles: "How I Love You" and "Just This Life".

More Pics & Brochures

அல்லேலூயா.
இயேசு இரட்சிக்கிறார்!   இயேசு சுகமளி

அற்பத சுகமளிக்கும் கூட்ட

நாள் : 10—9—86 புதன் முதல் 14—9—86 ஞா
நேரம் : தினமும் மாலை 6 மணி.
இடம் : சீரணி கலையரங்கம், நம்பியூர் (சந்தைப் பேட்

செய்திபாளர்கள் :- Bro. **JOHN OW**

சகோ. ஜான் ஓவென் (அமெரிக்க
PASTOR: **S. SAMUEL MOSE**
பாஸ்டர்: எஸ். சாமுவேல் மோஸ
DR. **S. BENJAMIN** O.N.
டாக்டர். எஸ். பெஞ்சமீன் O.N.G
மற்றும் பலதேவ ஊழியர்க

குருடர் பார்வை அடைகிறார்கள்
சப்பாணிகள் நடக்கிறார்கள்
குஷ்டரோகிகள் சுத்தமடைகிறார்கள்
செவிடர்கள் கேட்கிறார்கள்

வந்து பாருங்கள்.   யோவா: 1:46

சகல வியாதிஸ்தர்களையும் பில்லி சூனிய க
கட்டப்பட்டுள்ளவர்களையும் அசுத்த ஆவியின்
கஷ்டப்படுவோரையும் கொண்டு வாருங்கள். இயே
பார். யாவரையும் எவ்வித பாகுபாடின்றி இறைவ
வின் அன்பால் அன்புடன் அழைக்கிறோம்.

விபரங்களுக்கு,
S. சாமுவேல்மோ
தீ சர்ச் ஆப் காட்,
25, மலையப்பனையம் ரோடு,
நம்பியூர் - 638458.
பெரியார் மாவட்டம்

பாபு மின் அச்சகம், நம்பியூர். தொலைபேசி: 72.

Jesus Calls !   Jesus Saves !!   Jesus Comes !!!

All Night Prayer Meeting.

Place : Bethal Cottage, Valparai
(Govt. Hospital Road)
Date : 9 - 8 - 1986 Saturday
Time : 10 P.M (Night)

Special Messages Delivered by
Rev. JON OWEN   (U.S.A.)
Erg. J. P. SOLOMON (Madras)

Heart Touching Messages, Enjoy Sweet Music, Receive at Soul & Body Jesus Calls You Eternal Life. No caste, No creed, Come in large number. God's Blessings Await You.

| Special Prayers offered for sick people |

All Night - Prayer Fellowship
VALPARAI.

Chillin' with the Chilluns

Recommended Reading

A History of Missions: "to the ends of the Earth..."

by Walden L Owen Jr.
(Author)
Jonathan L Owen (Illustrator)

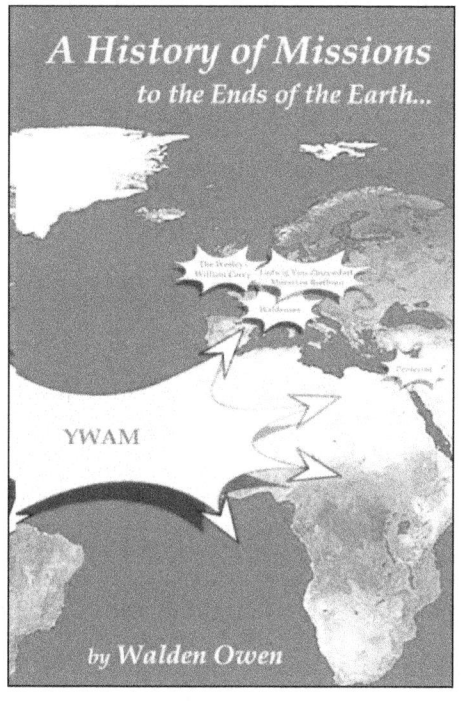

A History of Missions: God had missions on his heart from the very beginning. What I have written here is simply a short version of how missions has developed over the centuries. Angels could have done a better job, but God chose to use the people he had created.

Some ideas worked. Some ideas probably should have never been tried. However, as the task converges in our century, one has to admit that we are getting better at it by the grace of God. Who knows? After reading the book, you might even want to get involved.

Excerpt from the book:

We are very familiar with the "Tower of Babel" narrative recorded in Genesis 11. Prior to that dispersion, God dealt with mankind as a whole. People were not separated into language groups. The entire human race was a monolithic unity. They all spoke the same language.

In their determination to establish an idolatrous pantheon, they were able to strongly resist any message God might deliver. Mankind was determined to rebel against their Creator.

In the words of Genesis 11:6, we are given to understand that because all men spoke the same language and because they had chosen to reject God, "Now nothing that they propose to do will be withheld from them." No work of evil would be impossible to them. As a result of man's decision, God said in Genesis 11:7, "Come let us go down and there confuse their language, that they may not understand one another's speech." There is no question but that this was an act of judgment.

However, this move on God's part was also an act of tremendous mercy and included a wonderful strategy. He would not destroy all of mankind as He had done with the flood. Humanity was now resisting Him as a massive, singular entity. This time God would win them back family by family, clan by clan, people by people, and nation by nation. This is the Creator of the universe initiating a plan to "seek and to save that which was lost." This is our missionary God establishing the concept of Missions thousands of years before the Great Commission was delivered.

Church History: the Gates of Hell will Not Prevail

by Walden L Owen Jr. (Author)
Jonathan L Owen (Illustrator)

In Matthew 16:18 Jesus said, "I will build my church and the gates of hell will not prevail against it." The Church of Jesus Christ was born a very healthy baby. True, it had to grow and it did encounter opposition. However, the struggle did not drag through fifteen centuries until Martin Luther finally broke the chains. From the very beginning a vibrant group of believers formed in the Alpine region of southeastern France and northern Italy. From this secluded area, godly missionaries went throughout Europe proclaiming salvation in Christ Jesus. All through the centuries since Jesus' proclamation, the gates of Hell have not been able to stand against the Church of Jesus Christ.

Excerpt from the book:

As the blanket of Rome's apostasy draped itself over the plains of Lombardy that extended some 200 miles north of Rome toward the rising peaks of the Alps, hundreds of people who were unwilling to accept those errors began to flee to the safety of the mountains. There they would find a people ready to receive them who already believed as they did. Though the people of the plains had been overcome by apostasy, the people of the mountains had not. In a series of valleys, seemingly carved out by God for this very purpose, the ancient church of the Waldenses thrived. There were seven valleys that formed the territory of the Waldenses. Three of them extended like spokes of a wheel from a common entrance. One was 12 miles long by 2 miles wide. Another formed a huge cup, 50 miles in circumference. At the very ends of these three valleys were the other four which formed the rim of a wheel. Each valley had its own entrance and exit and was laced with caves and huge rocks that formed places of protection. Each valley is related to the other in such a way that one opens into the other, forming an impregnable fortress. Not only were these valleys difficult to invade, but they were also well-watered and fertile The antiquity of the Waldenses is strongly supported by history. An ancient poem dating from the year 1100, entitled, The Nobla Leycon, is not only a poem but is also a confession of faith that could only have been composed after a serious study of Christianity in contrast to the errors of Rome. An interesting passage from this early poem speaks of the godliness of the Waldenses, also known as Vaudois. "If there be an honest man, who desires to love God and fear Jesus Christ, who will neither slander, nor swear, nor lie, nor commit adultery, nor kill, nor steal, nor avenge himself of his enemies, they presently say of such a one he is a Vaudes and worthy of death." (Wylie, vol. i, p. 26; Sir Samuel Morland records the complete Nobla Leycon in his History of the Churches of the Waldenses.)

Let God Be True: In the beginning God created the Heavens and the Earth (Genesis 1:1)

by Walden L Owen Jr. (Author)
Jonathan L Owen (Illustrator)

Excerpt from the book:

I want you to look especially at the segment dealing with the explosion of Mt. St. Helens which has been called by many, "a miniature Genesis flood." Then ask yourself the question, "Does geology demand millions of years for certain features to form or could they happen quickly?"

With the explosion of Mt. St. Helens in Washington State, the catastrophe of the Genesis flood was replicated, only on a much smaller scale. As twenty million tons of TNT blast energy was released in the Mt. St. Helens explosion, a hundred sixty square miles of pine forest was blown down and scattered like match sticks. This took all of six minutes. The blast catapulted a huge bulk of debris into Spirit Lake creating a tidal wave that reached 860 feet above its normal level. The wave swept enough pine logs back into the lake to cover half its 4 square miles of surface. Another gigantic portion of debris swept down and blocked the north fork of the Toutle River drainage basin. Steam explosion pits were formed as many feet of hot ash covered glacier ice. The clash of 550 degree ash with cold, glacier ice produced steam where the ash and ice met. Steam continued to generate until enough pressure was produced to cause huge explosions. These explosions formed gigantic pits, some a hundred feet in depth. The intricate gully and rill effect looked exactly like what can be observed in our Western Badlands today. These formations were produced in just 5 days. Landslide material blocked the north fork of the Toutle River for two years. Without normal outflow, pressure continued to build up from a lake behind the lava dome. Eventually, on March 19, 1982, the pressure caused a huge mud flow that gauged out the blockage and cut a series of new channels for the river. A miniature Grand Canyon was created, involving a whole series of complex canyons, some of which were over a hundred feet deep. The canyon walls displayed the unusual, water-deposited layers so familiar to those who study the topography of the Grand Canyon. All of these features were carved out in just one day.